RAGE

OUTRAGE

OUTRAGE

OUTRAGE

OUTRAGE

OUTRAGE

OUTR

# OUTRAGE

# OUTRAGE

**Why the Fight for LGBTQ+ Equality Is Not
Yet Won and What We Can Do About It**

## Ellen Jones

BLUEBIRD

First published 2025 by Bluebird
an imprint of Pan Macmillan
The Smithson, 6 Briset Street, London EC1M 5NR
*EU representative:* Macmillan Publishers Ireland Ltd, 1st Floor,
The Liffey Trust Centre, 117–126 Sheriff Street Upper,
Dublin 1, D01 YC43
Associated companies throughout the world
www.panmacmillan.com

HB ISBN 978-1-0350-3060-6
TPB ISBN 978-1-0350-3061-3

Copyright © Ellen Jones 2025

The right of Ellen Jones to be identified as the
author of this work has been asserted by her in accordance
with the Copyright, Designs and Patents Act 1988.

All legal information in this book was correct at the time of publication but may subsequently
have changed. Regular research was disrupted during the coronavirus pandemic, meaning that some of
the data included is not up to date but we have included the latest available data. Personal
details of interviewees have been changed to protect anonymity.

1 3 5 7 9 8 6 4 2

A CIP catalogue record for this book is available from the British Library.

Typeset in Minion Pro by Palimpsest Book Production Limited, Falkirk, Stirlingshire
Printed and bound by CPI Group (UK) Ltd, Croydon, CR0 4YY

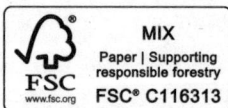

FSC
www.fsc.org
MIX
Paper | Supporting
responsible forestry
FSC® C116313

Visit **www.panmacmillan.com/bluebird** to read more about all our books
and to buy them. You will also find features, author interviews and
news of any author events, and you can sign up for e-newsletters
so that you're always first to hear about our new releases.

*For my parents Gill and Chris for their unwavering love and support.*

*In memory of my friends Shay, Immy, Oli. Mourn the dead, fight like hell for the living.*

# Contents

# Outraged

'If you're queer and you're not angry in 1992,
you're not paying attention; if you're straight it
might be hard to figure out what all the
shouting is about.'[1]

I was flicking through magazine archives when I found this quote
– about queer activism and organizing around the AIDS crisis –
from future Pulitzer Prize-winning author and screenwriter
Michael Cunningham, at that time a member of direct action
group ACT UP.[2]

How astonishing and agonizing it is that over thirty years later his
words still feel so relevant.

I began writing this book with a very different intention – to
explore representation and how it shaped understanding of LGBTQ+
lives, if it did. But, the more I spoke to people, the more I wrote, the
more political and social events unfurled, the more I knew I had to
write something less theoretical and more practical. When I first
started writing this book, there were no drag bans in the US.[3] There
were fewer trans children murdered or taking their own lives.[4] The
Conservative UK government, which left office in 2024, hadn't tried
to pull apart the Equality Act to remove rights from trans people.

There's an adage in the queer community that it gets better.

Whilst, over the past decade, I have become far more confident in my identity as a queer person, I have also become more scared, more furious. When I came out, it was 2012. Summer had brought the Olympic spirit to the UK, and with it, a sense of community, conviviality and hope. I was picking my GCSE options and trying to survive the ruthless day-to-day antics of an all-girls school, knowing that I was probably gay, that it would come out or I would come out and then – potentially – everything would change forever. The uncertainty of it all was crushing but, in general, I felt relatively safe.

I wasn't aware of it as a teenager, but back then, in 2012, I had the privilege of living in the country ranked top in Europe for its support of LGBTQ+ people. The Rainbow Map and Index is a study released each year by ILGA (the International Lesbian, Gay, Bisexual, Trans, and Intersex Association), which tracks the 'legal and policy' situation of all forty-nine European nations as they pertain to LGBTQ+ rights.[5] Until 2015, the UK was considered one of the most progressive in terms of the rights, protections and freedoms for queer people.[6] Since then, the UK has plummeted to seventeenth place at the time of writing. Whilst the ranking of countries in a comparative way risks positioning some countries as 'good' and others as 'bad', whereas the reality is usually far more nuanced, it's a useful tool for visualizing what many of us have felt deep in our bones: the sheer severity of the decline in LGBTQ+ equality in the UK and, most alarmingly, how rapidly it has happened. Hate crimes on the basis of sexuality have gone up by over 112% in just the last five years alone, and a staggering 186% for trans people.[7]

Whilst writing this book, I have spoken to hundreds of people – both within the UK and around the globe – about the advancement of LGBTQ+ equality and the threats to that progress. Broadly, I have found they fall into one of three groups.

There are people who believe that LGBTQ+ equality has gone too far, that we have it too good. Anti-LGBTQ+ sentiment exists on a spectrum and I have spoken to people all along it. I have been told by strangers that I – as a queer woman who supports trans rights –

am a predator, enabling child sex abuse. I have been told that people like me are responsible for the decline of our great nation. Frankly, I'm amazed they think LGBTQ+ people have that kind of power. It certainly doesn't feel like it.

Secondly, there are those who feel we are on a positive trajectory, that things are better than they used to be for LGBTQ+ people. These are people like Geoff, the queer housing innovator we will meet later, who was alive when homosexuality was still a criminal offence, and who lived through the AIDS crisis. This generation remembers a time when there were not only no legal protections but active persecution by the state and a public hatred of LGBTQ+ people. Comparatively, LGBTQ+ equality seems to be on an upward swing. I can't help thinking that, because of what they went through, they have come to accept a more marginalized experience.

Then there is the third group, people like Charlie, who we'll also meet later, who are keeping up to date with the latest information and are terrified about the trajectory we are on. They are scared for their safety. They are working out how they could get out of the UK if they ever needed to. They are stockpiling medications. Sometimes, they are accused of exaggerating the situation, the risks to their safety, security and dignity.

But it is not hyperbolic to say that the UK is *not* a safe place for LGBTQ+ people and particularly for those who are trans, non-binary or gender non-conforming. Granted, we do have some legal protections that other countries do not, but those protections are far from the whole story, and the notion that the UK is a global leader on LGBTQ+ equality is untrue and out of date.

The findings of ILGA Europe's report were echoed by the UN. Victor Madrigal-Borloz is the UN's independent expert on protection against violent discrimination based on sexual orientation and gender identity. In spring 2023, the UN undertook their first visit to the UK, in order to assess how LGBTQ+ rights were progressing.[8] The outcome was a damning indictment of the actions – and in-actions – of government, law enforcement and media. Not only was

Madrigal-Borloz alarmed at the immense surge in hate crimes, threats, harassment and anti-LGBTQ+ incidents, he noted that these could be 'attributed – by a wide range of stakeholders – to the toxic nature of the public debate surrounding sexual orientation and gender identity'. Madrigal-Borloz warned that these developments could endanger the very significant achievements, built over decades, that the UK has made to address violence and discrimination.

The UK must relinquish the idea that it is a safe, welcoming and progressive place for LGBTQ+ people. That narrative has lulled us into a place of complacency and inaction.

We must also recognize that the rise in anti-LGBTQ+ sentiment hasn't occurred in a vacuum. It's happened alongside the escalating vilification of migrants and particularly of refugees. It's happened alongside growing rates of religious hate crime.[9] And it's happened at a time when the NPCC reported that they expect nearly all forms of violence against women and girls to continue to rise.[10]

It has also come at the same time that the police have been given unprecedented powers under the Police, Crime, Sentencing and Courts Act 2022, resulting in protests and even just the potential for disruption being criminalized.[11] Peaceful protestors have found themselves detained and arrested simply for exercising their democratic rights to protest and even, in one instance, for unknowingly being stood next to protestors at the coronation of King Charles.[12]

Around the world, we are witnessing the active erasure of people and communities that have always existed. In the UK, we are seeing organizations that support LGBTQ+ people having their existence threatened. Human rights have been turned into topics of debate for the media in an epidemic of violent hate crime. In the US, even prior to the re-election of Donald Trump in 2024, families were fleeing to states[13] that are marginally safer for fear of losing their children – to suicide, to a lack of healthcare, or because authorities are being empowered to remove children from trans-supportive parents.[14] The re-election of convicted felon Donald Trump as President of the United States in 2024 struck terror into the hearts of LGBTQ+

people once again; not just because Trump has threatened to remove employment protections for LGBTQ+ people, ban trans healthcare and ban trans people from sports but because a large part of Trump's campaign platform was centred on attacking trans and queer people, yet millions of people voted him into power. In Italy, the induction of a far-right leader has created a hostile environment in which immigrants are presented as the threat from the outside and LGBTQ+ people are the threat from within.[15] In Uganda, there is a move to strengthen anti-LGBTQ+ laws in such a way that to even identify as an LGBTQ+ person is a crime.[16] In Ghana, a bill has been approved (though not yet entered into law) which would criminalize showing allyship to LGBTQ+ people.[17] As LGBTQ+ people, we might have some protections, we might have some freedoms, but we are nowhere near equal.

This is not to say there are not thriving LGBTQ+ communities doing incredible work in all of these places, or that they are not working hard enough. The truth is LGBTQ+ people statistically make up a small portion of the population.[18] But, as this book will show, the rights of LGBTQ+ people are deeply intertwined with the rights, freedoms and protections of everyone. Violence never operates in a vacuum.[19]

This book will be published less than a year after a new Labour government has come to power. Although there was reason to be optimistic about a left-leaning government, as these have often been more supportive of LGBTQ+ rights than their right-wing counterparts, the first acts of Keir Starmer's government have been to sustain the Conservative attacks on trans people. Indeed, the week of his landslide election, Starmer took the opportunity to condemn the existence of trans women in women's spaces (even with a Gender Recognition Certificate), a right they have had for twenty years. Upon election, Labour extended the puberty blocker ban for trans young people and refused to repeal proposed plans to limit discussion of LGBTQ+ topics in the classroom. And, on the day that much of the world was looking at the US and the election of Trump,

Labour secretly extended this ban further all whilst Keir Starmer welcomed in Trump as President, allying himself with a leader who was declared by his own Chief of Staff to be 'the general definition of a fascist'.

Our allies must not get complacent. Complacency is not only killing LGBTQ+ people, but it harms everyone. You ignore our plight at your peril. As we have seen repeatedly, the violence experienced by LGBTQ+ people never operates on its own – it goes hand in hand with attacks on reproductive rights, violence against women, white supremacy, anti-immigration rhetoric and entrenched ableism.[20]

I never expected to write such a political or, indeed, angry book. Then again, over the course of writing the book, I didn't expect to attend so many funerals for young LGBTQ+ people who deserved so much more than the world gave them either.

This book is not intended as a comprehensive guide to everything ever experienced by LGBTQ+ people, or to go over every battle ever faced or fought. It's a snapshot of where we are and, hopefully, where we can go. I wanted to write a book you could give to someone who is compassionate and curious but doesn't know enough. I wanted to write a book for the LGBTQ+ people who know and feel that something is wrong, but don't have the details at their fingertips. I want this book to help us work together. I wanted to write a book a queer kid can give to a parent to help them understand some of the things affecting them.

The topics in this book will affect people you know and love. That is certain.

The real question is whether you can find the courage to step up and do something to help. It has never been more urgent.

# CHAPTER I
# The Marriage Equality Myth

The first time I came out to my brother, I was wearing Lycra hot pants, fishnets and gaudy red lipstick. I had been prancing around the house singing songs from *Cabaret*, making particularly sure to sing the original show tunes and not – as I had become accustomed to doing – the *Glee* soundtrack cover versions. Despite having been out for months, my parents had asked me to not tell him that I was gay, in case he shared it more publicly than I was comfortable with. Some might wonder if coming out as gay was wholly necessary given the campness of the affair, but my brother was only eleven years old and not necessarily au fait with queer culture.

Mum was hanging out the washing, taking her time to carefully match the pegs by colour, just so. The early evening had brought little reprieve from the scorching summer heat. I bounded outside into the garden. 'Mum! Mum! I can get married.' She looked baffled.

The Marriage (Same Sex Couples) Act passed and the law was going to be amended. For the first time in the UK, same sex couples would be able to marry, as opposed to only taking part in civil partnerships. One day, I would be able to get married, if I wanted to. I was giddy, filled with a sense of joy and excitement I didn't know it was possible to feel about the world. I suspect if I hadn't been needed in the school production later that day, I would have spent the rest of it twirling around the garden, high and exuberant.

## Background to the Act

The year was 2013. Just decades earlier, the possibility of same sex marriage equality would have been inconceivable; it was only in 1967 that the Sexual Offences Act had decriminalized sex acts between men in England and Wales, albeit with a higher age of consent than for heterosexual couples, an exemption within the armed forces and merchant navy and the proviso that any acts could only take place in private.[1] It was only in 2003, the year I began primary school, that Section 28 – a law which prohibited the mentioning of LGBTQ+ people in classrooms – was repealed in England.[2]

A year later – 2004 – the Civil Partnership Bill was entered into the House of Lords.[3] The bill was announced by Jacqui Smith, Deputy Minister for Women and Equality, as opening 'the way to respect, recognition and justice for those who have been denied it for too long'. She continued: 'Same-sex couples often face a range of unnecessary problems in their everyday lives because of a lack of legal recognition in their relationships. The Civil Partnership Bill aims to eradicate this by providing same sex couples with the oppor-tunity to gain recognition of their relationship for the first time.'[4]

## Why the Marriage Act Is Important

It wasn't just recognition that the Civil Partnership Act provided, but protections which many LGBTQ+ people had been forced to live without. During the AIDS crisis of the 1980s, LGBTQ+ people were unable to make medical decisions on behalf of their partners or to have inheritance rights.[5] And whilst civil partnerships were far from perfect, they made a world of difference to those people denied the opportunity to be at the bedside of their partners, and to those who died alone because hospitals denied visitation to anyone considered 'not family'.[6]

There's an adage in my part of the LGBTQ+ community: lots done, lots still to do. Because, whilst they did grant similar rights, civil partnerships *weren't* marriage and there was much contention over whether they were sufficient. In June 2009, an opinion poll for *The Times* found that 61% of the public believed that 'gay couples should have an equal right to get married, not just to have civil partnerships'.[7]

Leadership at key campaign groups, including Stonewall, did not have marriage equality on their agendas, a fact which drew widespread criticisms, including from one of the organization's most high-profile co-founders, Sir Ian McKellen.[8] It took until 2010 for Stonewall to announce their support for same sex marriage.[9]

That year's general election made same sex marriage equality a campaign issue and, with every vote counting, politicians had to step up and show their support for LGBTQ+ people or risk losing votes. 'If the Conservatives and Liberals can get together in a national coalition and settle their differences, I don't see why you can't have gay marriage,' noted future prime minister Boris Johnson.

But there was significant contention over whether same sex marriage should be allowed in the UK, or whether civil partnerships were enough. Whilst there are innumerable issues with the historical institution of marriage and many still choose to have civil partnerships in light of this fact, the very existence of civil partnerships provided a convenient way for those who didn't really support LGBTQ+ people to claim they believed in their right to marry. Even UKIP, one of the UK's further right political parties at that time, ostensibly supported LGBTQ+ people's right to wed, but claimed that no action was needed because the right was already essentially there, in the form of civil partnerships, a right which they respected.[10]

Just a few months later, in October 2010, campaigner Peter Tatchell launched his 'Equal Love' campaign – a resurrection of a campaign originally attempted in 1992 – to file an appeal to the European Court of Human Rights in a bid to end sexual orientation discrimination in marriage and partnership law. To emphasize the difference in treatment of couples on the grounds of sexual orientation, during November and December, eight couples attempted to file applications at their local registry offices. The four same sex couples attempted to apply for civil marriages, and the four heterosexual couples applied for civil partnerships. All couples were denied: it was clear that civil partnerships and marriage were enforcing a policy akin to 'separate but equal'.[11]

The concept of the campaign was clever, and it resonated with the public; not everyone would necessarily know or be close to an LGBTQ+ person, but hopefully, everyone knows what it is to need love. One of the things people so often get wrong about changes to the law is that they feel it paves the way for cultural shifts. In reality, no politician will ever support changes that risk losing them votes and no government will ever support something that risks losing them power. The people – the electorate – have to be on-side first, and to be vocal about their support.

David Cameron's decision to support same sex marriage surprised me, but not as much as it surprised and infuriated many of his own MPs and party members. Bob Stewart, MP for Beckenham, asked in the House of Commons for an explanation of 'why the government is so hell-bent on upsetting so many thousands of our citizens in normal marriages at this time'.[12] For David Cameron to be willing to split his party in an election year for something which seemed inconsequential to the lives of many of those with conservative values is incredibly revealing.[13] Supporting same sex marriage, at a time when Conservative austerity had caused devastation within towns and cities across the UK and detriment to the most vulnerable, allowed the party to seem socially conscious and for the people.[14] In part, same sex marriage equality became a way for David Cameron to appeal to those who might have been expected to vote Labour or Liberal Democrat: a facade of inclusion. Years later, the Conservative Party still use the argument that they enacted same sex marriage as indicative of their support of LGBTQ+ people, despite their policies actively causing us harm.

Despite the protestations of many, the Marriage Equality Bill[15] was passed in the Commons with 400 ayes and 175 noes. It was later given Royal Assent and, in 2014, the first same sex couples were able to marry in the UK.

## Joy

What followed were widespread celebrations and parties. Stephen Fry narrated one of the earliest same sex weddings – incidentally musical-themed – when it was recorded for the television show *Our Gay Wedding: The Musical*. Elton John and David Furnish soon announced they would marry, despite having been in a civil partnership for nearly a decade. 'Having our civil partnership was an incredible breakthrough for people that have campaigned for a long time – through the '60s and the '50s in England when it was so hard to be gay and hard to be open about it,' said Elton on NBC's *Today Show*. 'And it was a criminal act.' He continued, 'So for this legislation to come through is joyous, and we should celebrate it. We shouldn't just say, "Oh, well we have a civil partnership. We're not going to bother to get married." We will get married.'[16]

I'll never forget the spring and summer of 2014 and seeing – for the first time – photos in the press of women getting married. I had assumed I would never get married, that it simply was not an option for me. Once, aged twelve, my class were given homework in which we had to mood-board our ideal wedding, complete with our ideal husbands. Many of the girls chose pop stars. For the first time in my ridiculously studious life, I 'forgot' to do my homework. I could have lied, sure, but I felt deflated. It was just another reminder that my life would have restrictions and that these would only continue into adulthood. I think that was why I was so jubilant the day the bill passed: it was the tantalizing nature of the opportunity, not just to get married, but to not be restricted by the ways things were.

For the first time, I believed that change, that progress, was possible.

## Contentions

The topic of marriage has been contentious for a long time within the LGBTQ+ community. Of course, there are many who will see equating all aspects of LGBTQ+ life with marriage equality as both heteronormative and anti-feminist. But I've chosen to begin this book with a discussion around so-called marriage equality because it is a fantastic encapsulation of the challenges the LGBTQ+ community is facing *right now*: incomplete protections being enforced by a system that actively harms the most marginalized members of our community, combined with a huge swell of mainstream visibility.

In the 1970s, gay liberationist and feminist movements alike had worked to not only challenge restrictive gender norms but also highlight how marriage functioned as a patriarchal act of possessiveness which, more often than not, rendered women the property of their husbands. Some might see this as an archaic notion, but it was not until 1975 that women in the UK could open bank accounts or receive loans in their own names without the permission of their husbands.

Queer theorists have often argued that legalizing same sex marriage would serve only to uplift *some* LGBTQ+ people whilst marginalizing those already facing the most persecution – it legitimizes LGBTQ+ people, but it does so selectively.

From some corners of the LGBTQ+ community, there is a deep resentment of the pursuit of marriage equality, resentment which seems largely aimed at the marriage equality campaigns. In 2009, MJ Kaufman and Katie Miles published an essay online condemning the pursuit of gay marriage, which quickly went viral, even gaining the attention of the *New York Times*. As young queer people raised in queer families they felt deeply that, as many queer theorists before them had,[17] the pursuit of same sex marriage came at the cost of other changes to society LGBTQ+ people need. They called out the way the gay marriage movement conveniently seemed to forget about the plurality and diversity of queer people and queer activism and instead pushed narratives akin to assimilation: 'This agenda fractures our communities, pits us against natural allies, supports unequal power structures, obscures urgent queer concerns, abandons the struggle for mutual sustainability inside queer communities and disregards our awesome fabulous queer history.'[18, 19]

A year later, Kaufman issued an addendum to the essay, acknowledging that there was more nuance in the conversation. 'I see the impulse to ask the state to validate your family and the impulse to ask for a more expansive solution as two sides of the same coin.' Keef and Deeg, members of the radical queer collective LA GAI, summarized it best: 'Of course, we too will be fighting to defeat the anti-queer marriage amendments. How can we not? But we resent having to do it, and we will not allow it to distract us from our real needs: equality, justice, self-determination and self-actualization for ALL.'[20]

## Some Marriages Are More Equal than Others

Some might argue that marriage equality does deliver on at least one of those needs and is, surely, a type of equality. Except, in the UK, we have never actually had marriage equality. Neither has the United States nor Argentina, Australia, Austria, Belgium, Brazil or Canada; the list goes on – almost every single country that describes itself as having marriage equality is misrepresenting reality. What they do have is *same sex marriage*, and that is distinctly different from *marriage equality*. When we use the term *marriage equality* to mean *same sex marriage*, we exclude the reality of two significant demographics within the LGBTQ+ community: transgender people and disabled people.

Given the visibility of the same sex marriage campaign in England, Wales and Scotland, one might imagine strong awareness of this fact. Yet, when I tell people about it, even conscientious, politically aware people, they're often shocked, baffled and appalled.

The visibility of the same sex marriage campaign might have made some difference in changing hearts and minds on the topic of queer people, but it left behind some of those who have been at the forefront of the LGBTQ+ movement.

You would assume transgender people are able to get married just like anybody else. However, in the UK, trans people are required to be married under their birth sex unless they apply for a Gender Recognition Certificate (GRC).[21] GRCs are crucial for many trans people, as having one means that they can have their gender legally recognized and stated on their birth certificate.[22] Marriages are dependent on birth certificates whereas, for example, passports are not. It doesn't matter who you are as an adult when you marry, just what a piece of paper says you were at just a few days old.

Despite the UK government estimating there to be between 200,000 and 500,000 transgender people living in the UK,[23] as of 2020, sixteen years after the Gender Recognition Act of 2004, fewer than six thousand people had successfully gained a GRC.[24] This is not – as many anti-trans voices would argue – because those claiming to be trans are not trans, it is because the process of obtaining a GRC is expensive and arbitrary and requires proving your identity to a panel of people who have never met you before. Many transgender people have been denied GRCs, despite undergoing invasive and expensive medical procedures.

There have been proposals to make relatively straightforward reforms to the Gender Recognition Act in recent years: removing the need for doctors to be arbiters of identity, simplifying the process and removing or significantly reducing the fee. These simple reforms have been met with widespread hysteria fuelled by the transphobic narrative that without a medical diagnosis and gatekeeping of identity, cisgender women will become the target of predators.

Over thirty regions and states around the world allow gender recognition based on self-declaration, including Ireland, which made this change in 2015 – allowing trans people to exist without bureaucracy. As a result of these changes, there has been no evidence of increased harm to women caused by trans people.[25]

It is worth noting that, in 2023, the UK removed Ireland along with many other countries, including New Zealand, Belgium, the Netherlands and some US states, from the list of countries it would accept GRCs from. Failure to recognize these GRCs is tantamount to a travel ban for many trans people.[26] It did, however, add countries including Kazakhstan, where trans people must be forcibly sterilized, China, where families and HR departments must approve of a person's transition, and countries like Iran and Sri Lanka, where parents must approve of a person's transition. The approaches to trans people in all these regions have been condemned by human rights organizations across the globe.[27]

In 2023, the Scottish Parliament voted in favour of making the process of gender recognition easier for trans people through the Gender Recognition Reform (Scotland) Bill by a majority of eighty-six to thirty-nine. This was a government-sponsored bill, opposed by just nine members of the SNP. Within a month, the UK government used an extraordinary power – Section 35 – to overrule the Scottish government. This was the first time such a power had ever been used in the history of the devolved nations and set an alarming precedent that if individual nations wanted to make improvements for LGBTQ+ people, the UK government could – and would – overrule them. Although the initial legal challenge failed, the Scottish government has stated its commitment to fighting the Section 35 order.[28]

As the author of *Yes, You Are Trans Enough*, Mia Violet, wrote in 2018: 'The real reason I'm not married right now is that I'm not allowed to be a bride. I'm a transgender woman, but my marriage certificate would list me as a husband, and the ceremony would misgender me as male. Despite my passport correctly listing my gender as female and the fact I started my transition over five years ago, I'm not permitted to become my fiancé's wife.'[29]

Even if you can get a GRC, the UK does not currently recognize non-binary people, and campaigns to recognize non-binary genders have been blocked. As a result, non-binary people also face challenges to getting married. Of course, this has not stopped everyone.[30]

Filmmakers and founders of *My Genderation*, a film and resource project that celebrates trans lives and trans experiences, Fox and Owl Fisher held a protest wedding – a mock ceremony with traditional elements.[31] The couple then began conducting an informal survey of non-binary people to find out whether many were interested in marrying one day. The responses were stark, with person after person saying they were upset by the fact they couldn't legally marry as themselves or that they had put their wedding on hold until non-binary people like them could be legally recognized.

'Owl and I know that marriage is not the biggest issue facing people like us, but the fact that we can't get married highlights how the lack of legal gender recognition stops us from participating in society in the same way as others,' wrote Fox. 'It doesn't really matter whether or not non-binary people want to get married; the fact remains that everyone should have the right to.'[32]

It's not just LGBTQ+ people who are affected by bureaucracy such as this; in the UK, disabled people who marry or indeed cohabit can lose essential income in the form of benefits, income which quite literally ensures they are able to live life. An assumption is made that a disabled person's partner would become financially responsible for them, were they to marry or live together. Given the high rates of disability in the LGBTQ+ community and – as explored later on – the high levels of poor health outcomes and poor mental health, the reality is that there are LGBTQ+ people still unable to marry. Given the fight for legal recognition of LGBTQ+ relationships was advanced by the AIDS crisis, it is particularly damning that we have left behind the community we endeavoured to create safety for.

## Marriage Woes

But what about when a marriage *doesn't* work out, or faces difficulties? Until the creation of no-fault divorces in 2022, there was no recognition of a same sex affair as adultery under the law.[33] This meant that, for eight years, even though same sex marriage was legal, without equal legal options in divorce, there was no equality. UK divorce law reduced people to their genitals and viewed adultery as only being possible when both a penis and a vagina were involved. Again, there has been no consideration for how this definition impacts transgender people and there is very little research available.

Section 12 of the Matrimonial Causes Act 1973 still requires transgender people with a GRC to disclose their 'gender history' to the person they are marrying.[34] Failure to do so can result in the annulment of the marriage. There will be many who feel it is essential that any transgender person discloses that they are transgender before marriage, seeing a person's experience as of essential importance but there are, as far as I can tell, no other lived experiences a person is forced to disclose to their partner before marriage. After all, the right to privacy is something which is enshrined in human rights laws, and it does not seem right to have one rule for trans people and one rule for other groups.[35]

Furthermore, there exists in the law a 'spousal veto',[36] which allows partners to prevent the legal transition of their spouse. There is an argument often made by anti-trans organizations that trans people are forcing cisgender people into relationships. This isn't the case, but what is the case is that (often cisgender) partners are able to control the legally recognized gender of a trans person they are married or civilly partnered to. This veto is intended to 'give a spouse a say in the future of the marriage' but in practice, it gives a spouse control over the autonomy and freedom of their trans partner. It does not take much imagination to consider how that might be used to abuse a partner.

## When Your Life Is Up for 'Debate'

I came out for the first time eight months before same sex marriage became legal in England. Alongside the relentless bullying I received, the soundtrack to those early months was constant debates about what I thought were fundamental rights. Just six weeks before the amendment was passed, there was a serious attempt to eradicate the same sex marriage bill in the House of Lords.[37] Whilst my friends were in the playground, I was on a computer in the library, listening to men in suits – and yes, it was predominantly men – talk about how letting people like me get married would be like enabling incest, polygamy, bestiality and lots of other words I didn't really understand but were said with such a tone of disgust. The impact of hearing that is something I have only begun to process more than a decade on. It was impossible to turn on the radio or open the papers and not see something derogatory about people like me. I was just a child, but the messages I received were clear: you are immoral, disgusting, perverted and predatory. These are the same arguments being employed today. Whilst marriage equality might have had a substantial impact on raising the profile of LGBTQ+ issues, visibility itself is a double-edged sword.

What's notable to me, on reflection, is that when same sex marriage equality was no longer a debate but a fact of law, a vacuum was created: something had to be the subject of tabloid furore whilst the rest of our rainy isle was celebrating. Gay people could not so easily be attacked and undermined when their rights, and more importantly legal protections, were enshrined in law. But transgender people? They were far less supported by people – or the law – in the UK at that time.

The result? Anti-trans rhetoric spread beyond the hard right-wing, beyond the right-wing journalists into every media outlet.

In the UK, we have seen – and continue to see – an obsessive focus in both mainstream and alternative news outlets on the 'debate' of trans rights to the extent we are now known internationally as 'TERF Island'.[38] The homophobic arguments employed in anti-same sex marriage debates are being used a decade later, only now it is trans rights being called into question. Even the former Equalities Minister and current leader of the Conservative Party Kemi Badenoch – who was instrumental in organizing anti-trans changes – has mocked marriage equality. In a leaked recording from 2018, *Vice* reported that Kemi said: 'It's not even about sexuality now, it's now like the whole transgender movement, where, OK well we've got gay marriage, and civil partnerships, so what are transsexuals looking for?'[39] Transsexual is a term that is largely considered outdated and offensive. For Badenoch, the inclusion of queer people is seen as a slippery slope, one that leads to the inclusion of trans people – people that, as Equalities Minister, she was supposed to represent the rights of. 'Now it's not just about being free to marry who you want, you now want to have men using women's bathrooms.'

'This evangelical kind of hysteria we are seeing about trans people is the same thing – so obviously the same – as what was said about gay people in the '80s. It's just recycled homophobia,' Charlie Craggs, author and campaigner tells me. Trans people are being presented as malicious, violent predators when they are just trying to get on with their lives. They are estimated to make up less than 1% of the population in the UK,[40] and yet in 2020, *The Daily Telegraph* published over three hundred pieces about transgender people, almost all negative and none written by an actual trans person. Meanwhile, research by the Independent Press Standards Organisation found that in the UK, an average of thirty-four stories were published a month about trans people in the five years prior to April 2014 and that this figure jumped 418% to 176 per month between May 2014 and 2019.[41] The timing of this is significant: less than twelve months after same sex marriage legislation was passed and our rights solidified, there was a surge in coverage of trans people in the press. This was no coincidence.

For those with conservative viewpoints, particularly religious conservatives, they had suddenly lost a position of strength when same sex marriage was legalized and had to find a new target for their vitriol. No more campaigning – either for or against – was needed and this created a gap. Coalitions of all sorts of different people had come together in favour of same sex marriage, and support for queer rights more broadly had been strengthened; opinions had shifted, demographics changed, and whilst conservatism was far from minoritized, conservatives felt as though their rights were being infringed upon. This is evidenced by the pursuit of religious exemptions.

Author and journalist Sasha Issenberg summarized it beautifully: 'because of [the success of same sex marriage campaigns], many of those activists had already begun to move to an area where they still had strength, where the public opinion looked a lot more like it did around gay marriage twenty years ago – which is trans issues. And so they basically said, "We have lost the gay marriage fight, but we have this nearby place where we can manufacture conflict from a position of strength." And many of the same institutions that had been fighting over gay marriage all of a sudden just started fighting over issues related to transgender people.'[42]

## The Visibility Issue

Trans people are not a new phenomenon; however, trans visibility has substantially grown. Since the 1970s, there has been a steady increase in the number of trans people we see in the media owing to high-profile individuals coming out or, as is unfortunately often the case, being outed.[43]

Film and television previously painted those who cross-dressed or whose gender was non-conforming as being sick, twisted and perverted. More recently, we've seen some more positive reactions. Hollywood celebrities, including Elliot Page and Laverne Cox, have been lauded for being out as transgender people – both featuring on

the front cover of *TIME* magazine.[44] Trans and non-binary characters not only exist in some shows and films but are slowly becoming
more than just plot points or trauma porn, a phrase used to describe
the representation or consumption of traumatic experiences which
feels exploitative or sensationalized. Visibility is positioned as a positive, and it is in many ways. However, we must reconcile ourselves
with the truth: visibility on its own will not bring about change.

Author and activist Sarah Schulman described how, during the
same sex marriage debate in the US, the disconnect between queer
people and their allies intensified: 'While some gay communities are
angry, frightened, alienated and hurt by these political events,
straight progressives are barely aware that any of this has happened.'[45]
And that is the fundamental issue: visibility is all a matter of
perspective. If you are a person who is constantly facing barriers,
seeing people with whom you identify be maligned in person,
online and in the press, you understand the immense pressure you
are under, feeling like your every move is being watched. If, however,
the rights of LGBTQ+ people are simply one issue of many you hear
about, that effect is lessened.  In the UK, I feel we have a particular
responsibility to support the fight for marriage equality and the
decriminalization of homosexuality across the world; British penal
codes were introduced in many countries during colonial times and
still have devastating effects on the lives of LGBTQ+ people – criminalizing their very existences. We might have made huge steps
towards marriage equality – but we must continue to advocate in
this country and support those across the world fighting regressive
laws we, as a nation, implemented.

A decade after it passed, the same sex marriage campaign in
England and Wales haunts me and my work. I have seen how the
passing of same sex marriage legislation has contributed to the
complacency of our so-called allies. 'But you can get married' has
become a catchphrase of sorts, a way to curtail discussions about the
barriers LGBTQ+ people are facing. Same sex marriage has also
become a barometer for how accepting of diversity a country is:

many consider the UK to be safe and tolerant, even though the government has deported asylum seekers, undermined global human rights laws and denied the right to protest. Andrew Wale and Neil Allard, one of the first same sex couples to be married, were interviewed a decade on from marriage equality and their conclusion was similar. Progress had 'reversed a bit'.[46] Recounting the way he was abused in the streets for being gay, Allard said, 'The way they shouted at me and used a funny slur reminded me of being in the '70s. I was just a bit shocked. It still happens.'

There are some within the LGBTQ+ community who find it difficult to reconcile the fact our fight for freedom, inclusion and equity is reliant on our allies because they want to believe that we are strong and capable – and we are. But, in the world we currently live in, the LGBTQ+ community, and particularly those of us who are able to be out and vocal, are a minority, albeit a growing one. History has demonstrated that it is only when those outside of a marginalized group get involved that progress is made, right or wrong though that may be. LGBTQ+ people are not in the majority anywhere, and we are rarely the decision-makers. We need our allies to be active, understand the barriers we face and commit to change, and not just for the types of campaigns that are most palatable.

## And What You Can Do About It

→   Find out what marriage equality provisions exist where you live.
    Are same sex couples permitted to get married? What provi-
    sions are there for transgender people? Are there any religious
    exclusions? Every nation has its legislation around marriage
    equality, with additional variation by state or county. The
    International Lesbian, Gay, Bisexual, Trans, and Intersex
    Association (ILGA) provides a substantial overview of the legal
    protections and limitations in many parts of the world and is
    therefore a good place to start. The Human Rights Campaign
    also tracks upcoming developments in marriage equality laws,
    both positive and negative, on a global level.

→   If it is safe for you to do so, be vocal about your support for
    marriage equality and LGBTQ+ people more broadly. Within the
    Australian Marriage Equality campaign, research demonstrated
    that the most effective messaging came not from LGBTQ+
    rights campaigners, but from predominantly straight parents,
    grandparents and other allies.

→   Support campaigns around GRC reform that ensure trans
    people are able to get the necessary paperwork with ease. In
    recent years, we've seen a number of instances of consult-
    ations being issued to better understand what all people think
    about different areas of trans life, including GRCs, and many
    anti-trans campaigners have organized around this, providing
    targeted responses. Take the time to learn from trans people
    and organizations that support them how to fill out these
    consultations and encourage those around you to do the same.
    You could also consider volunteering for or supporting organ-
    izations like the Trans Legal Clinic, which support trans people
    to get their relevant documents.

# Putting in the Work

## Chantelle Day (she/her)

Chantelle Day is a prominent figure in the fight for marriage equality in the Cayman Islands, one of fourteen British Overseas Territories. Day, alongside her partner, Vickie Bodden Bush, made history by challenging the Cayman Islands' ban on same sex marriage after their application for a marriage licence was denied in 2018. The denial prompted them to take their case to the Grand Court of the Cayman Islands. In March 2019, the Grand Court ruled in favour of Day and Bodden Bush, declaring the ban on same sex marriage unconstitutional and ordering the government to amend the law accordingly. This landmark ruling was a significant victory for LGBTQ+ rights in the Cayman Islands, reflecting the principles of equality and non-discrimination.

However, the victory was short-lived. The Cayman Islands government appealed the decision, and in November 2019, the Court of Appeal overturned the ruling, reinstating the ban on same sex marriage. Despite this setback, Day's courageous fight has galvanized support for marriage equality and highlighted the ongoing struggle for LGBTQ+ rights in British Overseas Territories. Her advocacy continues to inspire many within the LGBTQ+ community and beyond, emphasizing the importance of persistence and resilience in the fight for equal rights

## John O'Doherty (he/him)

John O'Doherty is a leading LGBTQ+ rights activist and the founder of the Love Equality campaign in Northern Ireland. Same sex marriage equality came to Northern Ireland much later than the rest of the UK – passing into law in 2019 and coming into effect in 2020. For nearly fifteen years, O'Doherty was the director of The Rainbow Project, Northern Ireland's largest LGBTQ+ organization. In 2016, a coalition of organizations, including The Rainbow Project, Amnesty International, Irish Congress of Trade Unions and other advocacy groups, began the Love Equality campaign in a bid to get marriage equality in Northern Ireland. Under O'Doherty's leadership, the campaign mobilized public support, organized rallies and lobbied politicians to press for legislative change. In October 2019, their persistent efforts paid off when the UK government extended marriage equality to Northern Ireland, following the collapse of the devolved government at Stormont.

## Peter Tatchell (he/him)

Peter Tatchell is a founding member of the Gay Liberation Front, direct action group OutRage! and co-creator of the Equal Love campaign.

Tatchell's advocacy for marriage equality has been a significant part of his career. He argued that the exclusion of same sex couples from the institution of marriage was a form of discrimination that needed to be rectified. Through various campaigns, public demonstrations and legal challenges, Tatchell and his peers attempted to change public perception and push for legislative reform. The Equal Love campaign, which aimed to secure legal recognition for both same sex marriages and opposite-sex civil partnerships in the UK, was one of his most notable contributions to the fight for same sex marriage equality.

Although same sex marriage passed into law in England, Wales and Scotland in 2013, Tatchell has continued to campaign around the inequalities faced by LGBTQ+ people trying to get married, including discrimination faced in divorce, limitations on religious services and the barriers faced by transgender people.

# CHAPTER 2
# Home Sweet Home?

## Housing Crisis

One in five LGBTQ+ people have experienced homelessness at some point in their lives, rising to one in four for trans people.[1] For comparison, across England in 2023, around 309,000 people were experiencing homelessness,[2] equating to around 0.5% of the population. That's the closest comparison we can find: data is rarely collected about those who have *ever* been homeless when it comes to the wider population.

These statistics are shocking, but they exist within the context of a much larger issue. That there is a housing crisis in the UK comes as no surprise to anyone. In London, the typical cost of renting has increased by £559 a month in just four years, between 2019 and 2023,[3] yet wages have stagnated and inflation increased. More concerning is the way housing insecurity is not just part of the system but that its absence is treated as a luxury. To have a safe home you can afford has become a rarity, and even then, the anxiety of becoming homeless is ever present, with half of private renters in England being 'one pay cheque' away from losing their homes.[4] This is unsurprising, given that 11.3 million people spend more than 40% of their household income on their homes – more than any other country in Europe.[5]

You need only look at escalating rents, the number of people sleeping rough and the even greater number of precarious or outright unsafe housing situations people find themselves in through no fault of their own. According to the charity Shelter in 2021, one in three adults in the UK, or 17.5 million people, were impacted by the housing emergency – and that is to say nothing of the children and adolescents struggling with the same problem.[6]

For LGBTQ+ people, finding safe housing is even more of a challenge and homelessness even more of a risk. Nearly one in five LGBTQ+ private renters have experienced discrimination from a landlord or a letting agency because of their gender identity or sexuality.[7] The same survey found that 43% of LGBTQ+ respondents had been forced to live in unsuitable accommodation which was affecting their health, compared to just 29% of non-LGBTQ+ respondents. They were more likely to be living in houses impacted by dampness and mould, with 11% more LGBTQ+ respondents struggling to get repairs completed by landlords and letting agents than their non-LGBTQ+ counterparts.

These are not issues specific just to LGBTQ+ people – in the UK, three in four renters report being afraid to ask for repairs of any kind because some private landlords take steps to evict tenants who dare to request them.[8] This is perfectly legal behaviour on behalf of landlords, and whilst there are proposed changes under a Renters (Reform) Bill, this is not law yet at the time of writing. In the UK – with no reason given – private renters can be evicted and given just eight weeks to pack up and move out, though many landlords demand (illegally) an even faster egress.[9] And, if you feel your landlord has discriminated against you based on your gender or sexuality, there is very little you can do about it because, in reality, no one controls the landlords and no one protects the tenants from exploitation. Repairs to a property often involve being visited by either the landlord directly or a tradesperson; there is no requirement to be out to your landlord, and having that realization occur – that a tenant is an LGBTQ+ person – whilst standing in their home, can be genuinely dangerous. There is no guarantee that these landlords will be inclusive or tolerant of LGBTQ+ people. Whilst some LGBTQ+ people's gender or sexuality might be less obvious, hiding it is not always an option and, frankly, nor should it be.

Recently, I found a local electrician who advertised himself as specifically LGBTQ+ friendly (as well as anti-racist, feminist and mental health aware) and was struck by how unusual that was – I had never seen a contractor, outside those at specific organizations built on inclusion – be as clear as that about their values. 'I don't want anyone to feel like they might be unsafe or can't be who they are in their own home,' he told me, whilst checking the heating element in my shower. 'It's about respect and dignity. It shouldn't be hard.' It made a real difference, not only to me wanting to employ him in the first place but also to my feeling of safety when he visited.

## Power Imbalance

Max, a thirty-year-old transgender lesbian living in Brighton, tells me that, although their landlord knows that they are queer and trans, they still live in fear of losing their housing: 'It's so easy for him to make assumptions about me that could threaten my housing. We are seen as inherently unstable tenants who won't be able to pay rent on time or in the long term.' According to Max, this situation has worsened recently, even in one of the most accepting cities in the UK. 'It has become worse since the government has started talking about transgender people as having a mental illness.'

Research by Generation Rent and the Albert Kennedy Trust (now akt) also revealed the overt discrimination people faced.[10] One person explained: 'When searching for houses with my partner, houses seemed to disappear very quickly "because of other renters" but then remain on the market.'

Matt, twenty-eight, a non-binary queer person living in the West Midlands, has direct experience of housing discrimination. 'The first indicator that things might not be great with my flatmates – all of whom were nursing students – came when they'd been to a social event with a trans person who was living in the flat downstairs. They started saying horrible things about them and their gender presentation, not knowing about my identity. One of them turned to me and said some horrendously transphobic things, describing trans people as freakish, saying that a man can't be a woman and a woman can't be a man – Rishi Sunak could have taken it word for word.'

It was just the start of things to come for Matt.

'I was sexually active at the time and went and got tested. My HIV test came back with a mixed result, so I had to get tested again. I confided in one of the people I was living with that I was waiting on the repeated tests because of this mixed result. Word got around the flat and, after that, people would go silent when I entered a room. They would deep-clean and sanitize everything I'd touched. Remember, these are future nurses!'

The situation escalated rapidly: 'I came back after visiting family and overheard them shouting "faggot" and other slurs in the kitchen. A few days later – after they went out drinking – they came back and started shouting "fuck that faggot" and other nasty, homophobic things.'

Matt left that night, in their pyjamas and a hoodie, and thankfully was supported by a friend nearby. 'I expected some drama, especially living with students, some of whom were younger than me. But I wasn't expecting outright homophobia and transphobia, especially from nursing students, who should have known better both about LGBTQ+ people and about someone getting tested for HIV.'

As a result of that experience, Matt no longer shares much of their personal life with new people, especially the people they live with.

In a hypercompetitive market, and in a world where people are still biased against LGBTQ+ people, it is not an unreasonable leap to make that, whilst overt discrimination against LGBTQ+ people might be illegal, landlords can perpetuate housing inequality by just not taking on LGBTQ+ tenants. Particularly when the financial situation alone created by the hypercompetitive rental market is much more likely to exclude LGBTQ+ people, who are more likely to experience financial disparities, including being in insecure work, underemployed or underpaid.[11] In the private rental market, many people who are deemed 'risky' to rent to rely on having a guarantor – a wealthy person who is responsible for paying rent in the event you cannot. For most, this is a parent or family member – connections some young LGBTQ+ people don't have, especially if they've been ostracized from their families.

Offering over the asking price is now an expectation; it's not uncommon to see people offering to pay a year's rent up front, in cash, to secure a place to live. It's not just about money, either – several landlords require cover letters or interviews – akin to an audition process – to access what is a basic right. Research by Stonewall found that one in four trans people and one in five non-binary people had been discriminated against when looking for a flat to rent or buy.[12] The system leads to discrimination not only against LGBTQ+ people, but other minorities, too. Non-white British households are more than twice as likely to rent in the private sector than white British households, and more than half of migrant households are in the private sector, with research suggesting that people of colour and migrant renters are more commonly subjected to poor standards of living, overcrowding and abuse by landlords.[13] Not only does this result in even poorer experiences for LGBTQ+ people of colour and migrants, but it demonstrates the fundamental truth: everyone is harmed by poor housing but it is communities that have been historically and are presently marginalized and undermined that are impacted most.[14] Housing is a basic human right, not a luxury, but it is one that is easy to deny to people maligned in the media every day.

## The Safety ~~Net~~ Not

One of the more bizarre experiences I've had as a queer person living in London was sleeping tucked up next to people I had met only twice three years prior, and chatted to online, because they had nowhere else to go. For me, the LGBTQ+ community is about sharing what you have. In hindsight, it might not have been the safest approach, but in the absence of safety nets, what else are we to do? My then-acquaintance was forced to leave the flat they had rented because it was completely uninhabitable due to the flat crawling – quite literally – with mice, cockroaches and bedbugs. And that's not to mention the walls, which were more mould than paint. This was a tenancy secured through a so-called reputable letting agency, one with offices across the UK. Like many people moving to London for their first jobs, they had to agree to a tenancy without being able to see the property in person because they lived hundreds of miles away. The image of them shoving the food from their freezer into my own crammed drawers because they couldn't afford to replace it if it defrosted will stay with me forever.

Whether situations like this are because of corrupt letting agencies and landlords or families kicking a person out after they come out, the outcome – at least in the immediate term – is the same: LGBTQ+ people with nowhere to go. I don't want people I consider community put in harm's way if there are things I can do to help.

The cost-of-living crisis and lack of housing means that 30% of twenty-five- to twenty-nine-year-olds and 10% of thirty- to thirty-four-year-olds still live with their parents.[15] Whilst for some this is a genuine choice or there are other circumstances such as caring needs within the family, it's clear that many still live at 'home' because there's nowhere else to go. And this takes on a different nuance when it comes to LGBTQ+ community members, who may be being forced to live with parents or other family members who are not supportive because they simply have no other choice. Recent research by the charity Just Like Us revealed that almost half of young LGBTQ+ young adults are estranged from at least one family member and a third are not confident their parents or guardian will accept them as being LGBTQ+.[16]

## Structural Survey

There's a legitimate question to be raised about whether the housing available in the UK is structured correctly for LGBTQ+ people and the changing nature of the market more broadly. Many properties are designed – in theory – for a family in which two generations live together, but increasingly we are seeing a rise in intergenerational living and people not having children. I spoke to Amelia, a queer woman of twenty-seven from Plymouth, who told me that she rented what was advertised as a two-bedroom flat with a friend, only to be forced to leave because the second bedroom didn't meet legal requirements. The landlord had assumed that the pair were a queer couple, who would use the second room as an office space, as opposed to a second bedroom, and was too scared to ask about whether the pair were in a relationship together.

If you are new to or outside of the LGBTQ+ scene – which tends to be centered around cities, it can be particularly challenging to find safe housing because many queer houseshares and spare rooms are advertised through private WhatsApp groups, Facebook groups or other community forums.

Lynne Nicholls (she/her) is a social housing expert, part of First Brick, an LGBTQ+ housing group, and HouseProud, an LGBTQ+ housing network for people who work in the social housing sector. Social housing is housing rented from housing associations, cooperatives and councils and purports to provide eligible tenants with genuinely affordable places to live, secure long-term tenancies and protected rights. She's been instrumental in driving change, bringing together housing associations, local authorities, management organizations and care providers to talk about issues affecting LGBTQ+ tenants.

'We've been going for ten years now, and we have around fifty represented organizations from around the UK,' she tells me.

HouseProud[17] was responsible for the largest-ever study into the experiences of LGBTQ+ people in social housing, discovering in the process that 60% of trans people and a third of LGBTQ+ people did not feel safe in their neighbourhood.[18] Harassment from neighbours and, perhaps more significantly, the failures in addressing that harassment were also issues raised – a pattern seen across all types of housing. When she was a housing association chair, Lynne worked hard to make sure the board actually understood that they had an equality and diversity duty and that they had an equity, diversity and inclusion policy.

She says: 'I was also really proud that we created a residents board training, so residents could undergo training and sit on the board themselves.'

## Young, Free and Homeless

As we've seen, the lack of affordable housing in the private market or in social housing combined with a skyrocketing cost of living has resulted in an increasing number of people becoming homeless across the UK, with young people being particularly vulnerable. Of all homeless young people aged 16–25, just under a quarter are LGBTQ+,[19] compared to 3–5% of the general population. Of these young people, 77% believe coming out to their parents was the main reason they became homeless.[20] Young people in the UK are entitled to a lower minimum wage and are not entitled to housing benefits, which only exacerbates the problem.

When people think of homelessness, they tend to think of people sleeping rough in the street, but it is so much more than that. It's being forced to sofa surf; live in B&Bs, hostels or hotels; or stay in sheds and garages.[21]

Many people are forced to engage in survival sex. Quite literally what it sounds like: having sex with people to have somewhere to stay for a night, food or other essentials. Research by youth homelessness charity akt found that almost one in five LGBTQ+ young people aged 18–25 felt they had to have casual sex to find some-where to stay whilst they were homeless and that 16% of LGBTQ+ young people had engaged in sex work as a direct impact of their homelessness.[22]

There is a prevailing myth that you can tell if someone is experiencing homelessness, but many people hide it well and, even more, might not acknowledge themselves as being homeless in the first place. Most people couldn't imagine themselves becoming homeless, but, for many, only a few things need to come apart for them to fall through the cracks: a redundancy, an unexpected bill, an illness, a family member going into care, a sick child.

Whilst some LGBTQ+ people become homeless because of reasons related to their identity – for example, family abandonment or disapproval – there's a diverse range of reasons that someone might find themselves in this situation.

When I speak to Jordan (she/they), she is living in temporary accommodation in South East England. Jordan spent her teenage years in foster care, before being helped into supported accommodation. This past summer, whilst thousands flocked to the seaside town in which she lives, Jordan was grappling with a terrifying reality: turning twenty and, as such, ageing out of the care system. Although they had a job, it wasn't enough to keep a roof over their head. Jordan became homeless, with no family support to rely on and disabilities which prevented them from working full time.

'As a whole, my LGBTQ+ identity has not been a barrier in my housing, but this has been because I haven't disclosed it to anyone from housing, my social services team or my previous placement.' I ask her if it was a choice to hide her pansexuality, or whether it was something she felt she had to do. 'I have always been treated differently due to my disabilities, which is something I can't hide. My LGBTQ+ identity is something I can keep private, so I have, to prevent discrimination.'

Jordan has come to accept that to get support, they have to hide their LGBTQ+ identity – something which many LGBTQ+ people might not be able to do so easily. It is easy to understand, when Jordan explains the process of trying to get support and the sheer number of appointments, phone calls and forms to fill in, why they would not wish to add anything into the process which might be seen as a complication.

The process of declaring oneself homeless is, in theory, fairly simple. And yet, the system seems designed to make the lives of those navigating it a living hell. Despite Jordan having a 'high priority' status within the system, as a care leaver with complex health issues, they were initially told they were being sent to a property fifty miles from the area they grew up in which wasn't accessible to them. She tells me of the endless hoops she must jump through, work that is more laborious than most people's jobs. Jordan's experience with navigating housing support has been, to put it lightly, abysmal and yet they are still better off than some. 'If I didn't have internet or know how to navigate the endless calls, emails and evidence submissions, then I would be in a tent, as they don't accept anything but digital copies.'

As a disabled LGBTQ+ person, Jordan would be at extremely high risk were they to become a rough sleeper, but that remains a constant threat in their life: 'All that changed for me to become homeless was my age and my health, neither of which I can control.'

## Service Issues

Services for those experiencing homelessness should be equipped to support all people, but it is particularly concerning that they're often ill-equipped to support those who are the most vulnerable. Research by akt found that less than half of young LGBTQ+ people knew of any housing support available to them. What's more, 59% of LGBTQ+ youth who did reach out to their local authority for support were subject to discrimination and harassment.[23]

It was more feasible for Quinnley (she/he/they), twenty-one, to emigrate than to access housing in the UK. It's been wonderful – if crushing – to watch her thrive on the other side of the world. I can't help but feel like the UK has let them down. Quinnley became homeless as a result of a cocktail of factors, putting him in at best precarious and at worst downright dangerous positions. 'In shared rooms and when sofa surfing you have the added challenge of no privacy, which makes life as a trans person extremely difficult, especially as you have no control over the people you are sharing the space with,' they tell me. 'Their morals and perspective on life could negatively impact your day-to-day safety and mental health.'

Quinnley highlights the difficulty of finding places to wash and clean yourself when homeless and trans, too. And getting their period adds another level of distress – and danger. 'When a dorm or housing space is split into male and female spaces, it can pose safety risks and discomfort. I am more comfortable in a women's space than I am in a men's space, especially since I get my period and that impacts me and my work life significantly. It's already difficult enough in a women's space where menstruation is a taboo discussion. I don't need the added challenge of my safety being put at risk and feeling like I have something to hide.'

## Home Life

Home is much more than the structures we live in – that's something I've come to learn all too well. So many LGBTQ+ people I meet are living in accommodation that is technically safe, but they still feel like an outsider, that they have to hide themselves. It's not uncommon for me to have people in the local community ask if they can come round and *just be* in my flat because they know there are no expectations, no prerequisites. I have every kind of tea and coffee and milk. One day, a friend came by with decaf teabags as though I wouldn't keep them fully stocked, just in case. I also have toiletries of all types, two different-weighted blankets, spare clothes and an amount of cash if people need to go and get things in their size or style. It's far from a perfect solution, but it's something.

The housing crisis has multiple potential solutions, none of which, so far, any government has managed to implement. These include the introduction of rent controls, the abolition of Section 21 'no-fault evictions', which allow landlords to get rid of tenants for no good reason in a very short space of time. There must also be proper investment in council housing – refurbishing and repairing so these properties provide a good quality of life for those who live in them. That dry, safe, warm homes are an aspiration and not a given in one of the world's wealthiest nations is a disgrace. These are all things that the newly elected Labour Party has promised as part of their manifesto; however, at the time of writing it remains to be seen whether this will happen, particularly at a time when their approach since entering power has been akin to austerity measures.

The housing crisis is an excellent example of why we cannot focus just on the LGBTQ+ community when it comes to driving change, nor can we pursue so-called apolitical stances. It's as a direct result of the housing-for-profit approach, which has been exacerbated by Conservative policies over the last decade. The fact of the matter is that it's incredibly difficult to maintain wellbeing, relationships, employment and everything else you need to make your life a life if you don't know where you will be sleeping.

LGBTQ+ people are disproportionately affected, but we are far from the only group that suffers as a result of a shambolic, greedy approach to housing – one which sacrifices the health and wellbeing of the most vulnerable for a cash grab.

## And What You Can Do About It

→ Donate to and fundraise for organizations that support LGBTQ+ people experiencing homelessness. Key organizations in the UK include Stonewall Housing, akt and The Outside Project.

→ Make it clear when advertising a property, a room or even a trade if you are LGBTQ+ friendly. Many LGBTQ+ people will not apply unless it is clear that you are welcoming.

→ If you work in providing services in housing or homelessness, ensure you are treating people with respect, including using the correct name and pronouns and ensuring that there are appropriate toilets available. Be aware of and research the particular vulnerabilities LGBTQ+ people have when it comes to housing discrimination and homelessness.

→ Join or financially support your local renter's union. These unions can help renters with local support if they experience landlord harassment or illegal eviction. ACORN are a UK-wide direct action union, whilst the London Renters Union and Greater Manchester Tenants Union represent tenants in their respective cities.

→ Vote for politicians who advocate for and protect safe housing for all, including LGBTQ+ people. This means looking at whether your local MP and other politicians support decent standards in housing, rent control measures, the ending of nationality requirements and the ending of discrimination against people on benefits or who have children.

# Putting in the Work

## Carla Ecola (they/them)

Carla Ecola is a queer homelessness activist who in 2017 founded The Outside Project, the UK's first Community Shelter, Centre and Domestic Abuse Refuge for LGBTQ+ people. Ecola established The Outside Project in response to the acute housing crisis faced by LGBTQ+ individuals, including those who were 'hidden' homeless, who were endangered and who felt excluded by mainstream services.

Ecola's work was influenced by their own experiences of being homeless in London after moving from Birmingham in their twenties, as well as seeing the challenges faced by LGBTQ+ people facing homelessness in their job as an outreach worker.

The Outside Project's main HQ – The LGBTIQ+ Centre in London – is home to groups supporting homeless LGBTQ+ people, whether that's by providing a space to have breakfast and find community or by providing access to domestic violence support. Ecola's efforts have brought much-needed attention to the intersection of homelessness and LGBTQ+ rights, making them a significant figure in both the housing sector and the LGBTQ+ rights movement.

## Marsha P. Johnson (she/her)

Marsha P. Johnson, alongside Sylvia Rivera, co-founded the Street Transvestite Action Revolutionaries (STAR) in 1970, an organization dedicated to supporting homeless LGBTQ+ youth and sex workers in New York City. STAR was born out of the dire need for safe spaces and resources for the most marginalized members of the LGBTQ+ community, particularly transgender and gender non-conforming individuals, who faced widespread discrimination and violence.

STAR was instrumental in raising awareness about the issues facing transgender individuals and challenging the mainstream gay rights movement to be more inclusive. Despite limited resources and significant societal pushback, Johnson and Rivera's efforts laid the groundwork for future activism within the LGBTQ+ community. Their legacy continues to inspire contemporary movements that seek to address homelessness, discrimination and violence against transgender and gender non-conforming people.

## Cath Hall (she/her)

Cath Hall is the founder of the Albert Kennedy Trust (now akt), an organization established in 1989 to support LGBTQ+ youth facing homelessness or living in hostile environments. Hall, a foster carer, was moved to action after the tragic death of Albert Kennedy, a young gay man who fell to his death whilst trying to escape a violent attack.

This event highlighted to Hall, a straight ally, the urgent need for a dedicated support system for vulnerable LGBTQ+ young people who were being rejected by their families and communities, leading to homelessness and increased risk of exploitation and violence. She founded akt to provide safe housing, support and advocacy, and – thirty-five years later – the organization continues to offer a range of services, including emergency accommodation, mentoring and assistance with finding long-term housing solutions for young LGBTQ+ people.

# CHAPTER 3
# Edu-gay-tion

## Section 28

'I started my teaching career in a girls' convent school in Liverpool, in 1988, just when Section 28 came in,' Professor Catherine Lee tells me. Not only is Catherine an expert in inclusive education and the author of *Pretended: Schools and Section 28*, but she's also the inspiration behind *Blue Jean*, the critically acclaimed film directed by Georgia Oakley and starring Rosy McEwen. The film tells the story of a lesbian PE teacher as she navigates life, balancing being a teacher with her sexuality, until one day her worlds collide when a student comes into the gay bar she frequents.

Section 28 of the Local Government Act 1988 may well have been the most pernicious piece of legislation affecting LGBTQ+ people in the UK in the twentieth century. Although laws that aggressively criminalized homosexuality were in place until 1967, at least they were clear and direct about what it was they were prohibiting. There was no room for miscommunication. Section 28, on the other hand, was intentionally vague in its language:

'A local authority shall not intentionally promote homosexuality or publish material with the intention of promoting homosexuality.'[1] It followed with: 'a local authority shall not promote the teaching in any maintained school of the acceptability of homosexuality as a pretended family relationship.' It remained in place for fifteen years in England and Wales – until 2003 – when it was repealed under Tony Blair's Labour government, though its effects were felt for far longer. One of the most troubling aspects of Section 28 is that many people educated under its edict were unaware it existed. Many grew up understanding that to be queer was too shameful even to mention, and believing that nobody who felt the way they did had ever existed before. Even now, it's often assumed that LGBTQ+ people were not mentioned due to pervasive social stigma rather than an outright ban.

For many teachers, including Professor Lee, it was unclear what 'promoting' homosexuality actually meant. As a result of this ambiguity in the language, to be safe, many LGBTQ+ figures were removed from the curriculum, or their identity was erased altogether. You could still teach the writings of Oscar Wilde, but you couldn't dare mention that he was persecuted for homosexuality. It was as though mentioning LGBTQ+ people might lead to more of them appearing. Sir Ian McKellen decried the clause: 'The truth is that homosexuality cannot be taught any more than it can be caught. Everywhere in the media, in the church, in the teaching of literature, language, art and politics, heterosexuality is daily, hourly promoted. I still haven't been persuaded.'[2]

The law was not well publicized. Like most of the educators I spoke to, Catherine tells me that actually, no, there was no big announcement. 'This was a Local Government Act, not a Schools Act, so it wasn't included in the list of things schools had to do, it wasn't on the regular circulars.' The lack of promotion did little to allay the fears of teachers.

'The majority of the staff in the school knew very little, if anything, about it. Those of us who were gay were terrified. And, at the school I worked at, every single one of the senior leadership team was a nun.'

'What about other PE teachers?' I ask. There's something of a stereotype that female PE teachers are queer, but it's one that chimes with my personal experience.

Catherine agrees. 'Most of us at the PE college were gay. And then we went on to get jobs in the local area. We'd hang out together on a Saturday night in the women's bar down in the centre of Liverpool and then, when we saw each other at the netball and hockey fixtures, pretend we hadn't ever met. The predominant emotion was just one of fear.'

It's interesting to think about the effect of that fear on those teachers. I don't think anyone does their best work whilst terrified. I certainly don't.

Although Section 28 was repealed more than twenty years ago, I still regularly encounter teachers in the course of my work who are not certain if they can or should talk about queer and trans people in the classroom. This has been exacerbated by an increased hostility towards transgender people in the press and guidance from the Department of Education which has increasingly targeted transgender young people and discussions of gender and sexuality in schools.

## Usualizing

'Are we relevant to the subject you teach?' This is a question I often ask educators when I do school visits, or deliver training to staff on inclusion. LGBTQ+ people's work and achievements have shaped every area of society, and their experiences as people outside of dominant gender and sexuality expectations have an impact on that work. They've often been under-recognized or had their identity minimized; I was an avid reader at school and yet I didn't realize that Virginia Woolf was queer until I invigilated an exhibition at the Barbican Art Gallery in 2018, the year after I left. Section 28 was an attempt to rewrite the past, present and future, to erase the existence of LGBTQ+ people, not only from schools and educational settings but also from the minds of young people. It served to deny the reality: LGBTQ+ people have always existed and moreover that we have made profound and meaningful contributions to society.

Whether you like it or not, you have benefitted from the work of queer and trans people. The microchips in your phones, computers and coffee machines owe their existence to Lynn Conway,[3] a trans woman who co-developed a new microchip design which revolutionized tech forever. Alan Turing, whose code-breaking work at Bletchley Park helped shorten the Second World War by between two and four years, was later chemically castrated for his sexuality and forced into suicide. His work saved an estimated fourteen million lives.[4]

I started learning about the world wars at school aged nine, with trips to museums and memorials, explanations of different planes and weapons, and visits to an Anderson shelter. I was part of a code-breaking club where we did cyphers in our lunch break, but I didn't find out about Turing until many years later, when he was posthumously pardoned by the Queen in 2013.[5]

When I talk about LGBTQ+ inclusion in education, what I am asking for is for schools to acknowledge that we exist and that we can do great things. When I was in sixth form, students decorated the hallways for LGBTQ+ History Month with Pride flag bunting and posters with a range of LGBTQ+ role models from across all walks of life. From physics to maths to music to French, every block had posters emblazoned across the walls with people – past and present – who had made a positive impact on the world. But more than that, we advocated for mentioning that those people were LGBTQ+ when their names came up. This was not my idea, I confess. I had bribed my mother, a computing teacher, to go to a teachers' conference at a weekend so that I could sneak in with her and learn about LGBTQ+ education. I'm a nerd, what can I say?

It was here that I first encountered Emeritus Professor Sue Sanders, co-founder of Schools OUT and LGBTQ+ History Month. I was immediately captivated – she remains one of the most formidable people I have ever met. She talked passionately about the importance of 'usualizing' LGBTQ+ people in the classroom. 'Normal' and 'normalizing' had too much baggage (who's to say what's 'normal'?), and some feel that attempting to reclaim the terms to talk about LGBTQ+ people is problematic. But 'usualizing' is, instead, about the frequency and regularity with which LGBTQ+ people are mentioned in schools. Research in 2021 by LGBTQ+ young people's charity Just Like Us suggests that only a third of schools celebrate Pride, LGBTQ+ History Month or School Diversity Week, with 35% of pupils reporting that their school celebrates, and 38% of teachers reporting the same.[6]

What I like about 'usualizing' is that it stops the notion that LGBTQ+ people have not made meaningful contributions to society. It ensures we are understood and encountered in a wider context, beyond the confines of relationships and sex education. You cannot withdraw your children from maths, English or any other part of the curriculum, but parents can withdraw their children from lessons on sex and relationships specifically under current guidelines. Usualizing the existence of LGBTQ+ people by integrating it into the everyday makes it much more tricky for people who are against LGBTQ+ people to specifically target LGBTQ+ lessons or programmes. It also ensures inclusion can happen without placing *extra* responsibility for specific LGBTQ+ lessons onto the shoulders of teachers. To make it even easier, organizations like Schools OUT have created lesson plans and resources to support teaching across a range of subjects, age groups and settings.

## The Hypersexualization Trap

People often question whether it is appropriate for primary-age children to be exposed to LGBTQ+ topics because of fears about sexualization and inappropriateness. No one wants children exposed to anything inappropriate, but the idea that being LGBTQ+ is inherently more sexual than being straight is deeply flawed.

There is a long history of LGBTQ+ people being sexualized, even when they are not engaging in anything explicit. In general, hugging, kissing or holding hands has been deemed non-sexual when it applies to straight, cisgender people, whilst LGBTQ+ people are seen as not only sexual but hypersexual. As a teenage lesbian, one of the things I discovered upon coming out was the strange paradox that my kissing a boy was not just acceptable but everywhere in media, whilst holding hands with a girlfriend was seen as lewd and inappropriate.

In recent years, we have seen a massive rise in the number of states in the US attempting to implement bans on drag performances, though several have been made at least temporarily unenforceable due to federal court orders.[7] Drag is an art and, like all art, there are parts which children may not understand or might have questions about and parts which may be inappropriate for children, full stop. But saying all drag is an adult form of entertainment is like stopping children from watching *Finding Nemo* because of the existence of *Magic Mike*. The idea that drag is inherently adult entertainment is rooted in both a wilful misunderstanding of drag as an art form and a deeper fear of LGBTQ+ people as a whole. There is nothing inherently dangerous about drag, but there is something dangerous about people who do not want children exposed to diversity and inclusion in different areas of life.

What is incredibly telling about these bans is that they explicitly targeted anything which could be considered as 'sexual' or, under existing laws about 'prurience', acts which might arouse a person. In Texas, specifically, the law which was introduced and then blocked placed any venues that host drag performances – even libraries and care homes – in the same category as strip clubs[8]. Breaking the restrictions – which were incredibly vague and could also have applied to cheerleading events and karaoke nights, even musical theatre – could mean fines and criminal penalties of up to a year in jail.

Arizona went further, with its ban penalizing drag performers with at least ten years in prison and registration as a sex offender. One version of a drag ban in West Virginia included language that would criminalize 'transgender exposure, performances or display', essentially meaning transgender and non-binary people could have no interaction with children or young people at all without risking jail.[9] At the time of writing, these bans have been blocked or temporarily blocked by the Federal Supreme Court, but the harm has been done and the re-election of Trump's Republican Party, combined with a Republican-majority Senate means further attacks on LGBTQ+ people are almost certainly guaranteed.

This is not just an attitude in the law, but also something built into the fabric of technology. This phenomenon occurs not just in mainstream media, but within social media, too; in 2010, YouTube brought in its 'restricted mode', a feature still in place today. This is a mode which is auto-enabled on many accounts and was designed to filter out 'potentially inappropriate content' like violence, crime, terrorism or sex. What happened, however, was that large amounts of LGBTQ+ themed content became hidden on the platform because it was deemed to be inappropriate for children even when it did not contain anything that was concerning.[10] Content creators raised the issue in 2017 with YouTube, after the discovery that hundreds of thousands of videos – from a lesbian couple reading their wedding vows to each other to videos reviewing queer media – were hidden on the platform with no explanation. After a disappointing response from YouTube in which they denied the mode was removing content including LGBTQ+ people, they eventually admitted that this system – which was using machine learning to identify inappropriate content – had not been adequately set up to counteract the biases people had towards LGBTQ+ people. Quite literally, the system had learned that LGBTQ+ people were hypersexual and perpetuated this bias through the system. What is notable to me, as a gay woman, is that the hypersexualization of both drag and trans people we are seeing mirrors the exact arguments and attitudes we saw a decade ago regarding gay people. When I came out as a lesbian, the sexualization I experienced mostly came from straight, cis white women who suddenly thought that I was predatory and a threat to their daughters. I still instinctually refuse to hold hands with girlfriends when children or young people walk past us, even now. I wish I could say this was my own neurosis, but in fact, two-thirds of people who are LGBTQ+ in the UK will not hold hands with their partners in public, either.

One of the contradictions I have never understood is that the need to 'protect children' never extends to LGBTQ+ children and young people themselves. Arguments that LGBTQ+ people are perverted sexual deviants are unfounded, but they're deeply uncomfortable when you realize they are being applied to children, too. The same people campaigning against the sexualization of children are then causing the sexualization of children.

And as for the idea that we should not expose them to the idea of sexuality and gender – this is already happening: walk into any toy store and you will still see a section 'for girls' that radiates pink and a section 'for boys' in blue – what is that if not influencing a child's gender and gender expression? But – as with so much else – we see one rule for LGBTQ+ people and one rule for everyone else. In my experience children, in general, do not care what someone's gender or sexuality is because – loath though some parts of society are to admit it – children are not born with bigotry built in – it's a learned behaviour. But that learning can be avoided by including LGBTQ+ people in the wide context of discussions about the benefits of diversity and especially family diversity. Banning LGBTQ+ topics in schools is not going to stop children encountering LGBTQ+ people in their day-to-day lives, especially as some of them will themselves come from families with LGBTQ+ parents.

Amy Ashenden (she/her), Director of Communications at LGBTQ+ young people's charity Just Like Us, tells me: 'We like to believe things have got better because there's more visibility, but growing up LGBTQ+ is still unacceptably tough. LGBTQ+ young people are facing higher levels of tension at home, family estrangement, panic attacks, depression, anxiety, bullying in school, and then at work as young adults.'

## Don't Say Gay – Section 28 2.0?

I first heard the use of the word 'groomer' as a slur from Will Larkin (they/them) the day before they graduated from high school in Florida. Their school years had been shaped by a steep rise in anti-LGBTQ+ sentiment. Florida has a particularly fraught history with LGBTQ+ equality: in 1977, Anita Bryant – pop singer, evangelical Christian and orange juice spokesperson – launched the 'Save Our Children' campaign in the state, a pursuit that ultimately led to the repeal of a Dade County ordinance that protected the rights of lesbian, gay and bisexual residents.[11] Afraid that her children would be subjected to the 'perversion of gay teachers', Bryant campaigned to repeal a second ordinance that protected teachers from being fired due to their sexual orientation. According to her, these laws were not basic rights but instead 'special privileges', and teachers would be 'flaunting their homosexuality'. Her fear was that children could be harmed by being in the vicinity of queer people, either through 'perversion' or by converting them to be LGBTQ+ themselves. She said: 'Homosexuals cannot reproduce, so they must recruit.' This idea of 'recruitment', that LGBTQ+ people are either directly or indirectly influenced into becoming so, is one that has underpinned much anti-LGBTQ+ legislation.

'I've known that I was gay and non-binary before I knew that the queer community existed, before even kindergarten,' Will says, speaking out against HB 1557, dubbed the 'Don't Say Gay' bill.[12] Passed into law in 2022 by Florida Governor Ron DeSantis, its original purpose was to 'prohibit classroom discussion about sexual orientation or gender identity in certain grade levels or in a specified manner.' Further laws since have added provisions prohibiting the use of pronouns consistent with one's gender identity, expanding book bans and censoring the health curriculum and instruction.[13]

The first time I heard Will speak, it was on a viral TikTok video – one of hundreds featuring children, teenagers and adults pleading with politicians. That children are being forced to make impassioned pleas for recognition of their or their family's existence is unconscionable.

'We learned about Oscar Wilde; it's part of our English curriculum for seniors, for twelfth graders. Our teacher told us that this was the last year that we could say he was gay; he didn't even say he was gay, just the laws Wilde was prosecuted under.' Will goes on to explain which courses are being pulled from college (university) programmes across Florida, including Advanced Placement Psychology and African American Studies programmes.

It's difficult not to look at the rapid derailing of LGBTQ+ equality in the US education system and see it as a potential and increasingly realized future for the UK's. What is consistent across both is the focus on LGBTQ+ people coming at a time when there are real, practical problems that need addressing in schools and education but that would require a substantial overhaul to achieve.

'We were organizing a rally, which took months,' Will says when I interview them. 'We start speaking and someone comes up to us and says, "Hey, I need to let you know that whilst you were inside, twenty-eight kids were shot and killed at an elementary school in Texas." And it hit me: I'm fighting book bans, and kids are being murdered.'

I ask Will what impact they feel the new laws and the time they spent campaigning against them has had on their education. 'Oh, I haven't done classwork in like a year. It's not a good environment, I can't focus on it. If you talk to the average LGBTQ+ person in Florida, they will agree with me that no matter what you're doing, no matter where you are, no matter what you're focused on, there is a dark, scary cloud looming above you.'

Florida is something of a litmus test politically, because it has one of the earliest legislative sessions in the US, meaning it makes its laws before most of the other states. Of late, many of these have been anti-progressive: the Don't Say Gay bill, a fifteen-week abortion ban and a crackdown on critical race theory, which suggests race is a social construct and that racism is not merely the product of individual bias or prejudice, but instead systemic, embedded in legal systems and policies.

These are all laws that attack marginalized groups from all sides. Will believes that communities coming together will be essential for driving change. 'The opposition treat feminism, queer rights and Black Lives Matter as though they're separate movements, but they're not, they're all interconnected. We see that as young people, and I think that's why they try to keep it out of the classroom. They talk about indoctrination and how queer people are indoctrinating people, but it's the other way around.' Trump has made this clear several times, stating that no school should teach 'critical race theory, transgender insanity, and other inappropriate racial, sexual, or political content on our children', also taking steps to white-wash the history of slavery.

The day after we spoke, Will graduated and Governor DeSantis announced his plans to run for President of the United States, though subsequently dropped out. Will hid the rainbow Pride flag and the trans flag in the sleeves of their graduation gown, revealing them on stage as they shook hands with the school leadership, a final act of defiance against the school and education system.

It's difficult not to feel as though the world is ending in slow motion. Despite being on the other side of the Atlantic, I'm furious for and on behalf of all the young people in the US being denied a quality education, furious that in a country where there is so much wealth, schools are underfunded, children are dying in school shootings and those in charge are more interested in stoking culture wars than taking action. It's hard not to want to shriek 'Do something!' But it's not a problem specific to the US and, often, it feels that here in the UK, we are not much better.

Whilst writing this book, innumerable young LGBTQ+ people still of school age have died – many to suicide. There have also been several notable cases of violence against transgender teenagers in the UK, including the fatal stabbing of Brianna Ghey, aged sixteen.[14] Ghey's killers referred to her as 'it' throughout their interrogation and made jokes about Brianna's gender. Another girl, aged eighteen, had abuse hurled at her and was stabbed fourteen times on her way to a roller-skating party in London after being cornered by a group.[15] It's essential to remember when we talk about this inclusion in schools, it's not only for the benefit of LGBTQ+ children, or kids who come from families with LGBTQ+ parents, but for everyone.

'LGBTQ+ inclusive education benefits all young people, not just those who are LGBTQ+,' Amy Ashenden from Just Like Us reminds me. 'Our independent research shows that the rate of suicidal thoughts among non-LGBTQ+ young people is lower when there is positive messaging about LGBTQ+ people at school. We also have to remember that lots of young people in school come from LGBTQ+ families, or might have a trans sibling – regardless, everyone will one day leave school and enter a workplace, where they need to respect their LGBTQ+ colleagues.'

The risks of not having that respect taught – brutal bullying and vicious attacks – are symptomatic of a system that does not value LGBTQ+ lives and safety. And no matter how much schools promote anti-bullying initiatives or pledge their support for diversity, it's tricky to see this realized in a context in which elected officials and state departments are targeting children for simply being themselves.

## Don't Say They?

While the discrimination in the US and threats to LGBTQ+ people in education might be more obvious, it's not just in the US that this persecution is happening; in December 2023, the UK Department for Education released guidance for teachers on 'how best to support pupils questioning their gender in school'.[16] The guidance was promised much earlier in the year, but faced numerous legal issues before finally being released.

The new guidance for teachers was direct in its dismissal of trans inclusion in schools: 'social transition is not a neutral act' and 'social transition, in practice, should be extremely rare'. Social transition refers to actions like using a different name, cutting hair and wearing clothes that are gender-affirming – i.e. garments traditionally thought to be more likely worn by the gender you are, even if that doesn't match the gender you were assigned at birth. The restrictions placed on transgender and gender-questioning children as part of this guidance are tantamount to a ban on social transition in schools for the vast majority of young people. The outcome – if these rules are made statutory – would be the erasure and denial of trans students from the British education system. Whether this guidance is shelved by the new Labour government remains to be seen, though the early signs are not optimistic,[17] it's important to note how harmful it would be not only to transgender children but also to cisgender kids. What sort of democratic government dictates the hairstyles, names and clothing of children based on their assigned sex? It's a horrific precedent.

One of the most alarming parts of the guidance is the mandatory outing of trans and gender-questioning young people to their parents. Under the proposed guidance, if you are a young person who thinks you may be transgender and you share that with your teacher, they will be forced to tell your parents or carers. (There is some recognition that schools can choose not to inform the parents if they believe that doing so 'might raise a significant risk of harm to the child', but the guidance argues that this is 'exceptionally rare'.)

Outing someone without their consent is a gross violation of autonomy and personhood. I was fourteen and out to only a handful of my closest friends when I was forced to come out more widely. I was being blackmailed by some girls in my year group, who were threatening to out me unless I confessed to giving a blow job to a boy from another school. It was childish and petty: they didn't even think I was gay but, unknowingly, they put me in an impossible position.

It was mid-January and the playground was covered in snow and slush. I spent the afternoon in the office of the heads of years, who tried to pick apart the situation as delicately as they could. My form tutor, concerned for my wellbeing, emailed my mum with her concerns. The message was only a couple of sentences long and, whilst she did not explicitly out me, she revealed enough that it was impossible not to come out to my mum. Her actions – driven by her understanding of safeguarding procedure, as well as genuine compassion and concern – meant I had to come out to my parents well before I was ready, or knew I would be safe.

Knowing she had messed up, the next morning my teacher pulled me aside to apologize. 'I knew what I had done as soon as I sent it, but there was nothing I could do.' I could only shrug. It was done and there was nothing I could do, either. I'm aware that my experience is a million times better than that of many of my friends who were outed or forced to come out; my parents were incredibly supportive and there were no negative repercussions. It still felt horrible – like the floor had fallen away from underneath me. The moment I had played out in my head time and time again, hoping to get it right, was gone. I didn't get it wrong, I didn't get it any way – I wasn't in control. I wasn't really prepared, I needed more time. But things could have so easily gone another way.

The reality is many LGBTQ+ people don't receive a straightforward reaction from family members. Research by Just Like Us found that a quarter of LGBTQ+ young people are facing daily tension at home, compared to 15% of their peers, and that LGBTQ+ people are half as likely to be 'very close' to their family.

Indeed, the NSPCC – the UK's leading organization on child safety and wellbeing – are clear in their guidance that 'sharing a child or young person's gender identity or sexuality might put them at extra risk if the person you tell is unsupportive'. They also emphasize that adults risk losing the trust of a child whom they out without their consent.[18] And sadly, sometimes, a reaction is more serious than lack of support or someone to talk to: it can be abuse by family members.

A 2022 survey by Galop found that of those LGBTQ+ people who had experienced familial abuse, 63% were under eighteen when it first happened and that the majority of that maltreatment came from parents.[19] The abuse LGBTQ+ young people can face at the hands of their parents may not always be obvious to teachers and other adults, either. A child is highly unlikely to disclose anything to someone who has made, or could make, them less safe by outing them.

I have spoken with parents who believe they should be told about their child's gender and sexuality because they would 'want to know'. My feeling is that this should still come from the child. If, as a parent, you really want to know about your child's identity, then it is your responsibility to create a space which is supportive and in which your child feels safe telling you about their experiences.

In 2023, Rishi Sunak announced guidance that, if implemented, would prevent teachers from discussing trans matters in schools. This guidance was rooted in fears about safeguarding, the report upon which it was based arguing that the safeguarding of children was failing as a result of approaches that affirmed and supported trans, or potentially trans, children. The report found schools were not reliably informing parents as soon as a pupil expressed the wish to change gender and, generally, schools were being led by pupils. Several stated they would seek guidance from local authorities, many of which explicitly stated that children should not be outed without their consent.

Safeguarding involves an incredibly important set of measures that are designed to prevent harm to young people. It's a combination of holistic and statutory practices that apply to anyone working to provide services to children. In short, safeguarding is designed to serve the best interests of children. The Children Act of 1989 is one of the primary safeguarding laws and it emphasizes that parental involvement in the life of a child is important and should be prioritized. It also outlines several areas of parental responsibility, for example, providing a home for the child, agreeing to medical treatment, agreeing to name changes and more. Essentially, if a child discloses information that is not known by their parents, their school is required to share this information and act in accordance with the wishes of the parent, not the child.

Long before the 2024 General Election was announced I had spoken to Professor Catherine Lee about her expectations if, after fourteen years of Conservative government, Labour winning the general election would have an impact. 'I'm not sure that there'll be any particular change on all this,' Catherine told me. 'We were so hopeful when Tony Blair got in. But he looked so closely at the data about public attitudes and decided how to act based on that.' Her prediction seems to have come true, with the recently elected Labour Party continuing to avoid the question of whether they would support a proposed ban on teachers discussing trans issues with pupils. When asked prior to the election, Keir Starmer stated he would not remove the ban, stating: 'I'm not in favour of ideology being taught in our schools on gender.' The idea that a more left-leaning government inherently benefits all LGBTQ+ people is a fallacy and – as we did before – we must pressure the Labour Party to take action. As Catherine points out, it's the public who will be just as responsible for driving towards inclusive education for young people – making it clear to any politicians attempting to win votes that excluding young LGBTQ+ people will not help them to get into power, nor to keep it.

## Relationships and Sex Education

Just days before the general election was called in May 2024, the government also announced its draft Relationships, Sex and Health Education guidance, designed, in the words of Rishi Sunak, to protect 'our precious children'.[20]

'Most of the guidance actually seems pretty reasonable, because it's putting age limits on stuff that nobody was doing anyway,' Adam Beardwell (he/him), subject leader for Personal, Social and Health Education (PSHE) for years seven to twelve in a UK state school, tells me. For example, the guidance made clear that teachers were not allowed to teach pupils any form of sex education until the age of nine and ten (year five), and conversations about sex are prohibited until children are thirteen. 'No school had a policy of teaching about sexual intercourse to eight-year-olds, or trying to horrify eleven-year-olds with graphic descriptions of sexual assault. We teach around the topics in age-appropriate ways, like ensuring primary-school-age children understand about their bodies, about what positive relationships look like. When they're older, we ensure they know about reproduction, keeping safe, consent. But there are still some really sinister, horrible parts of the proposed guidance too.'

These include explicitly prohibiting discussing 'the concept of gender identity'. Attributing this as a 'concept' is commonly used to undermine the existence of trans and non-binary people, which the guidance describes as a 'contested theory'. However, much of the guidance put forward about lesbian, gay and bisexual matters remained very similar to that in previous iterations; put simply, the restrictions would predominantly target trans people.

'There's the very Section 28-flavoured "don't talk about gender identity" bit, which could have been lifted straight out of TERF [trans-exclusionary radical feminism][21] Twitter,' says Adam. 'It frames being trans or gender-questioning as some terrible thing that needs to be prevented at all costs.'

The guidance also places worrying age restrictions for conversations about important topics like contraception, sexually transmitted infections and abortions, which cannot be discussed until children are over the age of thirteen. The largest group affected by this issue are cisgender girls, who could find themselves pregnant due to a lack of appropriate advice. We know comprehensive sex education in schools reduces the rates of sexual activity, means children have less (unsafe) sex, and reduces rates of both teenage pregnancy and child sexual abuse, and yet this guidance places limitations on the conversations teachers can have.[22]

'The guidance doesn't define anywhere what "explicit" or "details of sexual acts" means, but I am worried that it means we can't teach proper lessons on condom use,' Adam continues. 'We don't like to think about it, but every school in the country is going to have [thirteen- and fourteen-year-olds] who are sexually active. And if they don't have proper safe sex education at school, they're going to find out what "normal" sex is like either from porn, or from their partner (who is the sort of person who's willing to have sex with a thirteen-year-old), and that's terrifying.' Adam is not wrong: the average age of children seeing pornography for the first time is thirteen years old, though many children are as young or eight or nine.[23] By the time schools get round to having important conversations about these topics – under this guidance – it will be far too late.

Once again, whilst the anti-trans brigade are celebrating restrictions placed on trans topics in schools, all young people are put at risk through the pursuit of an educational policy that is not evidence-based, not supported by teachers and driven by political motivations.

## Conflicting Information

One of the challenges of both the new guidance on trans matters and the sex and relationships guidance is how they interact with the curriculum's existing policy and values-based work. 'We have a duty to teach about the protected characteristics listed in the Equality Act 2010, but this guidance instructs us not to even mention gender identity, which is a contradiction,' Adam tells me. 'If we are asked questions about gender identity (which students already do), we have to just say "it's a highly contested issue" and "it's complex". If you've ever met a young person, you'll know that telling them it's too complicated for them to understand is never going to work.'

Indeed, some have suggested this guidance is not even legally sound, and it is expected that were schools to implement it, they would leave themselves open to legal challenges, particularly contraventions of the Equality Act.

'The very least we would expect from any government guidance is that it is legally sound,' Julie McCulloch, director of policy at the Association of School and College Leaders said. 'If the government cannot provide assurance that schools and colleges will not be leaving themselves open to legal challenge by following this guidance, then the government itself must commit to taking on any legal challenges that arise against schools.'

The Equality Act 2010 does not just protect LGBTQ+ people but ensures people are not being discriminated against because of their gender, race, disability, age or religion; the only way to implement this guidance would be to pull apart the Equality Act, which would, in turn, jeopardize all equalities laws. The guidance is in the interests of those who are racist and sexist and who want to be able to discriminate freely to attack transgender people and the laws that protect them from abuse because it opens the floodgates for the erosion of other protections. It's a terrifying thought, but is not just possible, but plausible.

Professor Catherine Lee is clear on this, too: 'I don't actually think we need guidance. Teachers are already used to holistically looking at pastoral care, dealing with individual needs. We need to look at a child and be able to say, "What does this kid need?" We don't go, "Oh, that kid's non-binary, let's chuck in the non-binary section." Most of the time, we're not "implementing policy", we are asking a very simple question: what does this kid need to be ready to learn? Whether that's a cereal bar or to know that they are safe or some equipment, we try to make that happen.'

There's always talk about LGBTQ+ inclusive education being somehow damaging to children, but like so many areas where LGBTQ+ people are targeted, it's those advocating for harmful measures who are responsible for implementing disastrous policies. If we want to look at the risks to young people's education, why are we not investing in education? Why are we not paying teachers properly?[24] Why are there schools where the majority of some classes are homeless?[25]

There *are* threats to children's wellbeing and education but they don't come from queer and trans people. We are – as Will in Florida pointed out – just a distraction. You can't talk about the need to protect young people when millions of young people are starving,[26] when they are being shot at their school desks in the US[27] and when they're experiencing mental health crises.[28] That's not rocket science, it's common sense.

## And What You Can Do About It

→ Everyone needs to be aware of how important LGBTQ+ education is and the extent to which educators are under pressure.
'Tell your local, former or current school that you'd love them to
support LGBTQ+ pupils,' Just Like Us advises, 'and show them
that you're willing to help make that happen too. Teachers are
under a lot of pressure, so it's important we don't enter a blame
game – Section 28 instigated a horrific culture that terrified
many teachers into silence, after all – so show your support
and be willing to be part of making the change.' There are also
lots of opportunities for people to provide support in schools.
Just Like Us runs an ambassador programme for LGBTQ+
people aged 18–25. and other organizations like Diversity Role
Models and Stonewall provide external role models and
speakers in schools.

→ If you are a teacher or other adult involved with young people,
take steps to support young LGBTQ+ people by listening to
them and by making it clear to everyone that you are a safe
person to talk to. There is sometimes a misconception that you
will 'know' who is LGBTQ+, but that is unlikely to be the case.
Make sure that you take the time to learn about some of the
common LGBTQ+ identities and resources you can signpost
people too. Sometimes the worst things are said not out of
malice but out of a lack of knowledge.

→ Several teaching unions and other educational organizations
across the globe are active in campaigning against restrictions
on LGBTQ+ education. Make sure you are supporting those
campaigns directly where you can, making it clear also to
elected officials that you will not support them if they fail to
support LGBTQ+ children.

# Putting in the Work

## Sue Sanders (she/her)

Sue Sanders is the co-founder of Schools OUT and creator of LGBTQ+ History Month, which she launched in 2005. Schools OUT – originally called The Gay Teachers Association – started in 1974 with the aim of helping schools become inclusive, safe and welcoming spaces for LGBTQ+ teachers, students, families and staff, from headteachers to dinner ladies. This became increasingly challenging with the introduction of Section 28, which Sanders passionately fought alongside the organization. Sanders' work primarily focused on challenging homophobia, biphobia and transphobia in schools through advocacy, training and the development of resources.

One of Sanders' most significant achievements is the creation of LGBTQ+ History Month in the UK. This annual event, celebrated every February, aims to promote equality and diversity by increasing the visibility of LGBTQ+ people, their history and their contributions to society. Through various activities, events and educational materials, LGBTQ+ History Month encourages schools, communities and organizations to recognize and celebrate the lives of LGBTQ+ individuals.

Sue Sanders has also been involved in numerous initiatives and campaigns to advance LGBTQ+ rights. She continues to work with organizations across the UK and the globe to improve policies and practices that affect LGBTQ+ people.

## Dr Adam Brett (he/him) and Jo Brassington (they/them)

Dr Adam Brett and Jo Brassington are leading advocates for LGBTQ+ inclusivity in education. As co-creators of *Pride & Progress*, they've built a platform that supports LGBTQ+

educators and promotes more inclusive schools. Their podcast features candid conversations with educators, offering real-world strategies to tackle issues like homophobia, transphobia and navigating identity in the classroom. Jo, a non-binary educator, focuses on non-binary visibility and challenges outdated gender norms, whilst Adam, an openly gay educator, blends personal experience with research to show how inclusive practices benefit students and staff. Together, they co-authored the book *Pride & Progress: Making Schools LGBT+ Inclusive Spaces*, a practical guide for educators committed to change.

# CHAPTER 4
# Health Conscious

## Life or Death Situation

It was a hot, smog-filled October in East London. The English summer seemed to have lasted about twelve years – another reminder that everything, including the planet, was on fire. Harper (they/she) and I first met at the funeral service of one of my queer and trans friends who had died, by suicide, in their early twenties. Over the last few years, we had kept in touch and finally had met for something other than a memorial or a march.

'Do you ever think?' I asked, licking around the edge of my ice cream, 'that if politics wasn't like this, there would be a lot less drink, drugs, smoking and addiction amongst our friends?'

'That, and we would stop having to bury people every three to six months.' That week, the Conservative Party had announced a swathe of proposed restrictions – including banning trans women from hospital wards, a policy subsequently endorsed by the Labour Party several months later.[1] They argued the move would 'protect women', by which they meant cisgender women. As a cisgender woman, I can safely say trans people do not pose a threat to me, but a government system intent on implementing a policy of segregation does. And it's not only me who thinks that. In 2022, Translucent – a group advocating for trans rights – published an investigation into 102 NHS trusts. Their research revealed that not a single woman assigned female at birth had made any sort of complaint about a transgender woman being cared for in the same ward within the last year.[2] It's almost as if – as we saw in the previous chapter – politicians are making policies not from an evidence-based or informed perspective but by preying on fears about protecting vulnerable people to win votes.

It was no surprise, then, that the celebrant at our dear friend's memorial spoke of barriers to accessing healthcare as a contributing factor in their death. It's a hard pill to swallow that if there were better access to inclusive healthcare – whether that's in mental health, gender-affirming care or just antibiotics for an infection – fewer people in my community would be dead.

It's true that some progress has been made. At least it's no longer the case that being queer is considered a sickness – homosexuality was delisted as a mental illness by the American Psychiatric Association in 1973 and later by the World Health Organization's International Classification of Diseases (ICD) – used by the NHS – in 1990. But it wasn't until 2018 that the World Health Organization declared the same for being transgender. But, as this chapter will show, there is still a long way to go. We should have confidence that when we seek medical treatment, we will receive the care we need, or be referred somewhere appropriate for more support. For many LGBTQ+ people, that is far from the case.

## Health Inequalities

Talking about the scope and scale of LGBTQ+ health inequalities is always a little difficult because, put simply, we don't have robust data collection and monitoring systems in place, an aspect I'll explore later in this chapter. I suspect the health of LGBTQ+ people is even worse than the numbers show – in part because so much research relies on self-reported data and therefore only includes information from people who have chosen to disclose. But doing so implies a level of safety that I'm not at all convinced every member of the queer community feels.

Much of the academic and scientific research that is available is outdated. Recent years have seen a massive uptick in hate crimes against LGBTQ+ people,[3] Brexit, a global pandemic, an escalation of the media and political hatred for LGBTQ+ people, a cost-of-living crisis and so much more. These issues have disproportionately impacted LGBTQ+ people and have doubtless increased stress, poor mental health and behaviours we know are detrimental to health, such as smoking and drinking. Research into LGBTQ+ matters is usually undertaken by LGBTQ+ organizations who – for the last five years – have been fighting not only for their survival against back-drops of mounting political and financial pressures, but also to keep those who use their services alive and well.

Still, the data we do have paints a grim picture. A 2020 review of data sources found that there was a heightened risk of long-term illness and health-related limitations in gay, bisexual and queer men in comparison to their heterosexual counterparts, whilst a study of over two million people, including over 27,000 LGB [lesbian, gay and bisexual] people, found that gay and bisexual men reported fair or poor general health in comparison to their heterosexual counter-parts, who more regularly scored higher.[4]

Meanwhile, a 2024 study of 100,000 nurses found that among them lesbian and bisexual women died 26% sooner than hetero-sexual women – with bisexual women dying 37% sooner and lesbian women dying 20% sooner. The study concluded that stigma, preju-dice, discrimination and chronic stress caused by existing in the world as gay and bisexual women worsened health outcomes and could cause early death. It was noted that bisexual people in the cohort faced exclusion not just from outside the LGBTQ+ commu-nity, but from within it too. The study also highlighted the need to tackle an 'increasingly hostile policy climate for LGBTQ+ people'. The statistics are stark, but they are also likely an underestimation of how bad things are, as nurses have, according to the study, 'protective factors the general population doesn't have' such as a stable job, education and an understanding of health and wellbeing.[5]

## Minority Stress

This is not the first time we have seen anti-LGBTQ+ sentiment affect queer and trans wellbeing. It's often discussed in the context of mental health, but that stress is also damaging to the physical body. Research has demonstrated the direct relationship between discrimination and psychological stress and shown that experiencing even mild anti-LGBTQ+ prejudice can have a negative effect, resulting in increased heart rate, blood pressure and cortisol.[6] Over time, responses like these can lead to heart disease, stroke, poor mental health outcomes and more.[7]

It doesn't require a medical degree to realize how hard it is to maintain good mental and physical health when your existence is continually subject to intense political and media debate and scrutiny. And then when health problems do manifest, we might not receive the care we need and deserve.

## Healthcare as a Human Right

Health – and access to healthcare – underpins so much of day-to-day life. Timely access to effective and robust healthcare can be the difference between getting treatment for a mild infection and dying of sepsis. It's the difference between having cancer that is detected, caught early and treated, and being given a terminal diagnosis. It's the difference between having well-managed pain and being in debilitating agony which prevents you from working or looking after yourself or others, putting your housing and even your ability to buy food at risk. When people are unable to access healthcare, it can upend, or simply just end, lives.

It's because of this that the right to health is enshrined in so many human rights organizations and statutes across the globe – including the International Covenant on Economic, Social and Cultural Rights. According to the World Health Organization, 'Every human being has the right to the highest attainable standard of physical and mental health.'[8] And that right to health is made up of five key parts: availability, accessibility, assessment, acceptability and quality. These are in addition to the human rights obligations of non-discrimination, participation and accountability.

But healthcare services in the UK and around the world are failing to meet their obligations to provide this care to many LGBTQ+ people through a lack of resources, education, information and provision, ultimately leading to worse outcomes. In some cases, we're even seeing a slide-back of previous progress.

## Culturally Competent Care

I was sixteen the first time I experienced homophobia in a healthcare setting. I had been cursed with the dreaded combination of a urinary tract infection and thrush, caused by the antibiotics used to treat the initial infection. After several days of trying to DIY some remedies – do not do this, I beg you – I reconciled myself to the fact I should probably tell my mum. She insisted I go to the local surgery.

The nurse was a brusque woman, her hair slicked back into an immaculate bun. She gave the impression that whatever you were about to say, it would annoy her. 'Is there any chance you could be pregnant?'

'Absolutely not,' I snorted.

'How can you be so sure?' She raised an eyebrow as if to say, 'I know what you young people get up to, and here you are with two infections. Don't try to pull the wool over my eyes.'

'Because I'm a lesbian.'

'You are not,' she shot back.

'Umm, I rather think I am,' I rebutted.

She sighed, looked me up and down once more and scrawled out a prescription.

At the time, I was mostly baffled and, more importantly, not feeling very well. I was feverish and tired. It was a while before I pieced together that I had just experienced homophobia. But why should my identity be undermined during a routine nurse's appointment? Why should I have to deal with that? Homophobia, as far as I know, is not a treatment for infection. I almost certainly wasn't the first person she had expressed those sentiments to, and I wouldn't be the last.

Sadly, I am not alone in having experienced this sort of discrimination. A 2017 survey of 108,000 LGBTQ+ people[9] found that at least 16% of respondents who accessed or tried to access public health services had a negative experience because of their sexual orientation and at least 38% had a negative experience because of their gender identity.[10]

General practitioners are the first port of call for healthcare in the UK, and their practices have changed significantly over the past decade as they have become increasingly overstretched and underfunded. As I was growing up, my GP knew me and my entire family well. Now, I almost never see the same doctor twice. This is problematic in terms of continuity of care, and it's worse for LGBTQ+ people, who are forced to repeatedly come out to new people due to a lack of centralized data-keeping. In 2022, only around half (56%) of LGBTQ+ patients said their needs were met by their GP which dropped to 47% for trans respondents.[11] LGBTQ+ people are less likely to have a regular healthcare provider, something which can be compounded by other factors such as not having consistent housing or a permanent fixed address.

A 2021 study by TransActual found that 45% of trans respondents said their GP lacked an understanding of their needs – increasing to 55% for non-binary people.[12] A shocking one in seven respondents said that their GP had refused to provide care or treatment on account of their trans status at least once. It is understandable, then, that 57% of trans people reported avoiding going to their doctor when unwell, and that 16% 'often' do this. The data was even more alarming for trans Black people and other trans people of colour, with 53% of Black people and people of colour reporting experiencing racism whilst accessing trans-specific healthcare services.

Across the board, 17% of LGBTQ+ people reported experiencing discrimination at the general practice, rising to 25% for trans people, with 58% saying that they felt unable to complain. It's unsurprising, therefore, that LGBTQ+ people are less likely to have access to a regular healthcare provider, and even when they do, the evidence suggests those healthcare providers are often unable to offer the necessary support in a culturally competent way.

## Mind the Knowledge Gap

It was only when writing this chapter that I realized that, since my experience with that nurse, I've never revealed my sexuality to a GP, even when it's been relevant. One question I'm often asked at the diversity and inclusion talks and workshops I give to companies is whether it's necessary to mention a person's sexuality or gender when at the doctor's, and my response is that I don't ever want someone to be forced to hide any part of themselves. Having a holistic overview of a person's wellbeing is important: who do they live with? Who looks after them? Do they get out into the community? Are they in a positive relationship? Do they have family? These questions are all relevant to a person's health and to their care, but they can put LGBTQ+ people in an uncomfortable position. Do they out themselves to a doctor they can't be sure will be knowledgeable, or worse, could be prejudiced? Or do they keep quiet, as I've done, and risk adversely affecting the quality of treatment provided?

Right now, many LGBTQ+ people are not receiving the same level of care as straight and cisgender people because the knowledge, skills and experience aren't there. It isn't there because it's not deemed a priority in training. Supporting LGBTQ+ people still makes up a minuscule part of training for healthcare professionals and is often extracurricular and therefore easily missed, and it often becomes the responsibility of patients to educate their doctors.[13]

It's particularly difficult for trans patients. Ayo (she/her), thirty-six, from the North East tells me that her GP repeatedly informed her that she was okay whilst she was feeling increasingly unwell. 'He only believed me when I almost died.' Ayo developed a blood clot, which embolized to her lungs, something there is an increased risk of when taking hormone therapy.[14] Although Ayo was being sent for blood tests – 'They're clear, they're clear!' the doctor would say. Because these results for trans people often fall outside the expected range for a diagnosis, trans people can end up becoming ill.[15]

I've heard repeatedly of trans people having to explain their blood test results to their doctors, who are clueless about the meanings, and of nurses insisting trans women take pregnancy tests when they do not have a uterus. Data suggests that there are around as many people in the UK with rheumatoid arthritis as there are trans people.[16] The NHS would not for a moment think about not including the former within their training. Whilst there may have been a time in which healthcare professionals were less likely to encounter a trans person in their practice, this is no longer the case, and they need to be prepared to provide care to patients. Failure to do this denies people their right to health.

## LGBTQ+ Healthcare and Eugenics

We can't have a meaningful conversation about LGBTQ+ healthcare today without first discussing eugenics. It's a scary word, but the reality is, throughout the nineteenth and twentieth centuries in the Western world, it was one of the most popular scientific approaches, if not the most popular approach, across a number of fields, including medicine. Coined initially by Francis Galton in the late nineteenth century, eugenics is the theory – rooted in white supremacy – that humans can be improved by the selective breeding of populations. It was widely adopted by the governments of the US, Great Britain, Italy, Mexico and Canada.[17]

In the 1930s and 1940s, the Nazi Party attempted to 'cleanse' the German people and Nazi state of those who were considered undesirable – around six million Jews and a further five million prisoners of war who were from other ethnic minorities, as well as disabled and LGBTQ+ people.[18]

After the tragedy of the Holocaust, eugenics became less overtly popular, but it was still actively in place as policy, for example by the US government through forced sterilization[19] of 'undesirable' populations – namely immigrants, people of colour, Indigenous people, unmarried mothers and disabled people. It's vital to understand that these were not political acts in isolation. At the time, eugenics was endorsed by intellectuals around the world: leading scientists, academics and political leaders perpetuated eugenic beliefs and policies, many of which still exist today – typified perhaps most strongly by the rhetoric espoused in lockdown that things were okay because Covid-19 only killed the disabled, sick and old.[20] Although much of the original theory was centred on producing white, non-disabled people, it also targeted homosexuality and gender non-conformity. R. W. Shufeldt – a reputed doctor and scientist during the early twentieth century – felt it essential to prevent the breeding of 'sexual perverts and inverts – psychopathic types'.[21]

To be queer or trans was considered, by Shufeldt, an inbuilt trait that was heritable. It could not be cured but it could be prevented. Over time, attitudes shifted; homosexuality was then still punishable under the law, but it was also viewed as a disease, a psychiatric disorder, and that meant it could be treated. The dichotomy in these perspectives can be seen in the way judges were given the option to hand down prison sentences to those they considered criminal or treatment to those considered mentally ill. These so-called cures varied from chemical castration to electric shock treatment, but all were barbaric. Known as the 'Father of Lobotomies', Dr Walter Jackson Freeman II performed such operations across the US up until the mid-1960s, with around 40% of his patients being gay men; given that he performed over four thousand lobotomies – that's a huge number of gay men – all without any formal surgical training. Slicing the pre-frontal cortex's connections, Freeman was attempting to 'cure' homosexuality by tackling the supposed schizophrenia that it was believed to be a side effect of. 'It would appear that homosexuality is of little practical importance after frontal lobotomy,' he wrote.

The 'treatment' of homosexuality continued long after decriminalization – peaking in the 1960s and 1970s.[22] So-called therapies included electroshock therapy, prescription of oestrogen, psychoanalysis and much more. As recently as the 1990s, those serving in the UK armed forces were offered conversion therapy[23] – a practice in which LGBTQ+ people are forced to attempt to change their gender or sexuality. There's a tragic, and horrific, irony in the fact that very similar hormones to the ones we often deny transgender people were forced on queer men to feminize them, because medicine – for a long time and to this day – is rooted in reinforcing conformity.

## The AIDS Crisis and its Lasting Impact

The legacy of the AIDS crisis looms large in many LGBTQ+ people's experiences of health and healthcare. So many queer and trans people I have spoken to told me of the deeply entrenched shame they still feel about their sexuality. They know they should not, but they do because others have treated them as dirty, quite literally.

In 1981, the US Centers for Disease Control (CDC) published an article describing the prevalence of a rare type of lung infection, usually only seen in immunocompromised people, in five previously healthy gay men in Los Angeles, California.[24] The same day, the CDC received reports that groups of gay men in New York and California were experiencing a rare and aggressive cancer, again associated only with those with suppressed immune systems.[25] Within days, news grew of queer men being attacked by infections which ordinarily their bodies would fight off, and less than a fortnight later, the first man to be diagnosed with AIDS was admitted to the National Institutes of Health, aged thirty-five. He died in October 1981.[26] Just a few weeks later, the UK's *Gay News* ran the headline, 'Gay cancer or mass media scare?'[27] It was largely ignored. After all, homophobes had spread so many scaremongering stories about gay cancer during the 1960s and 1970s, this was nothing new.

No one could have predicted the impact that HIV and AIDS would have on the world, nor indeed for how long. Since the beginning of the epidemic, 85.6 million people have been infected with HIV and about 40.4 million people have died of AIDS-related illness, many of them people living in Africa. And, whilst queer men were one of the first communities affected by HIV – and held responsible for the epidemic – anyone can get HIV. In fact, in the UK, straight people are more likely to receive a new HIV diagnosis than gay and bisexual men.[28] For a long time, though, it was deemed to only affect LGBTQ+ people, to the extent it was referred to as 'gay-related immune deficiency', or GRIDS.

Over forty years since the epidemic began, the impacts have been huge – people lost innumerable friends, lovers, community, family and so much more. The experience of living through the AIDS crisis, whether HIV+ or not, has resulted in many people developing what has become known as AIDS survivor syndrome, which is used to articulate the physical, psychological and emotional impact of living through the grief and trauma of the AIDS epidemic.[29]

Yet, despite its influence and impact on older generations, so many young people I know – LGBTQ+ or not – have never heard of the AIDS crisis. For many, the Russell T. Davies series *It's a Sin*, starring Olly Alexander, was the first exposure they had to it. In fact, the first episode alone led to people searching in their droves for more information, with a 3,100% jump in searches for 'Why was AIDS so deadly in the 80s?' and a 2,150% rise for 'Can women get AIDS?'[30]

I found out about AIDS when I was fourteen, the day I came out – was forced out – to my mum. It turns out, I should have a gay uncle. My grandfather died of a sudden and catastrophic heart attack when my mum was just thirteen years old, and it was her cousin who stepped in as a father figure in her life. He was supposed to walk her down the aisle and be there for those important life moments.

But, like so many queer men in the 1980s, he contracted HIV and subsequently died of AIDS in the winter of 1986, aged forty-two. Until I came out, I didn't know he had ever existed.

'I tried to block it out,' Mum tells me. 'I'd lost my dad suddenly. Arthur came into our lives and was a massive support for four years, and then . . . he was gone too.' At the time, Mum was just seventeen. Arthur died a month before her eighteenth birthday, and – although she spoke to Arthur's ex-partner very briefly – she was not allowed to know at the time what had killed him, though she suspected it might have been HIV.

'It was all too painful.' The heartbreak of what had happened to Arthur never left my mother. The day I came out, she told me how she had sat at his bedside in St Mary's Hospital in Paddington as he wasted away and spoke of the catastrophic failures of the medical and political systems which contributed to his death. St Mary's undertook pioneering research which went on to pave the way for the creation of antiretroviral treatment, with some of the most significant studies published just months after Arthur's death.

Our understanding of HIV has improved significantly since the 1980s, and there are medicines available – namely PrEP and PEP – which can be taken to prevent the contraction of HIV after exposure (PEP), or to reduce the likelihood of contracting HIV for higher-risk groups (PrEP). People living with HIV in the UK now have a life expectancy in line with those not living with it.[31] But despite this, the shame and stigma persist, with long-lasting impacts on health.

During the 1980s, men who had sex with men were placed under a lifetime ban on donating blood, due to fears about the spread of AIDS.[32] It wasn't until forty years later that the NHS made significant changes to who could give blood, focusing not on identity but instead on actual sexual practice and individualized risk factors.[33] But these changes came far too late, when we knew as early as the mid-1990s that blood could be safely taken from queer men. The policy contributed to the stigma of people with HIV, and, by association, queer and trans people, as 'dirty'.

'I still get people who lived through that time period who feel they need to apologize to me because I have to touch their body when they have HIV,' says Ana Bott (she/they), the world's only advanced clinical massage therapist specializing in trans anatomy. People flock from across the world – Canada, America, Germany, Norway – to attend their clinic in Brighton. 'Older people still feel that shame because they've had such bad experiences of healthcare, of the stigma associated with their condition. And you just think – my god, how long has this stigma and shame lived in this person's body? What other healthcare are they not seeking?'

Ana tells me she wishes she could reassure and comfort their clients, but the reality is that the fears have a strong foundation: although it is illegal under the Equality Act, healthcare professionals have been known to deny care or provide a lesser standard to someone living with HIV. In the words of one doctor, as reported in one study, the stigma is 'pervasive, and it is something that has to be constantly battled'.[34] At another hospital, a senior doctor reflected that there was a reluctance to care for patients with HIV for fear of getting HIV themselves, even though this is not possible.

## Delaying Care

We see that when LGBTQ+ people arrive in healthcare settings, those settings have historically been – and often still are – sites of discrimination and harm. It's unsurprising, then, that queer people regularly avoid routine appointments and screening, if they are even invited to attend in the first place.

'The system does not compute trans people, it was not designed with them in mind, and it leads to health issues because people are getting missed,' Ana tells me. For example, if you are a trans man and the system lists you as male, you will not be invited for a smear test, even though many trans men still have a cervix. This means trans men can miss out on being invited for important screening tests which can help prevent the development of cancer.

'Trans people will come to my clinic and I might start to feel a mass at the back of their organs. And that's a really poignant and carefully managed moment when you have to tell someone, "Hey, there's something here and you need to see a doctor." For some, the fear of interacting with healthcare staff is greater than the fear of a malignant tumour.'

It's not just fear that prevents trans people from getting the care they need. In 2023, then Conservative Health Secretary Steve Barclay stated that, as part of ensuring the 'privacy, dignity and safety of all patients', he had 'ordered a reversal of unacceptable changes to the NHS website that erased references to women for conditions such as cervical cancer'. It's worth pointing out that at no point were women erased from the NHS website; there was simply language that acknowledged that not all women have a cervix (for example, as a result of having a hysterectomy) and not all people with cervixes are women. Robert Music, the chief executive of Jo's Cervical Cancer Trust, is clear: 'Cervical cancer can affect anyone born with a cervix, regardless of gender or sexual identity. Addressing harmful myths, such as cervical screening being less important for the LGBTQ+ community must be urgently addressed.'[35]

I don't speak for all women, but I know for a fact my womanhood is defined by far more than my reproductive organs – that seems a little bit anti-feminist to me, not least because there are many women who do not have ovaries due to hysterectomy. Are they less of a woman?

Gender-inclusive language does not cause tangible harm, but do you know what does? Excluding trans people from getting the care they need. When it comes to accessing gender- or sex-specific care, 29% of respondents to TransActual's survey reported having been refused care from gender- or sex-specific NHS services they needed, because they are trans.[36]

Not only trans people are affected. A lack of understanding has meant that lesbian, bisexual and queer women have been refused the HPV vaccination and smear tests.[37] As Sarah (she/they) recalled: 'I was told by a nurse once that I didn't need a smear as I was gay, even though in my past I had slept with men but didn't at the time of the smear. She refused to give me a smear, saying I didn't warrant one.'

## Can't Compute

'Without data, you are invisible,' said Michelle Ross, founder of CliniQ, a holistic sexual health and wellbeing service for trans people, partners and friends.[38] 'But right now, healthcare systems are unable to recognize and process data relating to gender diversity. In the UK currently, there is no system which can consistently record the existence of trans people – with the exception of the HIV and acquired immunodeficiency reporting system. This demonstrates that the failures of trans inclusion are not the responsibility of individual doctors or indeed even different trusts, but are baked into the infrastructure.'

Not all trans people will feel safe to disclose they are trans, but if they do, that should – with permission – be recorded on the system so that other clinicians can see it. It would ensure people could be addressed with the correct name and pronouns, as well as be invited to the appropriate screenings and their medical results viewed in context.

When it comes to the healthcare needs of trans people, 'the lack of data identification in general practice is one of the main barriers', says Dr Kamilla Kamaruddin. 'I have tried very hard to introduce transgender monitoring in general practice, but it is a system that is failing us.' As they go on to explain, the only code available is 'trans-sexual' – outdated and potentially offensive language.[39]

Whilst there are valid concerns about the way this data could be used to harm trans people, not being counted is dangerous, too. It leads to the argument that inclusive or specialist services designed to meet the needs of the trans community are not required because no one knows how many people the services would benefit. Accessing funding becomes almost impossible when there isn't enough data to make decisions on, especially in a system that is both resource-deprived and risk-averse.

## Race Relations

LGBTQ+ people are having to navigate an imperfect, sometimes biased, system when seeking care. But there's more to good health than issues which can be solved in a doctor's surgery. Increasingly, we're learning how important social determinants – those aspects of *society* which impact a person's life – are to their health.

A 2016 report by the Race Equality Foundation revealed that trans and non-binary people of colour faced particularly 'extreme barriers in accessing physical and behaviour care' because of the combined impacts of endemic transphobia and racism.[40]

Harvey Kennedy-Pitt founded Black Beetle Health, a public health community organization dedicated to promoting health, wellbeing and equality for LGBTQ+ people of colour, in recognition that racism, stigma and misinformation directly drive negative health outcomes experienced by this community. 'You can ensure people have housing and education and an ability to stay in employ-ment, and those are all really fantastic things, but it won't address the wider determinants of health, like structural racism and bias.' Harvey says. 'There is no help from the outside, so we have to really use the creativity that we innately have.' That creativity has spawned a range of resources across a range of health aspects, designed by and for LGBTQ+ Black people and people of colour. The organization also provides training for healthcare professionals, covering topics from decolonization to the impact of racism on health and much more.

## Beyond Textbooks

The barriers faced by LGBTQ+ people are due not only to the lack of funding, or the lack of knowledge on the part of practitioners. 'People's bodies are no longer the body that is in the textbook,' Ana Bott tells me. 'Maybe they have been microdosing on oestrogen or they have had a phalloplasty.'

Textbooks and other educational resources generally do not show queer and trans bodies – just as they still predominantly show white bodies – and there is important information simply missing out of not just ignorance, but a continual choice to exclude. We are not the only community excluded in textbooks; people of colour are still under-represented, meaning doctors miss important diagnoses because they do not recognize conditions in bodies outside of the white bodies that are the focus of textbooks, something which has been normalized.[41]

When I speak to other clinicians or therapists, they say, 'I would never turn a trans person away.' And I should hope not, but at the same time, do you know how to work with them? Do you understand top surgery? Can you talk to me about how testosterone is going to alter muscle tissue? Sometimes people say, 'I treat everyone the same,' but that is not equitable care. You would never dream of treating every single person with arthritis or diabetes in the same way – that's not biopsychosocial healthcare, that's not looking at people's individual needs.

## And What You Can Do About It

→ If you are a health or wellbeing professional, be informed about how best to serve your LGBTQ+ patients and clients so that you can provide an equitable level of care. There are some things – like getting names and pronouns correct – that are absolute bare minimums, but there are also specific things, like understanding that bodies may look or respond differently from how you've understood or been trained in the past. This can include undertaking professional development specific to queer and trans people's health needs, researching the specific barriers LGBTQ+ people are faced with and speaking to LGBTQ+ groups within your field or area, of which many are in existence. It also means listening to your patients, who are sometimes very clued-up on their health because they are aware there may be a lack of support. It might also mean ensuring patients attend appointments and regular check-ups, which they may avoid if they do not feel comfortable attending.

→ Support organizations like the LGBT Foundation, which do incredible work looking at the health and wellbeing of a massive range of LGBTQ+ people. This is something anyone can get involved with – not just professionals – and there are lots of volunteering opportunities, which might include anything from working in sexual health outreach to sitting on an advisory board. Lots of organizations have a range of roles for all types of people, and many of them are remote and could be done from home, if you have an hour or two spare each week.

→ If you feel comfortable, ask your local GP surgery or medical practice how they include LGBTQ+ patients – not just if they do. In my experience, lots of places say they do, but making them articulate the how forces them to think through the tangible actions they take. You could even start with something as simple as, 'Do you have any information on how you support LGBTQ+ patients?' or more specific questions like, 'Is this a practice that supports bridging prescriptions?'

→ You could consider becoming a patient advocate, supporting LGBTQ+ people to be listened to during their medical appointments, understand their rights as patients and ensure they get the care they need. This is something I've done informally for people in the community, but there are organizations that specifically offer training to do this. Even volunteering to be with a person at an appointment can be a great help, especially if you know an LGBTQ+ person who does not have family or close friends who can attend with them.

# Putting in the Work

## Dr Ronx (they/them)

Dr Ronx is an emergency medicine doctor, TV presenter and LGBTQ+ figure best known for starring on the CBBC show *Operation Ouch*, a children's TV show which educates children about medical topics.

Dr Ronx identifies as a queer, Black, androgynous intersectional feminist and speaks passionately about the importance of representation both within the community and specifically in healthcare. Driven by the belief that 'you cannot be what you do not see', Dr Ronx uses their platform to ensure people like them and particularly young Black queer and trans people know that there are opportunities in the world and in medicine.

Dr Ronx's work in emergency medicine is marked by a deep commitment to patient care, and they often use their platform to talk about the healthcare challenges faced by LGBTQ+ people, particularly trans people and LGBTQ+ people of colour. Beyond their medical and television career, Dr Ronx is an outspoken advocate for social justice, addressing issues such as racial inequality, access to healthcare and mental health awareness.

## Greg Owen (he/him)

Greg Owen is a prominent advocate and founder of *iwantPrEPnow.co.uk*, a site that helps people who are seeking PrEP to access this medication, which can prevent the spread of HIV. His work has led to thousands of people, particularly queer men, not becoming infected with HIV to the extent that – in the space of twelve months – there was a 40% reduction in HIV rates across gay men in London. Owen was not a doctor, or working in the healthcare space, but was working as a barman and homeless in 2015, when his friend Alex came to the UK from the US, where PrEP was more widely available. Owen wanted to take it but needed an HIV test first. It was positive.

Owen was frustrated that a medication that was not available on the NHS might have prevented him from contracting the infection. Although countries such as the US had made PrEP available, it was not widely available for sale in the UK, with just a single clinic providing the drug and at a cost of nearly $700 a month. iwantPrEPnow.co.uk offered the drug at one-tenth of the cost. Owen suddenly became a community leader overnight. It was not just an oversight that meant the NHS would not offer PrEP, but an outright refusal to pay for the drug. A lengthy legal battle was launched by The National AIDS Trust, who took NHS England to Court and eventually won.

Owen's work has been described as 'absolutely critical' by Professor Sheena McCormack – whose life's work as an epi-demiologist has been to track and fight the virus; 'And if iWantPrEPNow hadn't come along, we would not have been able to signpost people, or to very quickly come together with Greg to work up a safety net to make sure the drugs people were accessing were real.'

# CHAPTER 5
# Mental Healthcare

The idea of peace for LGBTQ+ people shouldn't be far-fetched and yet, at times, it can feel like a distant reality.

I was fourteen when people started telling me to kill myself for being gay. Other suggestions included self-harm and starving myself. And when I say people, I mean anonymous classmates at school. The messages I received online were anonymous but would detail where I'd had lunch and what lessons I'd had, so I knew they came from my peers. I just never knew who; I still don't. The ones telling me that my parents wanted me dead were always the worst.

I did what you are encouraged to do in these situations – speak to a teacher – but no real action was taken. I was made to feel as though the bullying was my fault and, had I been quieter, less visible, perhaps I wouldn't have experienced it.

So, I shut up, especially on the days when I got horrendous messages. Only a handful of close friends knew that the hate continued.

By the time I was in sixth form, the bullying had mostly stopped, but it was too late to undo the damage of this early homophobia. My resilience had slowly been worn away in a relentless process of attrition. I was done. It took another two and a half years, but I ended up being sent to a mental health team, who realized I was a complex case. I was misdiagnosed with bipolar disorder – which happens fairly regularly to autistic women. But the misdiagnosis was also, in part, because I didn't know how to explain that experiencing homophobia was traumatic and that every time I went into the world I was triggered, expecting to encounter it again.

As an adult working as an activist for LGBTQ+ and disability issues, I probably receive more hate now than I ever did as a kid, but I can handle it better. Back then, I was a child who was scared, not out to most of my family and with fewer critical thinking skills. Yet the mental health system expected me, as a teenager, not only to recount the things that had happened to me to a stranger, but to articulate them in a way that made it clear they were traumatic when I didn't have the vocabulary to do that. I'd heard of the term PTSD, but that was the purview of people who'd experienced war or sexual violence or other horrendous things. I didn't think it applied to me. I never lied, but none of the experts I saw were able to join the dots and recognize that homophobia, especially when experienced as a child, was a serious experience.

And I didn't realize it myself because I was just getting on with life as best I could. I didn't think it strange that I walked around in a fugue state, constantly thinking I was better off dead because that was what I had been told.

## Getting Help

It took me a long time to get NHS mental health support. Eventually, though, I found myself in the waiting room of a specialist service in North London. Granted, the specialism was bipolar disorder, which it turned out I didn't have, but it was better resourced than most mental health teams and gave me access to the professional help I needed.

The waiting room looked more like a community centre than a hospital – it was a long white room with a semi-transparent roof that let the light in. The therapy rooms, by contrast, were small and dimly lit, housing god-awful lime and traffic-cone orange sofas with covers that were peeling away at the edges. The corners always had some disregarded children's toy that I would spend the entire hour pulling apart and putting back together. Despite the initial misdiagnosis, this service ended up giving me the biggest gift: a queer and trans care coordinator. Niamh had long dark hair, wore mostly black and stomped about in a pair of worn Doc Martens. She had a plethora of gothic tattoos across her forearm and under her clavicle. Instantly, I felt safe. She was one of the first people to realize that I didn't have bipolar disorder; I had experienced homophobia at a young age and that had changed how my brain operated. I'd seen dozens of practitioners by then – more specialist, more senior – and none of them had worked that out.

## Identity-aware Care

We never talked about her identity because that wasn't the point. But she would sometimes mention her partner or events she had been to, giving me the subtle signs I look for to help find fellow queer people. There are aspects of being LGBTQ+ I often have to explain to people who aren't in the community: what a TERF is, that there are still so many people who hate the existence of LGBTQ+ people and some of the reasons they cite for doing so, and the tangible impacts, like an escalation in hate crime, which come when the government questions your existence. Being able to talk without justification, without explanation, to a queer therapist was life-changing.

That's not to say that only LGBTQ+ people can deliver LGBTQ+ inclusive mental healthcare. Later, when I was twenty-one, struggling with depression and a nice smorgasbord of unhealthy coping mechanisms, I was lucky enough to see another psychologist, who I think genuinely saved my life. As far as I'm aware, she wasn't

LGBTQ+ but she took the time to research the things impacting me, respectfully asked questions if there was something I said which she didn't understand and spoke to other clinicians. It was not rocket science: it was what I would consider the most fundamental aspect of healthcare, but she was the first clinician with whom I consulted who recognized a gap in her knowledge and sought to rectify it.

I felt obligated to write about the mental health of LGBTQ+ people because I have buried more friends as a result of suicide than anything else. Suicide feels like a regular occurrence in my community. A recent report in *Culture, Health & Sexuality*, an international journal for research, intervention and care, pointed out how difficult it is to track suicide rates for LGBTQ+ people accurately compared to the wider population. 'In the UK,' the report reads, 'understandings are hampered as sexual orientation, trans identity, nor gender identity are collected when recording death.'

But statistics consistently show how much more often LGBTQ+ people experience suicidal thoughts. In 2018, Stonewall found that 42% of LGBTQ+ people had felt that their lives were not worth living at some point over the last year, rising to 43% for bisexual men, 50% for bisexual women, 60% for trans people and 64% for non-binary people.[1]

These statistics are more than numbers. They're real people, with hopes, dreams, aspirations and friendships. They're kids who loved *Doctor Who* and the colour yellow, like Corei Hall, who took his life in 2023.[2] They're young campaigners and activists working to change the role of media representation.[3] They include my friend and former flatmate who spent their evenings playing video games with people across the world and who cooked the best roast potatoes I have ever had – before or since. They are brilliant, ordinary people who deserved so much more than the world gave them.

We have a tendency to treat suicide as an individual problem – the actions of a single person who makes a decision and then takes action to end their own life. So often it is seen as a choice, with the world assuming that the psychological, and often actual, violence inflicted by others could have been endlessly endured. But it's impossible to be indefinitely resilient. We fail to recognize what has led a person to make that decision and, in doing so, we deny reality.

In the case of LGBTQ+ people, those factors look like all the issues explored in this book. How can you keep living in a world that makes it harder to exist? Where you are denied access to healthcare, housing, family, leisure or community? How are you supposed to maintain good mental health when people like you are routinely talked about as a threat to others, as predatory, as endangering the lives of women and children? We've talked already about the physical health effects: the effects on mental health go even deeper.

I have never been angry with my LGBTQ+ friends for killing themselves. But I can't deny there's a psychological toll to all of this death for those left behind. What effect will opening up Instagram in the morning and being met with a memorial post or a fundraiser page have on the rest of us? What is the mental health toll of worrying who will be gone next?

## The Kids Aren't Alright

It's generally thought that Gen Z (those born between the mid-1990s and about 2010) are more accepting of LGBTQ+ life, more open with whom they love and more fluid in their identities. That may be true, but, if it is, it's not filtering down into increased happiness for young LGBTQ+ folk.

NHS Digital reports that around one in ten young people self-harmed in the last year, which rises to almost one in two for LGBTQ+ people aged 18–24.[4] In addition, as reported by Stonewall, more than a third of trans people and 41% of non-binary people harmed themselves, compared to 14% of non-trans LGB people. Alarmingly, 68% of LGBTQ+ people have experienced suicidal thoughts and feelings in the last year.[5] Young LGBTQ+ people in the UK are also almost three times more likely to have an eating disorder than their peers – with 20% being affected in the UK.[6] In the US, research by the Trevor Project saw this number rise to a staggering 36%.[7]

Despite the ostensible increased acceptance of queer and trans identities in younger generations,[8] LGBTQ+ people are still struggling at unprecedented rates. It is essential to recognize that this is not due to some inherent weakness of young LGBTQ+ people but because of the challenges they face. To me, these numbers are particularly telling. They illustrate how much increased visibility, and top-line 'acceptance' aren't enough. This acceptance can only do so much to shore up young people's wellbeing. Younger LGBTQ+ people might not be so aware of why these challenges exist, but they're seeing the impact of them – in their friendship groups, in their schools. It is no wonder young LGBTQ+ people are twice as likely to experience anxiety, depression and panic attacks than their peers[9] when they are contending with so much and, worse, when so much of what they face is hidden behind a glittery veil of acceptance.

I'd call it a silent epidemic, but we talk about it openly; the research is there – it's just that no one seems to be listening.

## Finding a Therapist

Getting support for your mental health seems almost impossible now, irrespective of whether you are LGBTQ+ or not. Research conducted by Rethink Mental Illness, a charity for people severely affected by mental illness, found that 80% of people experienced a deterioration in their mental health as they waited for support, with the waiting lists for adult community mental healthcare being a staggering two years long (727 days). Waiting for care resulted in 64% of these people experiencing a mental health crisis, with a quarter attempting suicide.[10] No surprise, then, that almost four in five had sought help from emergency services.[11] It's a postcode lottery which can have deadly consequences.

It is clear that more people are choosing – or, more often, are forced – to seek care privately. If I sought mental healthcare on the NHS today in my local area, I might start treatment in the next year, if I am lucky. But if you can afford to pay, you can get a same-day or same-week appointment.

Across the globe, LGBTQ+ people are less likely to be able to afford private healthcare, but they are more likely to need it and there is no guarantee that mental health services will be equipped to support them.[12] The escalation in hate crime, worsening quality of life, increase in the cost of living and often hostile media and political landscape, combined with the fact that mental health support is not seen as an essential part of wellbeing for queer people, and therefore not funded sufficiently, is a real issue.

## A Controversial Diagnosis

In 2019, being transgender was finally declassified as a mental illness by the World Health Organization, and yet most trans people in the UK still require a diagnosis in order to access gender-affirming care, an umbrella term which refers to a combination of social, legal and medical measures that help people feel happy, healthy and safe in their gender. I'll explore gender-affirming care, and why it's so crucial to the happiness of so many, in more detail in the next chapter.

This means that it's still psychiatrists who have the power to determine whether someone is 'trans enough' to get the medical and social support that they need. To be given any one of a number of mostly synonymous diagnoses, including gender dysphoria, gender identity disorder and gender incongruence, in the UK you have to be seen at a gender clinic – whether privately or on the NHS. Although a diagnosis isn't needed for trans people to update their name, passport and NHS medical record; access single-gender spaces; or be protected under the Equality Act, it's an essential part of being approved for gender-affirming care and being given a Gender Recognition Certificate (GRC).[13]

If you want to get paperwork, such as GRCs, changed, or, as we saw in Chapter 1, get married under your correct gender, you will need to convince a psychiatrist. The system forces trans people to convince psychiatrists and psychologists not only that they are trans, but that they are in distress – but not too much distress – and that they deserve help. If they are considered to be in 'too much distress', it could be deemed by medicine that they are not transgender but experiencing a mental health issue.

But with waiting lists at between two and seven years for an appointment,[14] a two-tier system has developed, not only for mental healthcare for trans people, but for access to transition care in general, where only those who can afford to seek diagnosis privately can then take the next steps. I don't know about you, but the idea of a psychiatrist, who has often never met you before, deciding your identity and the essential path you can take in life is archaic. It reminds me of the ways psychiatrists would certify if women needed abortion care in the 1960s and 1970s in the US; if they did not believe that carrying a foetus was a risk to your wellbeing, you would be forced to carry.[15] And to be honest, to this day in the UK, abortion has still not been decriminalized, with doctors essentially holding the power over many women and pregnant people's reproductive systems.

I am, of course, not saying that trans people should not be offered the opportunity to speak to mental health professionals about their wellbeing or about their transition. I would love to see a world where trans people are able to have conversations with clinicians about their needs, fears and aspirations when it comes to their health. But that would require a radical overhaul of the current system, where psychiatrists are, more often than not, the guards with the keys.

The current set-up also reinforces binary views about gender:

you're either trans and want to 'switch' gender, or you're not. It's not uncommon for trans people to limit sharing the more fluid, but equally valid, parts of their experience in these meetings, playing into a more socially acceptable version of 'transness' they feel would be understood. They might emulate more binary characteristics (remembering that there is no legal recognition of non-binary people in the UK), avoiding talking about anything that seems outside of those conventions out of fear about what might happen if they do. As award-winning non-binary poet Harry Josephine Giles describes: 'psychiatry creates processes to deny trans healthcare, a tight mesh of restrictive ideas through which gender-diverse people are forced to squeeze themselves'.[16]

A knock-on effect of this system is that many trans people don't seek mental health support at all, worrying that disclosing any adverse mental health might result in the denial of treatment later down the line. And, vice versa, waiting to access gender-affirming care such as hormone therapy and surgery has mental health impacts for trans people, with surgery-related delays impacting four in five trans people according to TransActual's survey.[17]

## LGBTQ+ Care Without Psychiatry

With so many aspects of being LGBTQ+ having previously been considered mental health disorders, psychiatry and queer rights have a long and complicated history. As an establishment and as a practice, psychiatry has been instrumental in driving homophobia, biphobia, transphobia and oppression. We view asylums as a feature of the past, but we still have systems which force or coerce treatment, detain people indefinitely, place legal restrictions upon them and provide police with powers to detain people who are perceived as mentally ill. Abuse and medical neglect on wards is rife, or, as one person put it to me 'baked in'.[18]

We have seen how LGBTQ+ people are more likely to experience poor mental health and often less likely to have access to support. It follows that LGBTQ+ people are more likely to be sectioned or otherwise find themselves in a mental health crisis than our non-LGBTQ+ counterparts because problems get worse in the absence of appropriate support, although research into this area is somewhat limited because patients do not always feel safe to disclose their experiences. LGBTQ+ people report being prohibited from speaking about their gender or sexuality on inpatient wards, though their straight and cisgender counterparts could. Charli (they/them), twenty-three, from the West Midlands, describes how during their stay on a psychiatric ward they were not allowed to discuss their LGBTQ+ identity.

Charli tells me, 'We weren't allowed to share diagnoses, treatment plans or anything perceived by the unit as "too personal", which seemed to be an ever-changing list, but included our LGBTQ+ identities. Many of us were LGBTQ+ which we discovered in covert conversations. If we were found to be having such conversations, we were split up and not supposed to continue to interact. Straight, cisgender people were allowed to talk about their identities and relationships unpenalized.'

Several were also told by doctors and nurses that their identities were illegitimate because of their diagnosis; lesbians were told they were not lesbians because they had experienced sexual trauma, for example. According to Charli, 'Several of us – including myself – had been told by the doctors that our sexuality or gender was only due to being autistic.'

Mental health wards are – like many wards – often segregated by gender. Ash (he/they), twenty-eight, from London is a male non-binary person and whose paperwork states that he is male. Despite this, he has been placed on both female and male wards; in the female wards, he's struggled with that experience being incongruent with his identity. On the male wards, he was under such extensive threat from other patients that he was required to have a member of staff with him at all times because they were that worried he would be attacked. 'I was only on that ward for two days, but had the most vile things shouted at me in that time; patients asking if I had "chopped my fucking tits off", if I had a dick or not, what was I doing there and that I should fuck back off to the women's ward. I had three patients try to attack me even with the staff there.'

Despite being on a male ward and recognized as male on his paperwork, Ash was misgendered every single time and refused use of the men's shower as it was 'inappropriate', even though it was a single closed room with a lock on the door.

Ash was discharged not because they had recovered, but because it was so unsafe on the male ward and female ward alike. They were allowed back into the community, but was still – as he describes himself – 'severely mentally ill and homeless'.

Psychiatry as an institution sits at odds with a lot of abolitionist, feminist, disability justice and liberatory movements because of the ways in which it removes people from their communities for surveillance, restricts people's rights and freedoms, and submits them to involuntary treatment – which may well constitute torture, according to the UN.[19] And that is not to mention the direct parallels between the psychiatric system and the prison system: the over-representation of people of colour, forced medication (chemical restraint), lack of access to sunlight, fresh air, the restriction of movement, solitary confinement and much more.[20]

'I was unwell. I was very, very sick. I should have been free to recover in peace instead of being hounded for who I am and what is or is not in my pants,' Ash continues. 'I don't want special treatment. I just want to be treated with respect and humanity and empathy as you would expect with anyone.'

That shouldn't seem ambitious and yet it feels like a distant dream for the mental healthcare system right now. Although, as Micha Frazer-Carroll emphasizes in her book *Mad World*: 'I want to call on our imaginations to interrogate the idea that these systems still broadly "work" for many. Does calling the police in crisis situations "work" when it might result in death? Does restraint "work", when it destroys trust and traumatizes and kills people? Does the mental health system "work" when we are at the constant mercy of professionals, and will never be on equal footing? Does institutionalization "work" when people are removed from their families for years? When we all navigate the system under the threat of section, abuse or neglect?'[21]

The weaponization of mental healthcare was made even more evident when, in early 2024, leaked documents from NHS England revealed that all young people waiting for gender services appointments should be called in for a mental health assessment first. The letter, sent to healthcare providers, stated, 'We request all [children and young people] who have been allocated to your service for mental health review are assessed as soon as possible,' continuing to harmfully conflate being trans with being mentally ill.[22]

This assessment includes a 'gender experience summary form', which asks families whether young people are accessing private treatment, including hormone treatment – something which is nearly impossible to access on the NHS and increasingly difficult to access privately due to the mounting persecution of providers. As part of this letter, providers are told to stop prescribing puberty blockers or gender-affirming hormones and not to prescribe them going forward. If the trans child or young person and/or their family 'disregards your advice and you consider that this puts the child/young person at increased risk, then a safeguarding referral may also be appropriate in line with standard safeguarding approaches'.

In short, if children and their families do not comply with the limitations imposed on them – which may go against the best standard of treatment – they can be referred to social services. All of this is framed as a mental health assessment and as an offer of 'support' in recognition of waiting lists. But let me be clear: NHS England is purporting to offer trans people mental health support but instead limiting their access to the treatment they actually need.

The Good Law Project stated that 'we are concerned about what appears to be a misleading exercise in gathering data on which trans youth are obtaining private treatment . . . for the purposes of seeking to cause or compel them to stop treatment'.[23]

## Interconnected

One of the difficulties of writing a chapter like this is that mental healthcare can't be separated from other topics. Attempting to discuss mental health whilst remaining apolitical is like fiddling whilst Rome burns. Even with the best mental healthcare in the world, it's difficult to stay mentally well whilst you can't access housing. It's difficult to stay mentally well whilst fearing losing your close family and friends. It's difficult to stay mentally well when every time you try to watch the news or flick through a newspaper you're faced with your community being vilified and killed.

'We're not even coping, we're like, swinging from "oh, no, this is the end" to "okay, actually, I'm okay" before we swing back again,' says Ben Pechey (they/them), author of *The Book of Non-Binary Joy* and *Your Gender Book*,[24] as well as a speaker and trainer for businesses. They are a bold, immensely stylish human whose wardrobe epitomizes the phrase 'dopamine dressing'. They are also someone who has spoken very openly about the harsh realities of being a queer, trans person in the UK.

'We are asking truly for the bare minimum. We're asking for people, especially the trans people, that are alive right now to reach their potential and live to their expected age. That's, I think, all that anyone is asking for. I didn't realize the importance of that basic ask for a long time.

'And then I nearly died this year, in May. It made me realize I need to live. I need to live more. And I think asking for the bare minimum thing is important because I could scream and scream and scream about adoption of inclusive terms, changing the law to fully protect trans people and getting better documentation for genderless people but I know that's not going to happen right now. So I must move my focus on something that gives us all a bit more peace, and that is the bare minimum trans people deserve.'

## And What You Can Do About It

→ To make sure therapy and other treatments are culturally competent and accessible quickly, we need to push for mandatory training on LGBTQ+ matters for all mental health providers. Providers need to be equipped to ask the right questions, to be sensitive, to understand the seriousness of some of the challenges LGBTQ+ people face. We should support ongoing education about the unique mental health needs of LGBTQ+ individuals. Expanding access to LGBTQ+ friendly mental health services, including telehealth, is crucial, as well as promoting policies that reduce wait times and make care more affordable and accessible.

→ Advocate for the removal of psychiatric assessments in order for trans people to access GRCs and gender-affirming care and informed consent models. These models allow trans individuals to get the care they need without unnecessary evaluations that prioritize psychiatrists over people. We should support policies that respect the autonomy of trans individuals in their healthcare decisions and raise awareness about the harm the existence of these processes causes.

→ Donate to or fundraise for organizations that provide free mental health support to LGBTQ+ people in need. If you have spare money, donating to LGBTQ+ people to support with therapy costs is a brilliant way to support folks, particularly those who need a specific type of therapy not offered on the NHS or who are facing insurmountable waiting list times.

# Putting in the Work

## Dominic Davies (he/him)

Dominic Davies is a psychotherapist, clinical sexologist, practice consultant and founder of Pink Therapy, a directory of LGBTQ+ inclusive therapists. Davies (alongside Charles Neal) co-edited three of the first-ever British textbooks on working with LGBTQ+ clients, published in 1996 and 2000, and contributed numerous other papers and chapters to the literature of this emerging field and presented at many national and international conferences at a time when the topic of LGBTQ+ mental health was far from on the agenda even in healthcare settings.

In 2021, Davies was named as one of fifty Distinguished Gender and Sexual Health Revolutionaries as a result of his work. He, alongside Dr Meg-John Barker, coined the term GSRD therapy – a term which covers gender, sex and relationship diversities – giving psychotherapists a vocabulary and a framework for better supporting LGBTQ+ clients across the spectrum.

Davies has worked in the field for over forty years, but founded Pink Therapy in 1999 after seeing how challenging it was for LGBTQ+ people to find support that was inclusive. Each person listed on the site is accredited based on their level of training. For his work, Davies has also been made a Fellow of the National Council of Integrative Psychotherapists, the highest level of membership for this professional body.

## Vernon (he/him)

Vernon is the founder of TransSober, a community-led organization based in Brighton which supports trans and non-binary people who are trying to live drug- and alcohol-free. Vernon started TransSober after experiencing the negative consequences of having to hide parts of his identity as a gay trans person with a learning disability in order to access drug and alcohol services. He wanted to create a space that understood and catered for the specific experiences of trans and non-binary people, irrespective of their circumstances.

Now, TransSober offers three peer-support groups a week, all led by trans and non-binary people with a range of lived experiences of drug and/or alcohol misuse and its associated problems, but who are now living drug- and alcohol-free.

# CHAPTER 6
# The Life-changing Magic of Gender-affirming Care

## Wednesday's Story

'I feel that it was a very magical thing to feel, to experience,' the artist Wednesday Holmes (they/them) tells me, their right hand rubbing over their chest subconsciously whilst they talk. After thirty years of feeling uncomfortable, Wednesday was able to get a double incision mastectomy, a type of top surgery some trans people undergo, in which their breasts are removed, leaving behind a flat chest.

'When I got in the car on the way home, it was just the best feeling in my whole life,' Wednesday says, welling up. 'Yes, when you wake up from the surgery, you're in pain. You've got surgical drains coming out of your body. You take about a billion pills. But I went outside to the garden and it was sunny. The flowers were out. I just remember taking my hand and touching my chest. It [felt] like truly touching my real self for the first time. I'd been so utterly, utterly confused about who I was for such a long time. It wasn't until I was properly able to physically and mentally heal from that surgery that I felt like myself, something I hadn't done for over thirty years.'

Wednesday was twenty-five years old when they first told their doctor they were non-binary and that they would like to get top surgery, years after they'd been wanting it. Whilst their GP was receptive, they let them know they would need to achieve a medical diagnosis of gender dysphoria and there would be a wait for that. Speaking to other trans people in their area, Wednesday realized it would likely take between five and ten years to get the care they needed, if not longer. It ended up taking ten years for Wednesday to receive the appropriate treatment.

## What Is Gender-affirming Care?

Wednesday's experience – and the lived testimonies of thousands of trans people across the globe – could not be a sharper contrast to the headlines we often see regarding gender-affirming care. It's not uncommon to read stories about 'trans-ing' children and 'butchering' women; as one *New York Post* headline reads: "Gender-affirming surgery" puts a feel-good phrase on child butchery'.[1] Medical transition is repeatedly described as dangerous and experimental, and trans people who pursue gender-affirming care are maligned as crazy, unstable and doing intentional harm to themselves.

The media narratives surrounding trans healthcare are so far removed from any reality that I feel we need to start with the basics. Let's define gender-affirming care, because the reality is that most of the people having conversations about – and indeed, legislating and campaigning on – 'gender-affirming care' can not even accurately define it.

Although the phrase 'gender-affirming' is regularly applied to refer to transition-related care, transgender people are not the only people who receive it. Examples include:

- Oestrogen as a hormone replacement therapy for cisgender women and other menopausal people.

- Breast implants – for example, for cisgender women, transgender women and some non-binary people.

- Breast reductions – for cisgender women, non-binary people and cisgender men with gynaecomastia.

- Testosterone – for cisgender men experiencing low testosterone levels, some trans masculine and non-binary people, and some other LGBTQ+ people including lesbians.

- Laser hair removal – for anyone who has hair they want to remove.

- Hair grafts for balding – for cisgender men experiencing balding as well as trans and non-binary people, who can experience balding as a side effect of hormone treatment.

- Steroid usage in bodybuilding – for anyone; many anabolic steroids used by bodybuilding men also contain hormones.

- Botox – for anyone, cis or trans.

- Jaw-sculpting – likewise for anyone who wants to change the shape of their jaw.

- Liposuction – for anyone who wants to change their body's fat distribution or shape.

- Reconstructive surgeries after breast cancer – for anyone who has had breast cancer, which, although it affects cisgender women most commonly, can also happen in cisgender men and trans people.

- (Re)constructive surgeries of the testicles and penis – for cisgender men after an accident or injury, or for trans-masculine people.

Demonstrably, gender-affirming care is something cisgender people seek, too. And cisgender people are able to access that care with far greater ease than their transgender counterparts. The drug spironolactone is commonly used to treat 'excessive' hair growth in cisgender women experiencing polycystic ovary syndrome (PCOS).[2] It's a drug some trans women take to prevent hair growth. Whilst I have had cisgender friends be offered the drug without even being asked about whether their hair growth is something important to them, transgender women are often expected to see at least one psychologist before treatment would be considered; in fact, in the UK, transgender people are regularly expected to undertake several consultations with a psychologist before being allowed to make decisions about their own bodies. As we touched upon in Chapter 5, being able to access gender-related surgery in the UK requires a formal diagnosis of gender dysphoria, gender incongruence or gender identity disorder.[3]

One person who spoke to me – Ella (she/her) – was just twenty-five when a doctor referred her to an endocrinologist for spirono-lactone, despite her protestations that she did not want to take that medication. 'It was noted that there was hair on my face. I had to repeat myself several times.' The medical care trans people seek is regularly presented by its opponents as reinforcing gender norms, reinforcing that there is a singular way to be a woman or a man that comes with necessary physical characteristics, but this is something that society (and particularly patriarchy) perpetuates.

Not only do cisgender people also receive gender-affirming care, they receive treatment more often than trans people and with far greater ease than their transgender counterparts. As psychologist Jae Sevelius suggests, 'The need for gender affirmation is not unique to transgender individuals, but may take on a more prominent role in their lives due to their gender minority status.[4]' However, when cisgender people undertake efforts to affirm their gender – no one bats an eyelid. In fact, we often applaud them. We recognize they understand who they are. In the US, there is no state which crim-inalizes a cisgender woman seeking a boob job if she wants to be seen as more feminine, whereas a transgender person getting a similar procedure could be committing a crime in several parts of the coun-try.[5] All that trans person is doing is saying they feel like a woman and taking steps to more accurately reflect and convey that in public. As a society, we uplift cisgender people who change their expression – whether through plastic surgery, tattoos, haircuts, clothing – all the time, but we don't extend the same courtesy to trans people.

## But Why Would People Change Their Bodies?

It is worth emphasizing that many trans people will never medically transition – either because they don't want to or because financial, geographical, medical or legal barriers make doing so impossible. There is also no one way to undertake a medical transition – some people take hormones to feminize, masculinize or neutralize their features, whilst others don't. Some people take hormones indefinitely, some people take them for a shorter period. Some people have surgery – whether affecting their chests, genitals or face – and others do not. Even within these categories are a range of surgical options and decisions trans people can make in conjunction with their doctors.

So just as there's no one-size-fits-all medical transition, there's no one-size-fits-all reason why people want to do it. If you ask trans people directly, answers will range from feeling a deeper sense of comfort with themselves to increased safety at work. Alfie (he/him), a forty-two-year-old trans man living in London, told me of the joy of being able to swim topless for the first time: 'I grew up near Llandudno, North Wales, and a lot of my childhood I spent in and out of the sea. There wasn't a huge amount of things to do as a teenager, so we usually went to the beach when we weren't in school.'

He continued, 'I adored swimming, but I always felt uncomfortable in swimming costumes although I didn't know why – we didn't really talk about trans stuff in the nineties. Thankfully, it was cold enough a lot of the time that everyone would wear a wetsuit if they had one – which are pretty gender-neutral anyway – or you could

get away with not going in at all because it was too cold. By the time
I was sixteen, I had pretty much stopped swimming at all. It's only
decades later and now that I have had top surgery (as well as being
on testosterone) that I have felt able to go swimming again. When I
was just on testosterone, I had a full beard and was quite muscular.
Lots of people read me as a man, anyway, but only because I hid my
chest under a binder and lots of layers even in summer. If I had gone
swimming, it would have been clear that I was transgender because
there was no hiding my chest. And although my scars still reveal that
I might be trans, they're so much less obvious. It's opened up a whole
new world for me – of movement, but also things like trips with my
husband and child to the beach without being scared or missing out.
I was able to take my daughter to swimming lessons and to be there
with her with the other parents.'

The evidence base in favour of gender-affirming care is overwhelmingly strong despite opponents to the practices positioning it
as experimental and dangerous. The Society for Evidence-Based
Gender Medicine, which seems to work to halt gender-affirming
care for young people, says: 'The history of medicine has many
examples in which the well-meaning pursuit of short-term relief of
symptoms has led to devastating long-term results.' It then goes on
to compare gender-affirming care to lobotomy and thalidomide,
positing that 'patients, families, and clinicians cannot make informed
healthcare decisions without knowing the likely benefits and harms
of the various interventions'.

But that's simply not true. The evidence is there and it's resound-
ingly positive. A systematic review of *all* peer-reviewed articles
published in English between 1991 and June 2017 identified fifty-six
studies, 93% of which found that gender transition improves the
overall wellbeing of trans people, with 7% reporting mixed or null
findings. Zero studies were found concluding that transition causes
overall harm.[6] The outcomes were clear: gender transition resulted
in improved quality of life, better relationships, higher self-esteem
and confidence and a reduction in anxiety, depression, suicidality

and substance use. It is for these reasons that leading medical organizations around the world recognize that gender-affirming care is medically necessary and support transgender people's access through this.

In 2023, the World Health Organization announced its intention to provide a guideline on the health of trans and gender-diverse people, with the intention of ensuring the access to and quality of health services for transgender people across the globe.

## Non, Je ne Regrette Rien

Whilst it is true that some people regret their transition, it is exceptionally rare, with regret rates ranging from 0.3 to 3.8% and often attributed to a lack of social support post-transition or the use of older, less effective surgical techniques.[7] To put that into context, up to 20% regret getting a knee replacement[8] and 21% of people regret corrective spinal surgery.[9] Indeed, the regret rate across all surgeries is about 14%.[10] Additionally, nearly 72% of men and 54% of women have regrets about marriage[11] and up to 14% of people regret the decision to have children[12] – both life-changing decisions with long-term repercussions. No one is denying patients knee or back surgery, because, as a society, we generally understand that no decision, especially a medical decision, is entirely free from the risk of regret. When it comes to gender-affirming care, however, we deny transgender people the autonomy to make decisions which, evidence overwhelmingly suggests, they are highly unlikely to regret.

## Waitlists, Waitlists, Waitlists

A pervasive myth surrounding access to gender-affirming care is that it can be obtained easily and rapidly. There is a belief that a person can say that they are transgender, walk into a doctor's surgery and get a referral or access to treatment. This is far from the case – but would it be so radical if it was? Free, accessible healthcare is after all a human right, not a privilege.

The claim that patients are fast-tracked could not be further from the truth. In fact, according to a survey conducted by TransActual, fewer than 15% of patients referred to a gender identity clinic since 2017 had attended their first appointment by 2022.[13] That appointment is not one where care might be decided or prescribed, it's simply an initial meeting with a doctor to get them up to speed with your medical care. In the summer of 2023, the BBC reported that the only gender identity clinic in South West England had an average wait time of seven and a half years.[14] A person could become a qualified architect in the time it takes to get a first appointment at the clinic. Whilst that was the longest wait time, the shortest – at Nottingham Centre for Transgender Health – was still four and a half years.

According to the NHS: 'The maximum waiting time for non-urgent, consultant-led treatments is eighteen weeks from the day your appointment is booked through the NHS e-Referral Service, or when the hospital or service receives your referral letter.' Transgender patients, therefore, are waiting between twelve and twenty times longer than the NHS's own standards. One argument I hear, even from well-meaning people, is that the NHS waiting lists are long for everyone right now. It is no secret that the NHS has been catastrophically underfunded by the Conservative government as a result of austerity, resulting in increased waits, lower standards of care and increased privatization.[15] Many wait times for treatment are inexcusable, but they still pale in comparison to those for transition-related care. I struggle to think of a demographic for whom being expected to wait half a decade for a first appointment would be considered acceptable.

Difficulties accessing treatment are not just down to underfunding. They can also be the result of serious management failures and the structural organization of the NHS, information which should alarm everyone.

## The Commissioning Fuck-up

When it comes to examining the failures of transition-related care, we have to look at the situation with metoidioplasty and phalloplasty on the NHS, which reveals failures in not only trans healthcare but also the commissioning structure of the NHS as a whole and the lack of duty of care for trans people. Law firm Leigh Day is now pursuing a legal investigation on the basis that they 'consider that these failures may be negligent and a breach of our client's human rights'.

Phalloplasty and metoidioplasty are two surgeries which trans men, some non-binary people and intersex people might have to create a penis – sometimes referred to as 'bottom surgery' or 'lower surgery'. Both procedures involve a multistage process, meaning that one operation is performed before allowing the tissues to heal and mature before beginning the next stage. Usually, this process would take about a year, and that was what patients expected. Now, it may be up to a decade before their surgeries are complete, despite having entered into the process under the expectation that it would last a year, maybe a little more.

Until March 2020, a single clinic – St Peter's Andrology – was the only centre contracted by the NHS across the whole of the UK to provide phalloplasty and metoidioplasty, essentially creating a monopoly on this surgery.[16] In the UK, all transition-related surgeries are centrally funded by a single body – NHS Specialist Commissioning – and when its contract with St Peter's Andrology expired, trans people were left in limbo. Whilst this coincided with all non-emergency surgeries being cancelled as a result of the Covid-19 pandemic, the issues relating to commissioning were unrelated to this.

By March 2021, all masculinizing lower surgeries in the UK had halted.[17] There was no fanfare, no outcry, just the quiet withdrawal of essential care from trans people, many of whom were not even informed about the situation. In total, it took seventeen months before NHS Specialist Commissioning announced that they had awarded a contract to a new provider – the New Victoria Hospital – and that surgeries would recommence. Despite a new service being commissioned, there was still a wait time of eight years for a stage one surgery. Patients who were waiting for stage two or stage three repair surgeries received a letter informing them their care had been transferred, but many were not given any indication of when they could expect to receive an operation date.

Chay Brown, co-founder of TransActual, was one of the people impacted by the failures, which resulted in him being forced to seek care privately: 'I had my first stage of lower surgery in 2019. By the summer of 2022, I still hadn't been offered a second date, but I had already taken my transition into my own hands. And because I'm very fortunate, I was able to go overseas, and go private and finish it.'

Although I was aware of the issues with commissioning, it was what Chay revealed about the lack of actual trained medical staff which shocked me most. 'Part of the wait was due to the availability of people to perform the surgery. NHS England is now training two teams for phallo and meta, but the question is: why didn't they start trying earlier? Why didn't they start training earlier?' With between one and two thousand people on the waiting list, clearly, resources are needed.

For Chay and many other trans people, the impacts of these institutional failings have had significant consequences. Not only does waiting between surgeries impact physical health – including sexual intimacy and urinary incontinence and infection – but it has repercussions on mental wellbeing, relationships and employment. When asked about the impacts of waiting for surgery by TransActual, responses emphasized feeling 'trapped' and 'stuck' as a result of the failings, unable to move on with their lives. One person waiting for stage three phalloplasty and surgical repairs stated, 'I've been too distressed by my physical situation to engage in any physical relationship, and my marriage broke down partially due to this. I had to leave my job due to problems caused by stress and time off work.'

Speaking of his own personal distress, Keelin McCoy, a trans man who is waiting for surgery to fix a painful complication, spoke of the horrific consequences of living in limbo: 'I've been waiting for stage three for two years. I didn't consent to this amount of time, especially given the fact I was given an estimate of six months as a maximum. I need corrective surgery, and until this is done I'm on pain medication as I suffer from bladder spasms hourly. I feel the NHS has completely failed me and thousands of others who are stuck in limbo, some of which can't deal with this mentally, and the mere thought that fellow friends have contemplated suicide all due to failings in the NHS to negotiate a deal is disgusting beyond belief.'[18]

Matthew, who is also being represented by the legal investigation, says, 'I have now been living for three years with an incomplete penis reconstruction. This continues to have vast negative impact on my mental health. My confidence has disappeared. I haven't been able to socialize like I used to, travel or gain new employment. I find it hard to trust people now. I have been hugely affected by stress, which has resulted in other knock-on health issues such as anxiety, depression, insomnia, hair loss and suicidal ideation.'

The financial repercussions of this NHS mismanagement must be considered, too. Essentially, the failure by the NHS has resulted in people being unable to work, advance their careers or go abroad for work, and some people even using money set aside for retirement. As one retired person stated: 'Finding my own way through the lack of "health" services for trans people from the very beginning of transition, including paying for hormones and top surgery, has cost me nearly seven thousand pounds, which I could not afford and can never get back. This makes me depressed as I am never likely to earn again, and that money would have made a great difference in my retirement.'

Even if you are not trans, the experiences trans people face should alarm you, particularly if you rely on the NHS for treatment. This time it was trans people, but it could easily have happened to another group. Though I suspect if, for example, the NHS failed to train and commission people to do breast reconstruction surgeries for cancer patients, there would be an outcry. Every time trans people are subject to low standards of 'care' by the medical system, it legitimizes that standard for everyone.

## Socio-economic Implications

Financial barriers to transition-related healthcare exist across the board, not just within metoidioplasty and phalloplasty.

'The situation we found in our Transition Access Survey is that around half of people go private,' Chay tells me, 'at least for part of their transition, and it's exacerbating the socio-economic divide, especially when we consider all the factors that could impact someone's financial situation – intersecting forms of oppression and things like that.'

Indeed, the average amount for those who had incurred costs associated with their transition was £5,573.[19] Facial feminization surgery (FFS) is not currently available on the NHS, despite being one of the surgeries trans women and trans feminine people most often seek. This is one of the reasons the average surgery costs for trans women and people on the trans feminine spectrum were significantly higher at £17,276,[20] compared to £7,518 for trans masculine respondents. Stories of trans people skipping meals to pay for medication are not uncommon.

Put simply, the system in the UK is such that trans people are being put into a terrifying predicament: either pay or risk your well-being and material safety on a day-to-day basis. As a result, it is often only wealthy or otherwise privileged trans people who are able to transition. This system often excludes the most marginalized within the trans community, including those who are sex workers or experiencing homelessness. Many trans people around the world are forced to crowdfund in order to gain enough money to access care. So prevalent is the phenomenon that platforms like GoFundMe have created a hub for those raising money for gender-affirming care, verifying fundraisers to ensure that they are legitimate and non-profit organizations with funds which can be used for gender-affirming care.[21]

The ways in which gender identity clinics and clinicians operate have resulted in the perpetuation of racism, and the prioritization of Eurocentric features has been seen across gender-affirming care providers.[22] Eurocentric beauty standards refer to the ideals of physical appearance that prioritize traits associated with European features, including fairer skin, straight or wavy hair, narrow noses, high cheekbones, hourglass body shapes and less obvious body hair. Clinical psychotherapist Dr Gávi Ansara described how he met Black trans women who were denied hormones and surgeries on the basis that they were considered 'too "masculine" to be women according to non-Black cultural gender norms'. The concept of 'passability' has come up repeatedly in my conversations with transgender people. Beauty norms are impossible to disentangle from colonial attitudes which prioritize whiteness and white features but, in the case of transgender people of colour they lead to them having healthcare denied. Even if care is able to be accessed, it can be tricky to find surgeons who share results of patients of colour, which is why Travis (he/him) felt compelled to create a resource specifically for trans people of colour to come together and be better informed about surgeons who have had the best results on bodies that look like theirs in the UK.[23]

One study in 2019 found that fewer than one in ten referrals to the Gender Identity Development Service (known as GIDS) were for young trans people of colour.[24] The research attributed this low number of referrals, in part, to a lack of familial and particularly parental support. TransActual's survey found that 95% of trans people of colour reported that they had experienced transphobia from family members.[25]

## Trans Healthcare Bans

In the US, it is not just financial or medical barriers denying trans people their healthcare, but political decisions. Over the course of 2022 and 2023, several states in the US introduced bans on gender-affirming care, particularly focused on minors.[26] At the time of writing, twenty-one states have banned gender-affirming care for minors, with a further seven considering similar laws. Some states, such as Kentucky, Alabama, Arkansas, Florida and Indiana, have court injunctions ensuring people can continue to access care, which is still available for now. In five states, it is now a felony to provide medical care for trans youth.

Several laws have also been enacted that restrict healthcare for people of all ages. Seven states have banned Medicaid from covering some forms of gender-affirming care[27] – a decision impacting an average of 38,000 people.[28] The precedent being set by this kind of legislation should alarm everyone. It suggests that governments can single out groups of people and deny them healthcare, in effect controlling what they can and cannot do with their own bodies. On the surface, it might seem that politicians are simply looking out for their constituents, ensuring that medicine is rooted in evidence, but when the evidence from every reputable major medical organization in your country supports gender-affirming care and condemns your actions, that does not seem to be the case.

And whilst in the UK health services providing care for transgender people are not yet facing outright legal bans or bomb threats, they are being undermined, under-resourced and ultimately prevented from delivering essential care.

## The Cass Review

In 2024, Dr Hilary Cass published her review of trans-related healthcare services in a study commissioned by the NHS to look into GIDS.

The publication of the report was celebrated by anti-trans campaigners as a significant win, which was a very odd spectacle – how strange to see people gleefully celebrating denying healthcare for kids. Amnesty International – amongst other human rights organizations – condemned the way the report was being used: 'This review is being weaponized by people who revel in spreading disinformation and myths about healthcare for trans young people,' the charity stated.[29] The Cass Review was not a scientific review but a political document and one littered with problems or, as Novara Media put it, 'few have dared to fail so publicly'.[30] Very little data in the report was new (which is not inherently surprising as it was a systematic review), which made the new recommendations on restricting trans healthcare more alarming.

The report was worrying, not only because it excluded large swathes of existing evidence on trans people's healthcare but it also undermined important notions of legal competence around medical treatment.

## Methodological Flaws

A good example of this is the fact that Cass reported that 'the evidence base, particularly in relation to the use of puberty blockers and masculinizing/feminizing hormones, had already been shown to be weak.' How Cass came to this conclusion is alarming, but unsurprising given the ways evidence was graded. Of the 103 studies into puberty blockers and hormones, they deemed only two studies to be of high quality. That in and of itself is not wrong to do, but only

two guidelines were used for review, something which has been criticized by other health bodies across the globe as being out of line
with best practice.[31]

## Double-blinded Studies and Questionable Ethics

Several of the exclusions to the Cass Review were implemented due
to either the size of the study or the failure of not 'blinding' the
control group. It would be impossible, not to mention highly
unethical, to change someone's hormones and puberty without their
knowledge, given the impacts it would have on their bodies – let
alone to consider doing this without their knowledge. The question
of the study size and length of results is also strange, given just how
recently children and young people had access to medical support
and given how many other examples of medical care exist where we
have little long-term data and where sample sizes are small.

It's worth noting, too, that studies being of lower quality does not
mean the information within them is of lower quality: it might mean
the sample size is smaller, or results are written up in a different way.
Given that the trans population is small, and the number of people
getting access to gender-affirming care, especially young people, is
small, it follows that the research we have available may be on
smaller sample sizes. After all, you cannot have large, longitudinal
studies on communities if you are not delivering gender-affirming
care to many people over a long period.

Countless lives have been saved because of medical interventions
pursued in the absence of long-term data about their efficacy, or
safety, even. An excellent example of this is in the instance of
pandemics, such as Covid-19, in which, despite the lack of longitudinal evidence about the novel virus, there was a drive to create and
then roll out a vaccination because it was recognized to be in people's
best interest. Another comparison is what is known in pharmacy as
'orphan drugs' – drugs that are developed in small quantities to treat

a smaller number of people with rarer conditions. Examples of these drugs include those used to treat cystic fibrosis, leukaemia and haemophilia B. Even though the research on these drugs is on smaller populations, we don't automatically ban those medications or consider the evidence unsubstantiated because we recognize they serve a particular purpose for a community in need.

Cass suggests a need for a type of 'puberty blocker trial', implying that the drugs are in some way experimental or their risks are unknown. Doctors have been using puberty blockers as a treatment for over forty years, both as a way of limiting hormones in the treatment of some cancers, but also as a way of delaying puberty in very young children. In fact, although the NHS is now recommending that doctors stop prescribing puberty blockers for trans children, they continue to be prescribed for cisgender children. Both sets of children find their puberty distressing, and yet treatment is only available to cisgender children. One cannot help but feel it is not the drugs that are on trial. One of the suggestions of the report is the mandatory participation in medical trials as a condition of receiving care, which would be highly unethical – a kind of coercive consent. The Cass Review offers no explanations as to how the ethical challenges around studies might be circumnavigated because it isn't interested in them. 'The report does not appear to suggest how the ethical problems in the approach it calls for can be solved,' discrimination barrister Robin Moira White wrote for the *Independent*.[32]

The prioritization of randomized controlled trials over other types of data – which we use in research where that methodology would be unethical or impossible – such as expert opinion and observational study, places the Cass Review at odds with the approaches of other studies. It is telling that in adopting this approach, the report was able to exclude widely used best practice from around the world, including that of the World Professional Association for Transgender Health (WPATH), the leading global authority in trans healthcare.

## Excluding Trans People

One of the most alarming things about this research is that transgender researchers were explicitly excluded from the design and research team.[33] And whilst the review is praised by some as being 'independent', that Cass had negligible prior experience or knowledge of trans and gender-diverse youth or indeed transgender medicine and surgery, is astonishing; it is hard to imagine another area of medicine where such an approach has been used.

If a team composed entirely of men – some of whom happened to be incels involved in anti-feminist organizing – created a report about women's healthcare, excluded women from the research team and made suggestions that contradicted the evidence of every other group, I would like to think society would dismiss their work as inherently flawed from the beginning.

What's even more concerning is that the Cass Review was also written in such a way that it excluded personal and professional experiences. One senior psychiatrist at a gender identity clinic put it: 'The terms of reference stated that the Cass Review "deliberately does not contain subject matter, experts or people with lived experience of gender services" and Dr Cass herself was explicitly selected as a senior clinician "with no prior involvement [. . .] in this area."' Essentially, ignorance of gender-affirming medicine was framed as a virtue. I can think of no comparable medical review of a process where those with experience or expertise of that process were summarily dismissed.[34] Dr Cass was the only person approached for the review, despite having no background in transgender healthcare or experience in paediatric gender care. There *are* times when it is appropriate to use an independent researcher to develop a perspective on a topic. But as the Cass Review excluded much professional knowledge and experience, this was not handled well.[35]

In fact, the Cass Review is out of step with the WPATH standards of care guidelines for trans people and has been criticized by

THE LIFE-CHANGING MAGIC OF GENDER-AFFIRMING CARE    125

countries across the globe including Canada, the Netherlands, Belgium, Germany, Austria, Switzerland and Australia.[36]

The Cass Review was never really about the health of trans people. Its commissioning was rooted in anti-trans hysteria: the idea that children were being sacrificed, experimented on and rushed through clinics before being given life-altering drugs. Cass's own results disproved that: of 3,499 GIDS patients Cass audited, only 27% had been referred to endocrinology for puberty blockers and hormone therapy, after an average of 6.7 appointments across what normally amounted to years of waiting. Only half of these patients ever received a prescription. Fewer than ten of them detransitioned, or less than one percent. What's even more frustrating is that the report uses a study conducted in 1985 to argue that 80% of transgender young people 'desist' from being trans; this study was conducted by a doctor later discovered to be using practices akin to conversion therapy[37] until just a few years ago, at which point his clinic was closed after complaints including coercive behaviour modification in children, photographing them without clothing with no purpose and regarding being cisgender and heterosexual as the 'best outcome'.

## Cass, Gillick and Fraser

The Cass Review treats trans children as an unfavourable outcome, when – and this shouldn't have to be said – there is nothing wrong with being trans. It also treats children as being unable to make informed decisions for themselves. This has hugely concerning ramifications. No medical intervention is without risk – both positive and negative – and yet when it comes to treating trans and gender-questioning children, the Cass Review (and indeed, many anti-trans campaigners) fundamentally denies children agency and bodily autonomy when they would in other contexts be able to give it.

In the UK, we have guidelines called the Gillick competency and Fraser guidelines[38,] which help those who work with children, including healthcare professionals, to determine if those who are under eighteen years of age are mature enough to consent. The Fraser guidelines and Gillick competency are different in nature; the former refers to treatment relating to contraception and sexual health, and the latter is often used in a wider context to understand if a child can consent and understand the implications of their decision. Both approaches come from the same legal case when, in 1982, Victoria Gillick took her local health authority and the Department of Health and Social Security to court in an attempt to block doctors from giving contraceptive advice or treatment to under-sixteens without [the parent's] consent. The case was dismissed in the High Court, reversed in the Court of Appeal and then, in 1985, the House of Lords and the Law Lords ruled in favour of the original judgement.[39] Now, in UK law, we had a standard for understanding when children and young people could consent, and that may be a different age depending on the child and their experiences:

'[W]hether or not a child is capable of giving the necessary consent will depend on the child's maturity and understanding and the nature of the consent required. The child must be capable of making a reasonable assessment of the advantages and disadvantages of the treatment proposed, so the consent, if given, can be properly and fairly described as true consent.'

Lord Scarman also commented, 'it is not enough that she should understand the nature of the advice which is being given: she must also have a sufficient maturity to understand what is involved.'

Importantly, though, 'parental rights yield to the child's right to make his own decisions when he reaches a sufficient understanding and intelligence to be capable of making up his own mind on the matter requiring decision.'

The Cass Review argues for 'extreme caution' to be used when prescribing gender-affirming hormones to sixteen- and seventeen-year-olds, which has already led to the review of prescription policy for all under-sixteens. These are the same sixteen- and seventeen-year-olds who could legally have sex, get pregnant, get a job, join the army, and yet, in this situation only, they are not able to have control over their bodies.

'I came out at thirteen and went to the Tavistock Clinic and started blockers at fifteen,' Jay (he/him) tells me. 'Then, I started testosterone with them at sixteen. I was under the NHS clinic until eighteen and moved to the adult one, where they supported me with HRT monitoring and surgery referral.'

Jay continues, 'It makes me so sad and angry that people are not able to get care. I had such a positive experience overall. I help run an LGBTQ+ group locally and it breaks my heart that young people can't get the support I had. I just left my job working at CAMHS [Child and Adolescent Mental Health Services] because it all got too much hearing the discussions about trans healthcare.'

Cass also goes beyond the scope of her research in recommending that young adults have access to a special service between the ages of seventeen and twenty-five before being referred to adult services, supposedly to provide support during, what Cass describes as, a 'vulnerable' stage. Whilst on the surface this seems positive – an opportunity for more support for trans people – there are concerns that this will result in limitations being placed on adults seeking gender-affirming care.

In the last eight hours before the UK parliament was dissolved ahead of the 2024 election, the then Health Secretary, Victoria Atkins, used 'extraordinary powers' to ban new private puberty blocker prescriptions with an effect lasting three months.[40] Given that the NHS had stopped delivering puberty blockers because of political pressures, it would now become impossible for any more trans children to access these medications, and any doctors that prescribed them risked committing a criminal offence. The final act of the Conservative government was – quite literally – one which inflicted immense harm and cruelty to children. Parents and families – being informed about the changes – were given support in the form of a suicide hotline. Even more shockingly, extending and supporting this ban became a priority of Wes Streeting, the Labour Party's Health

Secretary, as soon as Labour came into power, demonstrating that whilst we might have a supposedly left-wing government led by a party that has historically been better on LGBTQ+ rights, trans people cannot rely on their support. It is worth noting that Wes Streeting is a gay man – one who had briefly spoken out on trans equality before reneging this – emphasizing that the threats faced by trans people come from inside the community, too.

## Reproductive Rights

The restrictions being placed on trans children and young people are intrinsically linked with reproductive rights. Not only because the nature of informed consent, Gillick competency and the Fraser guidelines are rooted in a legal case about accessing contraception, but because so many of the arguments that deny trans people, including children, their autonomy are rooted in a belief that they do not know their own minds or their own bodies in a kind of medical paternalism.

Those who oppose reproductive rights are often those who oppose trans and queer rights and are described in the field as being anti-gender. This doesn't mean they are against the concept of gender, but it is a phrase used to describe organizations and people who are determined to erode women's rights, LGBTQ+ rights, reproductive healthcare, abortions and more. In 2023, the Good Law Project reported that the spending of the Alliance Defending Freedom (ADF), which 'campaigns to attack LGBTQ+ rights' and was 'the force behind the US Supreme Court's controversial decision to overturn Roe v Wade', had been ramping up its activity in the UK, including the spending of thousands more pounds lobbying the highest levels of government in the UK.[41] We do not know where this money comes from exactly – and we likely never will – only that the ADF is one of the 'most aggressive campaign groups on the Christian far right'.

A report released by the European Parliamentary Forum for Sexual and Reproductive Rights found that between 2009 and 2018, at least

707.2 million US dollars was spent on funding anti-gender movements in Europe alone and that most of this came from the US and the Russian Federation. This money was linked to anti-abortion initiatives in France, Italy, Poland, Slovakia and Spain and at EU level, whilst there were also links to anti-gay marriage movements in Austria, Croatia, France, Germany, Finland, Italy, Slovakia and Romania.

It's worth emphasizing that this money doesn't come from governments, but from individuals, with financing coming mainly from ten key right-wing Christian organizations in the US, including the ADF.[42]

When Roe v Wade was overturned by the Supreme Court in America, a decision instantly outlawing abortion in many US states, I felt numb. It was as if the world's revolutions had slowed and we were waiting for things to snap back into place, like a record that kept catching. I was disgusted and horrified but mostly – if I'm honest – really, really scared. For my friends, for my communities, for what this meant for other hard-won legal wins. I kept asking myself repeatedly: what's next? Who's next? Even the mainstream media – *The New York Times*, *Forbes*, CBS, AP – immediately recognized that it would be LGBTQ+ heads on the chopping block.

US Supreme Court Justice Clarence Thomas wrote, in a statement concurring with the decision to overturn Roe v Wade, that the state should also reconsider Griswold v Connecticut, Lawrence v Texas and Obergefell v Hodges.[43] As a Brit, those names meant very little to me when I first heard them. But then I realized, in one fell swoop, Clarence had lined up contraception, same sex relationships and same sex marriage as the next targets. His language made clear where he stood: the judgements were 'demonstrably erroneous' and there was a need to 'correct the error'.

Although it was made clear that despite the overruling of Roe v Wade, for now, and the precedents stated in the other cases still stood, many LGBTQ+ people were uneasy. Once the initial shock had settled, I realized I really ought not to have been surprised. After all, there are a plethora of right-wing Christian groups in the US whose hundreds of millions of dollars have been funnelled into both anti-abortion and anti-LGBTQ+ groups and legislation. Once Roe v Wade was overturned, it's no surprise to me that there was a massive rise in attacks on LGBTQ+ rights, in particular trans people and drag queens.[44] Several notable organizations including the ADF and the Family Research Council have raised tens of millions of dollars by campaigning against LGBTQ+ rights and against abortions. Jennifer Bauwens – writing for the Family Research Council – begins her article about transgender youth with a celebration of Roe v Wade being overturned: 'As we reflect on the possibility that this historic wrong of legalized elective abortion might be righted, and as we build the foundations of a world in which the unborn are protected and their mothers supported, let's extend this same hopeful expectation to our children who have been exposed to post-modern/transgender ideology.'[45]

'I think the fight against transgender healthcare all boils down to the controlling of cis women's bodies,' Wednesday tells me. 'I don't think this has anything to do with trans people at all.'

'Criticisms of my top surgery always revolve around the fact I could breastfeed in the future, because my purpose was seen as being someone who could have children. Many people think that if you took testosterone, you couldn't get pregnant – which is not true. But we are expected to reproduce if we have a uterus. We're destroying their idea of a nuclear family.' Similar, outdated-seeming arguments have been made for years by anti-queer campaigners, that because queer sex does not result in procreation, it is sinful.

## Going Backwards

It isn't only children and young people who have been affected by the Cass Review. Since its publication, we have seen reports of restrictions being placed on trans adults who have been prescribed hormones for a number of years as doctors become increasingly nervous, not due to new data but because of political actions.

'It's a scary time to be trans just in the collective, general sense but also in a personal sense,' transgender actress and activist Charlie Craggs tells me. 'I recently spoke on Instagram about how, after moving to a new area, my new GP surgery has refused to give me hormones.' Charlie had been on her medication for years, after jumping through hoops and being on waiting lists for over a decade.

'It was not just one GP, but the entire practice which denied me care. And they proudly told me they were within their rights to do so.'

Charlie shared her experience online, not expecting *The Daily Mail* to write it up, painting her as some sort of conniving villain for the simple act of getting medical care.[46] 'I'm being denied medication that I have every right to, that I pay a lot of taxes towards, that I have been on for a decade.' Charlie has, thankfully, been able to remain on her medication, but only as a result of the community showing up for her: 'I've been scrounging spare packs of hormones from kind trans friends and followers so that my hairline (something I've paid tens of thousands of pounds for) doesn't fall out again. The scariest thing to me is how helpless the trans people who don't have a platform feel.' In October 2024, TransActual reported on over 215 incidents of trans people being denied medication over the course of six months, in effect forcing them to medically detransition. In no instance was medical safety cited for the reason.

## DIY Transition

Denying trans people access to gender-affirming care will not eliminate the existence of trans people. The reality is that obstructions – political, financial, medical and societal – to healthcare access have forced many trans people to a 'DIY' transition. This might include obtaining hormones and other medications over the internet and self-administering them or going to underground places to access surgical interventions.

This might sound alarming, but the truth is that DIY transition has long since been a practice. According to TransActual's Transition Access Report, a quarter of those accessing HRT had done so through self-medication, often because of the extensive NHS waiting lists.[47] As one man put it: 'I thought I'd be dead before I'd access hormones through the NHS which is why I self-medicated and then went private.' With HRT in particular, it is worth noting that the medications are relatively easy to access – in theory, pretty much every pharmacy in the UK has them. And yet trans people are sometimes waiting up to a decade to access care, even when most HRT is not licensed for a specific indication, meaning it is not a medication for one thing in particular. At the moment there are HRT shortages, and I know of cisgender women being forced to DIY their treatment, just like trans people do.

I've sometimes heard the 'DIY' transition movement referred to as symptomatic of a digital age, but a cursory look over the archives revealed to me a rich tapestry dating back at least to the 1950s in America and probably longer. There are lots of documented stories about people going to Mexico with suitcases and bringing back oestrogen to distribute within the community. Zines on DIY transition and word of mouth were the tools before Reddit and Tumblr provided wider platforms for disseminating information including harm reduction practices. And around the globe, where healthcare access varies widely, let alone for transition-related care, DIY practices are sometimes the only option.[48]

The idea of DIY transition often makes people uncomfortable, but I think it should make them angry. Not at trans people, but at a medical system that has forced people into this predicament in the first place. The frustration that I feel when I hear of cisgender women struggling to control their reproductive health and resorting to extreme measures because of legal and geographical barriers is just the same.

There are several networks and organizations – both formal and informal – around the globe operating a harm reduction model for DIY transition, ensuring that if trans people are self-medicating they do so safely. Some organize laboratory testing for common HRT sources; some provide safe injection supplies like needles, syringes and alcohol swabs, as well as information about vial contamination and other important aspects. They also lobby healthcare providers and GPs to work to ensure that their trans patients are supported within – and often in spite of – the current system. There are two things GPs and other healthcare providers are recommended to undertake: firstly, to provide blood tests to those they think might be self-medicating to ensure that a person is taking the right dose for them and not at risk of harmful side effects.[49] The second thing is to prescribe HRT. In the UK, this can be done through a 'bridging prescription' – essentially allowing trans people to access care before they are seen at the gender clinic, which could take years and potentially even decades as recent estimates suggest.[50]

## Why Should You Care?

The exceptionalism presented in arguments about trans healthcare is at best nonsensical and at worst deeply dangerous, both for transgender people and wider society. By separating out healthcare for trans people from healthcare more broadly, it makes it seem as though trans people and cis people have nothing in common when it comes to the care they receive, which could not be further from the case.

The precedent being set by anti-trans legislation and process suggests that governments can single out groups of people, deny them healthcare and, in effect, control what they can and cannot do with their own bodies. It's an egregious denial of bodily autonomy and self-determination which should alarm anyone, especially those who are committed to protecting the rights of cisgender women. It comes as no surprise that several of the organizations instrumental in overturning Roe v Wade are similarly funding anti-trans politicians and banning trans healthcare.

Trump's 2024 re-election campaign included targeted attacks on gender-affirming care, including the proposed barring of physicians who offer gender-affirming care to young people, denial of federal Medicaid and Medicare funding, as well as directing the Department of Justice to investigate the provision of gender-affirming care. Additionally, his administration could seek to reverse the Biden–Harris administration's recent Title IX regulations, which aim to enhance protections for transgender students but are currently halted in about half of US states.

These attacks go hand in hand with the anticipated removal of reproductive and sexual health rights across the US. Project 2025, a Conservative agenda backed by the Trump–Vance administration, identified ways in which abortion rights could be revoked including reviving the nineteenth century Comstock Act to ban medications and abortion materials from being sent through the US Postal Service. The pitting of women and trans people against each other when we have a common enemy has never made sense to me as a white cisgender woman. Because I know – and history tells us – that the rights I have over my body are much easier to take away when others are stripped of them first.

And, in the same way that anti-abortion laws do not stop abortions from happening – they only stop them from happening safely – laws prohibiting gender-affirming care do not stop gender-affirming care from being sought or accessed. How do we know this? People have undergone medical transition without the support of the healthcare systems, financial support or the law.[51]

## Some Optimism?

It feels important to note that despite the desperate, dire situation of gender-affirming healthcare, there still are, as Chay puts it, 'some really good pockets of amazing practice'. The challenge is getting those practices adopted more widely, at a time when the provision of gender-affirming care is being extinguished bit by bit.

## And What You Can Do About It

→ Write to your local MP to speak in favour of trans healthcare and show your support for trans young people who are attempting to access gender-affirming care. Several organizations, including TransActual and Mermaids, have pre-existing templates with the key facts available, which you can edit and send to your MP.

→ Donate to trans people's fundraisers – these can be found through mutual aid groups and platforms like GoFundMe and are often shared on social media. Many trans people are unable to access the care they need through the NHS because it simply is not available (such as in the case of facial feminization surgery). You can also donate to organizations like US-based Point of Pride which distribute funds to trans people in need.

→ Show up to the relevant protests in support of trans healthcare and to protest against restrictions being forced onto trans people's healthcare without evidence. Advocate for listening to trans people's voices and experiences and remind people that currently the UK is out of step with international guidelines.

→ If you have a trans friend, family member or person in your community who is undergoing medical transition involving surgery, offer to support them, driving them to or from their surgery, getting groceries in, cooking for them, helping look after any family or pets they have. I used to hate the idea of supporting people after surgery because I am notoriously bad with bodily fluids, but I then realized that I am very good at being useful in other ways. Even friends that live the other side of the world from me I can support by purchasing supplies they will need during recovery – everything from compression garments to wet wipes – and just by checking in, too.

# Putting in the Work

## Travis Joseph (he/him)

Travis Joseph is the founder of the Black Trans Hub, an online resource for transgender people of colour struggling to find information about trans healthcare. After reflecting on and sharing his own experiences of medical racism and a lack of information about what gender-affirming care looked like for people of colour, Joseph started compiling resources and gathering testimonials, which ensured people could make informed decisions about their healthcare, with a particular focus on collecting top-surgery testimonials and results, as many other resources show only white bodies. Joseph also started a directory for QTIPOC (queer, trans people of colour) to ensure they could access support.

## Erin Reed (she/her)

Erin Reed is a prominent journalist and advocate fighting for justice and liberation for trans people in the US and across the globe. As a journalist, she methodically tracks the progress of anti-trans legislation and the large number of restrictive laws being placed on gender-affirming care. She is the creator of the Anti-Trans Legislative Risk Map, which helps to provide people concerned about their risk of staying in their state with information about the likelihood of anti-trans bills being passed within a two-year period.

Reed is also the creator of Erin's Informed Consent HRT Map, a map detailing healthcare providers who operate a model of informed consent and which do not require transgender people to have a letter from a therapist or go through gatekeeping to access healthcare. The map has been used nearly four million times in order to access this healthcare.

Reed uses her online platforms to educate others on the importance of inclusive and affirming healthcare for transgender individuals, highlighting the mental health disparities that exist within the community. She actively engages with policymakers, healthcare providers and organizations to push for improvements in transgender healthcare access and quality.

# CHAPTER 7
# Safe Space

## Other Places

'I used to go to a spot called The Other Place in Cork in the nineties,' writer Karen Cogan (she/her) tells me. 'It was down an alley and had a *tiny* faded rainbow flag sticker above the doorbell, but everyone knew what "that place" was. Or they thought they did. In reality, it was lots of things: a sexual health clinic, safe space, nightclub, sporadic – a haven.

'I went for the first time with my three queer pals on one of the Friday nights in the basement. We were nervy, with newly shorn hair and baggy combat pants and Tori Amos T-shirts. It was full of lesbians – must have been a dyke night. I was scared and delighted at the same time. Danced all night, met a girl and promised to meet everyone at the book club the following day. A ball. Went every week for years. It's not there any more but it was magic. Magic.'

The Other Place opened in 1991, two years before Ireland decriminalized homosexuality – and closed in 2015, the same year the country voted in favour of same sex marriage equality. The timing is an indication, perhaps, that increased rights for LGBTQ+ people don't always go hand in hand with more spaces in which the community can safely exist.

We might imagine that progress moves as one and that increased legal rights for LGBTQ+ people will automatically mean more of other things, like queer venues to hang out in. But the data tells a different story. In the US, there were 44% fewer gay bars and clubs in 2024 than in 2022,[1] and more than half of London's LGBTQ+ venues closed between 2006 and 2022.[2] Sydney's Oxford Street has been reported as having an 'identity crisis' as heterosexual clubbers take over spaces once frequented by LGBTQ+ crowds.[3] By contrast, even though modern Berlin is bucking the trend when it comes to current LGBTQ+ venues, the number of gay bars the German city houses today pales in comparison to how many it used to have. In fact, in the 1920s and early 1930s, Berlin boasted over a hundred gay bars – far more than any modern city and more than currently exist in the entirety of the United States.

We can partly attribute this to changes to the way communities gather over time. Bars historically served as a place to meet other LGBTQ+ people and, importantly, to hook up. When homosexuality was illegal, private spaces like bars or clubs that flew under the radar were crucial. Now, the invention of dating apps like Grindr has taken away the need for some LGBTQ+ folk to visit a specific place to meet potential partners or lovers. In many cities, rent continues to spiral, making it difficult for independent businesses to hold on to venues and keep them open.

This was certainly the experience of folk in Ireland. Karen tells me that there were an incredible number of LGBTQ+ spaces in Cork, going back decades. But when one bar – Le Chateau – was named by *PinkNews* as a 'gay friendly' location, the bar's owner banned those who were perceived as too 'obviously gay'.[4] In the 1970s, the Irish Gay Rights Movement's Cork branch set up its first Gay Centre – a space for the community to gather, have social activities and weekend discos and access support services. And in the early 1980s Cork got its first openly queer bars – the Quay Co-op and Loafers bar, with more spaces being formed, including the Cork Resource Centre and The Other Place. Despite the fact that being queer was still illegal, plenty of groups sprang up – including particular ones for lesbian, bisexual and trans people. There was even a weekend every year where queer women came and gathered from across Ireland and beyond. 'It was so vibrant – we had so much fun,' Karen remembers.

Fun isn't frivolous. It can feel difficult to experience and to prioritize when under threat. But fun is a kind of quiet (and, let's face it, at times, not so quiet) rebellion – finding joy not just in the face of hardship but *because* of it. Queer spaces become sanctuaries – the focus for expression, community, family and so much more. Wherever you look in the world, there will be LGBTQ+ people forging space – sometimes publicly and sometimes more secretively – but no less defiantly. Even some of the world's most hostile regions for LGBTQ+ people, like Georgia and Uganda, have thriving underground LGBTQ+ community spaces.

Surely, this is testament to the fact that community is not a luxury: not a nice-to-have but an essential human need and one that LGBTQ+ people should not be deprived of. LGBTQ+ people are more likely to be lonely, with LGBT HERO reporting that, prior to lockdown, 21% of LGBTQ+ people experienced loneliness very often or every day, a number that over doubled to 56% during lockdown.[5] Existing in the world as an LGBTQ+ person often means experiencing some level of rejection. For some, coming out means being rejected by their community, religion, family, friends, workplace and more. Queer spaces function as an antidote to this – a quiet reminder that there is space in which you are allowed to exist as you are and, actually, you can belong.

## Queer Bars

If we are to talk about LGBTQ+ spaces, then we must talk about bars, which have served queer people for centuries. In London, for example, there is evidence of LGBTQ+ nightlife dating back as far as the 1700s, when 'molly houses' – spaces for LGBTQ+ people to meet in coffee houses or pubs or private rooms in otherwise straight venues – began to appear.[6] They were often raided by the police, a trend that continued for hundreds of years. Because homosexuality was illegal, any place where LGBTQ+ people gathered had to remain a relative secret. Licensing laws and other requirements acted as impediments, too, but there were workarounds if you were feeling innovative: the Burleigh Arms in Cambridge would serve chips at midnight so as to appear as a 'supper club'.[7]

As we've seen, nowadays, only a tiny portion of the LGBTQ+ bars there once were are still in existence. There is an argument that in a world which accepts LGBTQ+ people more easily, specific LGBTQ+ spaces are less needed for the community to feel safe. But when hate crimes against trans people have increased by 186% and hate crimes based on sexual orientation are up 112% in the last five years, that's clearly not the case.[8] In fact, it's tricky to feel safe anywhere and – whilst not perfect – queer bars can offer that feeling of safety.

## Access Codes

Even when venues are still around, all too regularly, those who want to go to queer spaces can find themselves unable to access them because they are perceived as not queer enough or, it seems, simply for being women or people of colour. I personally have given up trying to get into what is probably the most well-known gay bar in London after being turned away on two separate occasions because I did not look 'queer enough'. As a teen, I watched an interview with Lea DeLaria, considered the first openly gay stand-up comedian to appear on US television, who described the feeling of relief that coming into a gay bar brought her, the shaking off of the utter physical and mental exhaustion she encountered just living in the world, but also the feeling of safety it brought her as a butch dyke. I find it so jarring that forty years later, I cannot see myself in that experience.[9]

Perhaps this is because dyke bars specifically are a rarity now and it doesn't seem like that's due to lack of demand – when La Camionera, a new lesbian bar in Hackney, opened for one night in April 2023, instead of the twenty or thirty people expected, hundreds and hundreds of lesbians and queer women filled the streets. Within days, over £50,000 was raised to secure a permanent space for the bar. It's hardly surprising that the event was so popular when you consider there are only three permanent lesbian bars in the entire country.[10]

That's not to say there aren't some good nights out for queer women, but there's a transience to them and many of us feel the struggle of waiting for the next event to roll around. It's clear the scene has changed, with bars morphing into 'nights' for specific sub-sections of the community. They're not rooted – they come and go. Have we simply moved on, and gone beyond the need for bricks and mortar? I think two things can be true at once: you can create an exceptional, inclusive space for a specific date and time, but also we need spaces where LGBTQ+ people can go any time of the day or night to feel safe, to find community and to have fun.

Of course, when bars and clubs are the main – or only – venues in which to do that, we have a problem. Their nature, often based on partying, dancing and alcohol, is inherently exclusionary to certain parts of the community. There are many reasons – including sobriety, religion, disability, age or childcare needs – that may mean people struggle with certain aspects of bar culture. Bars and clubs can also create exclusion on the basis of income. Essentially, if you can't afford to pay for a drink or a ticket, you may not be able to access community spaces, and although some have implemented sliding-scale prices and pay-it-forward schemes, they're not perfect solutions.

## Staying Safe

One way in which LGBTQ+ nights and venues are doing more for the community is by launching practices to help keep attendees safe. These include training workers on identifying and preventing sexual harassment, maintaining clear codes of conduct for guests, providing taxi funds for those who may be unable to get to the venue, implementing buddy systems, having quieter hours for newbies or solo attendees who might feel overwhelmed, establishing quieter areas for people to take time for a breather, and so, so much more. This is not to say LGBTQ+ nights are some kind of utopia, but there is something incredibly radical and uplifting about the care and attention given to people at some of them.

Pxssy Palace – a night created by and for Black, Indigenous and people of colour who are queer, intersex, trans or non-binary – is notable in having a policy that the night is 'not a safe space' because in a world which is structurally racist, anti-trans, anti-queer, 'it is impossible and irresponsible to guarantee safety'. That does not mean that they do not make efforts to build safety – far from it. They have between five and fifteen QTIPOC support people who are trained to look after the venue and guests, including training to ensure they are equipped to respond to sexual harassment and assault. There are strong policies which guide behaviour, ensuring the space remains intentional: providing taxis for people for whom public transport is unsafe, a chill space and tickets for people on low incomes. To many, this would seem like a 'safe space', but I have great admiration for the fact the organizers reject this label. 'The issues we fight against in our daily lives also translate into our experiences at the club. Whilst we will have systems to support you at our events, we do not have control over nor are we responsible for how people behave in, or outside the club.'[11]

There's a refreshing honesty to this admission: violence, discrimination and inappropriate behaviour can happen anywhere, and we are prepared for it if it does. I have been spiked and had a friend get spiked at a well-known LGBTQ+ night, and although both times the experience was terrifying, it was so much less scary knowing that there were people from the community trained to support me, who were invested in my wellbeing.

After all, that's what these nights out often are – part of our wellbeing. Prominent queer producer June Thomas once wrote that the defining aspect of the gay bar is the fact it has 'more literature' – sticky, beer-stained leaflets and garish posters. This is not because we are reading on our nights out (at least, not in that way – reading is fundamental, after all). It is because gay bars have historically been *more* than just bars – they're our community spaces, too.

LGBTQ+ spaces have a long history of being hubs for organizing and educating, even if that's on the dancefloor. 'Me and a lot of other community leaders within nightlife have been speaking about how we can galvanize and inspire – especially the kids – to go out and vote, register to vote,' Lewis G. Burton, founder of queer techno rave INFERNO, tells me.

Lewis has been at the heart of queer nightlife for over twelve years, founding INFERNO in 2015 as a response to the homogeneity they saw in the scene – both in terms of the dominance of white cis gay men organizing these spaces and the fact the music was all house and disco. I first went to INFERNO in my early twenties, somewhat reluctantly dragged along by friends who thought it would be good for me to get out of the house. A rave is my idea of hell – at least in theory. In practice, I found a group of wonderful, weird, creative and chaotic queer people who have become dear friends over time.

'What's so beautiful about nightlife,' Lewis tells me, 'is that you get to run away to these spaces with all of this shame, find a sense of community and start finding out what queer joy is, what queer celebration is. You get to figure out who you are – you know, gender identity, sexuality, who you're attracted to. There are so few opportunities to get to play with that – nightclubs are one of the few spaces queer people get to do that.'

So queer clubs and bars have a beautiful, amazing function and they deserve our support and patronage. But when they're not necessarily safe or accessible to all LGBTQ+ people, having them as our *only* spaces is a barrier to finding much-needed community.

## Third Spaces

Could more types of third spaces be the answer? A third space is somewhere which is separate from work and home – a library, museum, gym, pool or park. The effectiveness of these spaces is magnified when they don't require financial resources to go to them – whether that's directly, to enter the wider venue in which the space is housed, or to travel there.

Many – though not all – third spaces are subsidized by local governments, which means their survival is often dependent on political decisions. Since 2010, the Conservative government pursued a policy of austerity, which has resulted in the closure of thousands of spaces – including 800 libraries alone.[12]

Increasingly, queer people are taking matters into their own hands. In 2017, a group of LGBTQ+ friends decided they needed to create a space by and for the community, somewhere which was intersectional, sober and existed outside of a commercial, money-making model. The dream for the London LGBTQ+ Community Centre was born. The goal for the space was simple – somewhere LGBTQ+ people could just *be* – and hell, don't I wish that was not a radical notion. The team began researching the needs of the community and what they wanted to see from the space. They held five open meetings, each attended by between 150 and 200 members of the local community. And they found a real need. Research conducted by the centre into the needs of LGBTQ+ Londoners – online, through feedback forms and through interviews – showed that 85% said that there were too few LGBTQ+ spaces in London and 94% said that there were too few spaces that did not revolve around nightlife.[13]

By the time the centre finally opened its doors in 2021 – initially as a six-month pop up – the Covid-19 pandemic had had a devastating impact on the world and drastically altered people's situations. Many LGBTQ+ people had lost access to their community overnight and were forced, like everyone else, into isolation. For some, this meant going back into the closet, or being forced into unsafe living conditions; others had lost their jobs and been placed in precarious financial situations.

'The one thing I was determined to do,' Lip, the centre manager, tells me, 'was to make sure tea was still one pound. Because no one needs to charge more than one pound for a cup of tea – and we have very fancy teabags!' they exclaim. Although the centre offers a pay-it-forward scheme, some people are ashamed or embarrassed they cannot afford to pay full price for a coffee. The £1 cup of tea has become a small symbol of dignity.

They also have a pay-it-forward system for free drinks, something Lip emphasizes is not always used by people who are unemployed: 'Maybe your bike got stolen this week. Maybe your wages came in late. Maybe your landlord just upped the rent or you got a big diagnosis. You can have a free drink if you want a free drink. Even if you don't need one, it can be really nice to have a cup of coffee sometimes. It's like a security blanket. It gives you a reason to be somewhere and something to do. That's why we have the board games on the shelves, posters all over the walls, to give people something to make them feel like there's a reason to be here.'

One thing I love about the centre is that you can literally just walk in off the street and do whatever – read, work, chat to people, get some information. It is the only place I can think of where, concurrently, you could get directed to support for chemsex addiction, attend a queer yoga class and join a Welsh Language LGBTQ+ meetup at the same time. One Saturday, my friend Donna and I popped in on our walk from the South Bank. There was a book group on, people playing board games and a clothing sale. I ended up leaving with the perfect purple skirt-suit, information about sexual health services and a very nice glow-in-the-dark sperm key ring, which I promptly turned into an exceedingly camp earring.

The breadth of activities also means that people who may feel ashamed or stigmatized about needing mental or sexual health support feel more able to seek it out, because no one can really tell what you are looking at.

'The language, culture and faith-based groups are the most important things we have because that's where your background, your culture and your history can really intersect,' Lip tells me. 'I've been able to witness people being overwhelmed by emotion when they're there. They come up to me and say, "This is the first time I've ever spoken to another queer person from the country I'm from, in the language that I grew up speaking." Seeing that connection reminds me of how rare spaces like this are.'

LGBTQ+ spaces, by their very nature, walk the very fine line between creating a space explicitly for LGBTQ+ people and potentially excluding those who are not able to be 'out'. The inclusion of allies in LGBTQ+ spaces is somewhat contentious but, in my experience, when allies are welcome, it has enabled friends who are LGBTQ+ but cannot come out to show up in the space anyway, with less risk to their safety.

## Going Underground

Creating an LGBTQ+ inclusive space somewhere like London, where, despite the serious challenges faced by the community, it is legal to be a queer person, is one thing. But how do you create community spaces when your very existence is unlawful?

In 2023, hundreds of people walked past a picture of Matthew Blaise (they/them), a young queer Nigerian activist displayed in the Museum of Modern Art. Their photo, taken by Yagazie Emezi during the height of the #EndSARS movement, shows Matthew in a black T-shirt tied at the waist and holding a banner above their head. In red writing, the banner said: 'Why Do I Get Beaten up 4 Being Femme Perceived Gay" At the bottom were two messages: 'EndSARS' and '#Queerlivesmatter'. Just weeks earlier, Matthew had been arrested on the streets of Lagos on the suspicion of perceived homosexuality. They were verbally and physically assaulted by the police before being released. Not two weeks later, they were arrested for 'looking like a lesbian'. In Nigeria, the Same Sex Marriage Prohibition Act criminalizes homosexuality and exacerbates a culture where homophobia and transphobia are endemic.

Now, aged twenty-four, Matthew is the founder of Obodo, a youth-led organization which helps build community and advocates for LGBTQ+ rights and education across Nigeria. 'In Igbo [the local language],' Matthew tells me, 'Obodo means a group of people who have existed since time immemorial, who have helped each other in times of hardship, and who have shared joy in times of triumph.' The organization has many threads – from monthly film and book clubs and spaces which host queer art to campaigns which directly counter homophobic rhetoric and encourage the wellbeing of queer Nigerians. They also operate a queer emergency fund, allowing them to provide mutual aid for any young LGBTQ+ people facing homelessness or needing other forms of support. It is an ambitious – but essential – undertaking, one rooted in giving young LGBTQ+ Nigerians their humanity back.

Matthew tells me in Nigeria it is not only the police and government who are violent towards LGBTQ+ folk, it is everyday people, too. 'They believe queer people need to be pushed away from society. How do they ensure that? By beating up their queer neighbours and by pushing them out. It's just layers and layers of violence.' Indeed, a survey released in 2019 revealed that 60% of Nigerians surveyed said they would not accept a family member who is LGBTQ+, and 75% were in support of the laws discriminating against queer people.[14] 'With Obodo, we want to organize queerness as much as possible, because it is not what you see in the world today. We want to live lives, through art, through mediums, through the work of people. And we want to also call it the dream of a future, the future we can all paint together.'

One of the biggest barriers Matthew has faced is obtaining funding for Obodo. There is little money available for any projects relating to the LGBTQ+ community, and what does exist goes to a handful of well-known organizations which do not necessarily serve the whole community. It's a story that I am all too familiar with, even in the UK.

Matthew raises an essential point about the ways in which funding applications are not only inaccessible to new or smaller groups, but that their set-up is inherently colonial. 'These funding applications are still based on colonial ideas and the capitalist idea of expecting something in return. They give you money and then they give you targets. They are forgetting they are dealing with human beings with lives. There should be ways to measure impact other than organizing people and treating them as outcomes. It's a very colonial idea, putting results over people.'

'I also realize how important it is to build your own community in a place like this, where you do not necessarily have the assets. Community for me is not just a group of people you can follow when you're in a time of distress, it is a group of people who need healing from trauma.'

## A Violent Noise

Even now, in spaces where it is not illegal to be LGBTQ+, we are not guaranteed safety. The first time I went to the now-closed bar G-A-Y, one of London's most well-known gay bars, I was eighteen. I have never really been one for going 'out out', but it felt like a rite of passage for me as a young queer person. As a member of my university's LGBTQ+ society, it was somewhat obligatory to attend at least some of the nights out.

I couldn't relax, though. I was too busy looking for exits, for escape routes. Just a year earlier – in 2016 – a gunman opened fire at Pulse, an LGBTQ+ club in Orlando, Florida. The result was the violent murder of at least forty-nine people with a further fifty injured. At that time, it was the deadliest mass shooting the US had ever seen, one which targeted not only LGBTQ+ people but Latinx LGBTQ+ who had gathered to party for Latin Night.[15] In G-A-Y, every time the bass pounded, I wondered if the way it made my body vibrate would obscure an attack. There had also been a series of recent terror attacks in London and the bombing at the Manchester Arena, which had claimed over twenty lives. In general, violence in the UK takes different forms to the mass-death events in the US. We have strict gun controls, meaning that mass shootings are a rarity – we haven't had a school shooting here since 1996, for example. But damage can still be done and, if anything, violence against LGBTQ+ people in LGBTQ+ venues seems to be escalating.

In August 2023, two men were stabbed outside the Two Brewers pub in Clapham. The Honor Oak pub in Lewisham, south London, has been subject to protests and overt violence from fascists and the far right after hosting a storytelling session by a drag queen. And when I say fascists, I am talking about extreme far-right organizations such as Patriotic Alternative and the Independent Nationalist Network. What is more, the Metropolitan Police protected the fascists by arresting counter-protestors – with reports of people being knocked to the floor, kicked and even their ribs being cracked. The 500 to 700 anti-fascist protestors and defenders of LGBTQ+ rights far outnumbered the fascists, but the police repeatedly tried to give the fascists more space and the counter-protestors less, even so far as placing the fascists outside a primary school.[16]

## The Future of Queer Spaces

The land on which Colour Factory – where I attended INFERNO – stands has now been sold to developers. Soon what was a key venue for so many queer and trans-led nights will have disappeared into the background, in favour of luxury flats, along with the dissipation of another space queer and trans people could have found hope and community in. This is true for dozens of venues in cities across the UK – land is being sold, rents raised, or it has become commercially unviable to keep doors open, especially when the cost of living is so high.

One of the miraculous things about moving to Margate, a small town on England's Kent coast, is that despite having only around 50,000 residents we have several LGBTQ+ venues – at least three LGBTQ+ bars and clubs and a plethora of other businesses owned and operated by LGBTQ+ people, not to mention the many other nights that exist. On my second day living by the sea and barely unpacked, I found myself at Queer Cuntry – which is very much what it says on the tin: a queer country night. Held in the basement of a Caribbean restaurant, it boasts live music, drag and performances to rival any of the big London venues. I genuinely couldn't believe that such a thing existed in such a small town – after all, my home town was larger than that and the closest thing to an LGBTQ+ space we managed to create was a semi-clandestine meeting in the corner of Caffè Nero on periodic afternoons. A few months later, when 15,000 people showed up for Margate Pride, I wept. I never imagined it was possible to have a life where I could live away from the city and still remain embedded in the LGBTQ+ community. I suspect the reason Margate's community has been able to flourish is in part because it attracts the type of people who are willing to get up and make something happen if it's not happening already. It's hard to convey just how many groups, clubs and activities there are most days of the week, predominantly run by the community.

There's something about living in a town where the winters are grim and grey and oh-so-wet, and when even in the summer almost everything shuts Monday to Wednesday, that makes you get creative about how you spend your time, because there are dark, damp evenings when your options would be to sit at home in the dry or walk to the pub in the rain – even our big supermarket closes at 8 p.m.! I also suspect we take in folk who didn't fit elsewhere; it's a real hotchpotch of people from all different backgrounds and ages just out and about in the town, and because it's so small, lots of us know each other.

What's glorious, too, is that these spaces have been intentionally created, often trying to counter many of the issues facing LGBTQ+ spaces that I've outlined. CAMP, for example, is a bar, but it's also a space which hosts local groups that organize projects or need support. There's a legendary quiz and brilliant music and it allows dogs. It's a place to go to celebrate, to have an incredible night out with friends. But it's also been a place I've been when I'm feeling lonely and unsure of myself and just want to be surrounded by people who get it. When one of my queer trans friends died and I was still deeply shaken by the sudden news, it was somewhere I could go, just to be. And maybe that's why queer spaces are so important: they allow us just to exist – without explanation or apology. They meet us where we are at – wherever we are: fresh out of the closet and quaking in our Doc Martens or coming from a march after years of protesting for our rights. Their existence helps us to keep going, and they must be preserved.

## And What You Can Do About It

→ Support your local LGBTQ+ spaces, whether that's through sharing events or volunteering your time, skills or resources. Many LGBTQ+ spaces, particularly those that are charitable or volunteer-led, will have lists of things they need, which could range from anything as small as a kettle to something larger, like a laptop.

→ If you are outside of the LGBTQ+ community, be mindful of the space you take up within LGBTQ+ venues such as bars and clubs. Most spaces welcome allies within them, especially when you are supporting another LGBTQ+ person, though always check as some events are exclusive to certain communities.

→ Put your money where your mouth is – whether that is buying a drink through a pay-it-forward scheme, making a regular donation to a taxi fund for trans people getting home from events or helping to subsidize free and lower-cost tickets by paying slightly more; all of these actions make a world of difference to LGBTQ+ people and spaces, who face significant financial barriers.

→ Recognize that going to explicitly LGBTQ+ spaces – even being seen in a context that might be construed as LGBTQ+ – can be dangerous for some folks. Be mindful that sometimes LGBTQ+ groups, clubs and activities might be subtler – it's not all glitter and rainbows. It might be a gathering of people at a coffee shop, or a trip to the cinema or a walk. The strengths of connection and visibility are not always the same thing. Likewise, be mindful of mentioning seeing a person at an LGBTQ+ space if you do not know their preferences and be mindful of posting anything identifying online, too.

# Putting in the Work

## Lady Phyll (she/her)

Lady Phyll is a formidable force in the LGBTQ+ and social justice movements. She is widely recognized as a co-founder and executive director of UK Black Pride, an organization that has created a vibrant and essential space for LGBTQ+ people of African, Asian, Caribbean, Middle Eastern and Latin American descent. UK Black Pride, under her leadership, has grown from a small gathering into one of the largest celebrations of its kind in Europe, drawing thousands of attendees each year.

Lady Phyll's activism is deeply rooted in her own experiences and the intersections of race, gender and sexuality. She has been a vocal advocate for the rights of marginalized communities, tirelessly working to ensure that their voices are heard and their rights are upheld. Beyond her work with UK Black Pride, she serves as the executive director of Kaleidoscope Trust, an organization dedicated to fighting for the human rights of LGBTQ+ people across the Commonwealth.

Her contributions extend into the literary world, where she has edited and contributed to various publications that highlight the experiences and struggles of LGBTQ+ people of colour. Lady Phyll is also known for her advocacy within the trade union movement, where she has worked to improve conditions and rights for workers.

## Reeta Loi (they/she/he)

Reeta Loi is a prominent British-Indian activist, writer and musician who co-founded Gaysians, an organization dedicated to amplifying the voices of South Asian LGBTQ+ individuals, creating spaces by and for the community.

Although they were writing about the experience of being queer and South Asian for several years, it was only in 2017 that they publicly came forward to use their name and face for *DIVA*, the lesbian and bi women's magazine.

In 2017, recognizing the need for a unified platform to address the unique issues faced by LGBTQ+ South Asians, Loi launched Gaysians. The organization aims to provide visibility, support and advocacy for South Asian LGBTQ+ communities. Gaysians quickly grew into a vital network, connecting individuals and organizations across the UK and beyond.

Gaysians advocated for the UK prime minister to apply pressure for Section 377 to be scrapped in India – a law introduced by the British during its colonial occupation, and in 2018 this law was removed. Loi and Gaysians hosted the UK celebration of the scrapping of Section 377; within a couple of weeks of the announcement, they had organized an event filled with dance, poetry, film, music performances and DJ-ing, which collided with food and drink to provide a never-before-seen experience, where over 200 Gaysians celebrated and also raised £5,000 for two LGBTQ+ charities in India.

# CHAPTER 8
# Queer Families

'Growing up in the 1990s, I never felt weird or different,' Freya (she/her) tells me. Freya grew up as the child of two mums – her biological mum and her other mum – who used a sperm donor to conceive. Now an adult herself, Freya and her wife are parents to two children, whom they also conceived using donor sperm and are raising in North West England.

'My parents were good at involving us in organizations with other queer families, so I grew up around families like mine. But my parents did have their share of issues. One of my mums was scared to tell anyone for a long time about my conception and so acted like she had gone it alone as a single mum. There was a lot of internalized homophobia for her.'

## Unfit Mothers?

This internalized homophobia is incredibly understandable, particularly at a time in which LGBTQ+ parents were under careful scrutiny. During the 1980s and 1990s, queer parenthood, and especially lesbian motherhood, was still considered highly contentious. In 1982, Rights of Women formed a Lesbian Custody Group, aiming to provide advice and support to queer mothers whose identity was used as evidence that they were unfit parents.[1] Their research showed that, at its worst, 90% of lesbian mothers were losing custody battles in the courts.[2]

'The judge said you won't have custody of your daughters because you're a lesbian and unfit to mother them.'[3] These were the words of Sandi Hughes – filmmaker, poet, DJ and activist – who went on to spend more than forty years documenting political spaces across Merseyside. Having moved to Liverpool in 1963 with her children and husband, she was mostly at home alone with the kids whilst her husband was at sea. When he returned, he treated her poorly. By this time, she had also realized she was lesbian and was going to leave him. After coming out in the 1970s and going through divorce proceedings, the judge made the decision that Sandi was unfit to raise her daughters but could raise her son. She made what I can only describe as the impossible choice to let them stay together as a family. She went back to her bedsit and was forced to start her life again, but this time without her four children or a partner.

There's no definitive record of how many queer parents, particularly lesbian and bisexual women, had their children removed by the British judicial system, but we know Sandi's experience was far from an isolated incident. It's a deep-seated fear, one that I can see still wracks some of the older queer women in my life. It's very hard to feel like a good mother when the state has deemed people like you not fit to raise your children.

The introduction of Section 28 in 1988 only exacerbated the issue. Not only did it prohibit the discussion of LGBTQ+ topics in schools but it also introduced the notion of a 'pretended family relationship' which permeated throughout the law. It was not until 2002, when the Adoption and Children Act[4] was introduced, and 2003, when Section 28 was abolished, that new types of LGBTQ+ families were recognized and formed.

# Better Times?

Is the situation better now? In many ways, yes, absolutely. From the sitcom *Modern Family* to children's books like *Grandad's Camper*, *The Accidental Diary of B.U.G.* and *The Last Firefox*, there are far more families with same sex parents (and grandparents) on our screens and in the pages of our literature. The Adoption and Children Act, which allowed same sex couples to adopt for the first time, came into effect in 2005 in England and Wales, and in 2007 in Scotland. But, despite some outliers, media representation remains relatively scant, and, as we will see, for everyday queer people wanting to start families there's still a long way to go.

Since coming out as a teenager, I've been asked repeatedly whether I'll have kids. It seems that as soon as I removed the possibility of having sex with men from my life, my desire and capacity to carry and bear a child moved to the top of people's agenda. It's been interesting to watch even the most strident of feminists – women who had raised me to be independent and bold – suddenly be concerned about my having children, as if that's the only purpose my life holds.

In truth, so far, I've not wanted children. Even when I was a child myself, I didn't like kids; they are sticky and loud and require a lot of attention. Ironically, children adore me and I can halt a toddler meltdown with a stern glance. My feelings might change; my mum tells me she was never that fussed about children and then one day woke up and really wanted them. But, as a lesbian, I can't just get casually interested in having a baby because the barriers to it happening remain immense. It's certainly not a situation I foresee finding myself in, but getting medical help for an LGBTQ+ person to start a family is far from straightforward.

## Fertility Treatment Inequality

A study of LGBTQ+ women and non-binary people, conducted in 2021 by Stonewall and DIVA magazine, found that 36% of respondents who had children experienced barriers or challenges with starting a family, but that the number jumped to a staggering 85% of those who used a medical intervention like IVF (in vitro fertilization, where an egg is fertilized by a sperm outside of the body to create an embryo, which is then implanted) and IUI (where sperm is placed directly into the uterus using a small catheter).[5]

It's essential to recognize that plenty of LGBTQ+ families can conceive without medical intervention. For example, a cis gay man and a bisexual trans man might have a child together, or an intersex woman and a cis woman could fall pregnant. But for lots of people, some medical intervention is necessary.

Ordering sperm for home insemination has been banned in the UK since 2005 and, as such, it is not possible to have sperm from sperm banks shipped to private homes, necessitating trips to either NHS or private clinics. 'We did originally want to make it as "unclinical" as possible,' Freya, twenty-nine, tells me, 'and wanted to do home insemination, but then banks stopped shipping to home addresses, so we had to switch it up and go with a clinic. In the end we still had the least invasive method, IUI with no meds needed at all, and it worked first time both times.'

Not everyone is quite as lucky in being able to conceive on the first try or without medication. In the UK, there are significant disparities for people trying to conceive using the NHS, with each devolved nation offering different levels of care. For same sex couples in England, the National Institute for Health and Care Excellence (NICE) guidance has resulted in an unfair and unlawful situation for LGBTQ+ couples. Most regions, but not all, stipulate that single women and female (cisgender) same sex couples must self-fund for the first six to twelve rounds of artificial insemination through private clinics[6] – often at a cost of tens of thousands of pounds – before they are eligible for any fertility treatment on the NHS. This is because they have to prove infertility, whereas straight cisgender people qualify after two years of unprotected sex, with no financial cost to them.

In 2021, wives Megan and Whitney Bacon-Evans took a case to the High Court after experiencing discrimination in the IVF process. As a result of being a same sex couple, they were required by their local trust – Frimley ICB – to undertake twelve rounds of fertility treatment including six intrauterine inseminations – at a cost of around £25,000 to £30,000, whereas most heterosexual couples could access some form of help for free. They went on to claim victory in their case when Frimley ICB recognized the 'need to update their policy to remove the inequality between same sex female couples and cis heterosexual couples'.[7]

Indeed, in 2022, the Women's Health Strategy committed to removing the need for self-funded artificial insemination.[8] However, local care boards have not necessarily implemented these new rules, with analysis by Stonewall revealing that, as of April 2024, 90% of care boards were failing to meet those targets.[9] One in five local care boards (19%) do not even adhere to NICE guidelines introduced over a decade ago in 2013 and require twelve, rather than six, self-funded rounds. The implementation of these outdated policies means that people may have to spend £60,000 before they can access healthcare.[10] That figure does not include the cost of buying sperm from a sperm bank, with average costs at well over £1,000 for one vial, rising with the level of motility (which indicates quality in terms of likelihood of falling pregnant). In the UK, donors are required to be anonymous until the child is eighteen.[11] The ramifications of this process are huge, making it financially impossible for the vast majority of LGBTQ+ people to access the fertility care they need.

## Two Mums, Two Dads

In the UK, a child can only have two legal parents.[12] A legal parent is someone who is named on the birth certificate and has financial responsibility for the child. This is true, irrespective of whether a legal parent holds parental responsibility, which is the legal obligation relating to important decisions for a child, such as where they go to school.[13]

Currently, the way the system works is that the person who gives birth is defined as the mother, even if a donated egg is used. When it comes to fertility treatment, if you are a woman who is married or in a civil partnership with a birth mother before fertility treatment starts, you are automatically considered the other legal parent.[14] However, if you are not married or in a civil partnership, both of you must give formal consent, in partnership with a registered UK fertility clinic, for the person donating the eggs for their partner to carry to become the other parent legally. If you are male and father a child through sex, you are the legal parent irrespective of your relationship with the mother.

It's important, if complicated and time-consuming, to keep abreast of the subtleties of the law here, as there are some same-sex families who seek legal resolution through the courts when they don't officially have to.

## Transparent

In the summer of 2023, author Logan Brown appeared on the cover of *Glamour* magazine.[15] Against a terracotta backdrop, Logan stands tall and proud, his right hand resting underneath his pregnant belly, his body painted to mimic a suit with the buttons burst open, and the magazine cover was emblazoned with three simple words: 'Trans Pregnant Proud'. The interview came after Logan began sharing his experiences of pregnancy online. Several famous creators on Instagram and TikTok took issue with this, sharing repeatedly that 'men can't get pregnant', that he was a woman, and encouraging their audiences to send hate towards Logan. 'At the end of the day, I'm a trans pregnant man and I do exist,' Logan responded. 'No matter what anyone says, I am literally living proof.'

There has been a furore in the media over the use of phrases like 'pregnant people', with detractors claiming that the wording erases women.[16] This seems odd to me. To my mind, women *are* people, so how are they excluded? The wording is there to include those trans men and non-binary people who are biologically able to get pregnant and give birth. In doing so, we are not excluding those cis women who are able to do the same. This is language that affirms people and respects their boundaries. I remain unsure of why so many people are so incredibly stressed about things that literally have no impact on them whatsoever. The idea that trans men giving birth somehow erases womanhood is incredibly sexist. Not only does it imply that cisgender women simply disappear into the ether when someone with a different life experience to them exists, it also conflates womanhood with the capacity (and desire) to carry and birth a child. To me, this feels rather reminiscent of Gilead – the dystopian anti-feminist world of Margaret Atwood's *The Handmaid's Tale*.

If we are going to get pernickety about language, we might as well talk about something that has *does* have harmful impact: calling trans men 'mothers'. Even if you have a GRC if you give birth to a child in England or Wales, you are legally defined as the child's mother. The same is true, of course, if you are non-binary. Why? Because of an antiquated law from the 1950s[17] which recognizes that only mothers give birth – and automatically gives them parental rights. That's right, laws created before the invention of the pill or before women could open their own bank accounts without their husband's approval are determining the ways in which we can, or rather, can't be recognized as parents.

That's not to say that some people aren't attempting to change things. In 2019, trans man Freddy McConnell asked to be recorded as 'parent' or 'father' on his child's birth certificate, but authorities refused and legal challenges to the High Court and Court of Appeal failed.[18] Where does this leave trans parents? Put simply, trans parents in the UK have no formal, legal recognition. A person can be a man in the eyes of the law until they give birth, in which case they suddenly become recognized as female again.

It is astonishing to think, therefore, that we have a legal system in this country that defines people not by who they are, but by if they have birthed a child. Trans men who carry a pregnancy are considered female when they give birth; trans men who do not carry a pregnancy have no right to register as a father, either. Trans women can't register as a mother or parent, either, irrespective of any biological link to a child; she might only register as a father. It's a system that makes no sense, particularly when all UK adopters are listed as a 'parent'. Surrogacy parental orders are similarly gender-neutral. Evidently, we can build inclusive systems when we feel like it matters.

To be fair to the lawmakers, when the Gender Recognition Act was introduced in 2004, there was significantly less recognition of trans people within society, and the idea that they might have families probably didn't enter into the heads of many of them. But it's not just the parents this impacts – it's children, too. Kids may be forced to go through life with no birth certificate, or an inaccurate one. In most contexts involving such vital documentation, providing false or misleading information would be considered fraudulent and, as such, punishable. And yet trans and non-binary parents are forced into a situation where they must give inaccurate details or are unable to update information.

The only option for trans and non-binary parents in the UK is to travel abroad to give birth in a country where birth certificates are not required to gender the parents, such as in Sweden.[19] But this is neither practical nor accessible for most people, particularly given that trans people are more likely to be financially disadvantaged.

Changes to the way birth certificates operate have been implemented already; for example, it is now possible to list a second parent on the certificate who is not a 'mother', which was created to allow two mothers to be included on the document. So why is it not possible to do the same for trans and non-binary parents? The situation shows how flawed the legal system is when it comes to supporting the T in LGBTQ+.

## Raising (LGBTQ+) Children

I am exceptionally fortunate to have two incredibly supportive parents who embraced having me as a daughter. They took all my quirks and foibles – not to mention me being an autistic lesbian – in their stride. And yet even they didn't do everything right, although never due to malice. Instead, if they did get anything wrong, it was down to only having had limited information and guidance.

When I came out, aged fourteen, the one thing I found incredibly difficult was that my parents insisted I didn't post publicly about being LGBTQ+ and asked me not to tell my little brother, who was eleven at the time. From their perspective, they were giving me time to better understand myself and the space to change my mind or to find a new label that better reflected me, which some LGBTQ+ people do. After all, I was still very young. They wanted to have a conversation with the wider family and give me space to control the narrative. My brother couldn't keep a secret to save his life and they didn't think he would understand. They had only positive intentions – attempting to keep me safe, secure and protected – and yet it made me feel as though being gay was something I ought to be ashamed of and couldn't share with people.

Raga D'Silva (she/her) is someone I admire deeply. She is the co-founder of OutSpoken, a speaking agency for LGBTQ+ women and non-binary people, and something of a powerhouse. She's passionate, seemingly indomitable and puts up with no nonsense.

'My children, they are your age,' Raga told me. 'And if either one or both of them were to come out to me, I would, of course, love them unconditionally – my mum didn't. And I know the trauma of that kind of rejection. But I would still hesitate. I would love them unconditionally. I would hold them. I would say that's fine.

'But I think I would grieve inside. Because for me, whatever I've been through and what I see others going through, I wouldn't want anybody to have to face that. Every day, we have to tell people, educate people, make people feel that they can accept us, not to reject us. You know, every day is like, we have to fight for our space. And I would hate for my children to have to go through that.'

This sentiment is echoed by Amelia (she/they), thirty-two, another parent who is queer themselves and has a queer stepkid. 'I feel a mixture of disappointment and hope. My stepkid is being bullied and I find myself being quite disheartened that kids these days are, in some ways, more progressive and tolerant, and in others still capable of being incredibly cruel.'

Bullying is something both LGBTQ+ children and the straight or cisgender children of LGBTQ+ parents can face. In fact, one of the biggest fears many queer parents have is that their children will experience discrimination because of their LGBTQ+ identity.[20] A 2020 survey of LGBTQ+ women found that of those with children, 36% had experienced homophobia from other parents and the same number claimed their children had experienced homophobia because of their parent's sexuality.[21]

'My children were very upset because they stopped wanting to go to school because of the bullying,' one parent shared. 'We felt anger it was not dealt with by the school and also guilty for feeling like we were the root of the kid's upset.' Discrimination faced by parents extends beyond just schools, too, with parents reporting being denied access to services and youth organizations, too.[22]

It's no wonder some LGBTQ+ parents, or potential parents, worry that there will be long-term harm to their children if they are raised by LGBTQ+ parents, a fear often rooted in the hatred thrown at their children by others. However, research consistently finds that their wellbeing does not differ from that of other children. A 2023 report comparing thirty-four studies from countries where same sex relationships are legal showed that children brought up by lesbian, gay, bisexual and trans parents fared just as well as those brought up by heterosexual parents.[23] In some areas, children of LGBTQ+ parents did significantly better, with a higher parent–child relationship quality, such as higher levels of warmth, greater amounts of interaction and more supportive behaviour, than that found in heterosexual parent groups.

## Rights Roll-backs

Despite what the data says about the wellbeing of children brought up by queer parents, in some parts of the world we're seeing rights go backwards. In Chapter 3, we saw how parts of the US are leading the way when it comes to removing LGBTQ+ representation, including representations of two-mum and two-dad families, from classrooms.

In 2021, Poland banned same sex couples from adopting, with lesbian couples already not eligible for IVF treatment in the country. Just two years later, Hungary, where it is already illegal for same sex potential parents to adopt or access fertility treatment, proposed a bill enabling and encouraging citizens to report same sex couples to the state authorities. Thankfully, it was vetoed before it became law.

In 2023, the government of Padua, Italy, began systematically removing the names of lesbian mothers from their children's birth certificates. This included birth certificates of children with lesbian parents being cancelled and recalled – essentially erasing the names of non-biological parents. Italy has some other incredibly troubling laws in place when it comes to LGBTQ+ families; artificial insemination is prohibited for same sex couples, and they are likewise only able to adopt their stepchildren. At present, individual cities within

Italy can choose their own laws when it comes to the legal protections of same sex parents. In 2017, laws were relaxed to allow same sex couples to go abroad and then register their children with the city upon their return. However, in 2023, the city of Padua decided to remove parental rights from the non-biological parents by cancelling their birth certificates retroactively.

## Parental Rights and LGBTQ+ Equality

We have seen that, for some, LGBTQ+ families represent a threat to society. One of the ways this manifests is when the existence of those families is set in direct opposition to other parents' rights. Whilst the Floridian bill which forbids the discussion of gender and sexuality in the classroom is often dubbed 'Don't Say Gay', its *actual* name is the Parental Rights in Education Bill[24] – although clearly it's not protecting the rights of queer parents to be seen and recognized. So-called parental rights have become a proxy for targeting LGBTQ+ people's existence and limiting children's 'exposure' to us, as though we might somehow be contagious.

Anti-LGBTQ+ campaigners are attempting to flip the narrative, casting themselves as the victims of oppression. As Antonia Tully of the Society for the Protection of Unborn Children, the largest and oldest pro-life group in the UK, puts it: 'The might of the political and educational establishment has closed ranks against these parents . . . I'm beginning to see a pattern here. Parents who dare to challenge the new orthodoxy in relation to relationships, marriage and family are intolerant, narrow-minded and cannot be trusted to educate their own children in these matters . . . And worse, the state duly believes they own our children.'[25]

So-called parental rights are used to prevent discussions of not only LGBTQ+ matters but also topics of race, feminism and reproduction. In 2023, the American Library Association documented 4,200 attempts to ban or restrict books in libraries and a total of

1,648 books that were banned.[26] Nearly half of filings, 43%, targeted titles with LGBTQ+ characters or themes, whilst 36% targeted titles featuring characters of colour or dealing with issues of race and racism. The top reason people challenged books was 'sexual' content; 61% of challenges referenced this concern. Almost none of these books were 'required reading' and could be chosen by young people and their families – or not – and yet still, they were banned. One interesting, and possibly heartening, thing to note is that polling consistently shows that Americans of all political alignments oppose book bans, which are often being implemented by a very vocal minority. These include Christian groups, who seek not just book bans but total educational reform to focus on so-called traditional values, removing discussions of not only LGBTQ+ people but racial diversity, social equality and relationship education. What's also staggering is the power given to the weight of one individual parent complaining: in Wisconsin, for example, one school district banned over 400 books on the basis of a single parent's challenge.[27] Across the US, 60% of book challenges were made by just eleven people.[28]

These attitudes aren't only coming from the US. I have spoken with UK school librarians who are regularly sent complaints about stocking inclusive materials, as well as texts which promote anti-LGBTQ+ sentiments or which reinforce 'gender critical' thinking. Blessing (she/her), forty-eight, a librarian at a school in the Midlands, tells me, 'What's really disturbing is that some of these books are not obviously against LGBTQ+ people, against trans people especially. To the untrained eye, they appear to be about celebrating difference, understanding yourself, but they have been written specifically to undermine trans people's existence.'

I do sometimes wonder what the world would look like if children were viewed as people and not property. It seems to me that a lot of those who place an emphasis on parental rights aren't going to achieve the best outcomes for their children. They're treating their children as objects – things to control.

Being queer is often attributed to social contagion or outside influence, and there are large parts of society that still believe if you don't mention being LGBTQ+ to children, they will not become LGBTQ+. I like to think I am anathema to that: never knew LGBTQ+ people existed, still ended up a massive lesbian.

Here's the thing: parental rights are important, and we should talk about them. The problem is that the phrase 'parental rights' has been co-opted to argue that parents have the right to control a child and everything they have access to. If we really care about parental rights, we should be looking at how the current system denies LGBTQ+ parents the same rights as other families.[29]

## The New Nuclear Family

In some ways, this idea of control is hardly surprising when the notion of a nuclear family has often been tied up with preserving wealth, bloodlines and property. Many LGBTQ+ people believe in updating the concept of family, or at least the traditional, nuclear version of it, in favour of an approach that celebrates everyone, not just those people they are biologically related to. The concept of 'found family' – friends who accept you just as you are, but whom you love and care for as deeply as family, is incredibly important to many queer people.

As Amelia reminded me, 'It's always strange to me that I have both my found family and my blood relatives. And under the system we have, the people who are most important to me are not recognized at all unless I were to write them into my will, for example.'

This isn't about individual families being broken up, but modernizing a society that makes a traditional family the only accepted set-up. Repeatedly during same sex marriage debates, opponents have leveraged supposed 'common-sense arguments' that the heterosexual, nuclear family with children is the 'natural truth' and better for society or, to quote one traditionalist outlet, 'central to a healthy, stable society'.[30]

In Great Britain, the Christian Medical Fellowship argued that:

'Stable marriage and families headed by a mother and a father are the bedrock of society and the state has a duty to protect the uniqueness of these key institutions. There is considerable evidence to show that marriage leads to better family relationships, less economic dependence, better physical health and longevity, improved mental health and emotional wellbeing and reduced crime and domestic violence. Same sex marriage, in comparison with marriage, is an unproven and experimental social mode.'[31]

Not only are LGBTQ+ families considered by opponents not to be families at all, but their mere existence is said to cause irrevocable harm, capable of eradicating other family structures in their entirety, and as a knock-on effect being responsible for the collapse of society. But, as we have discussed, children in families in same sex relationships can do even better than those in families with a mother and a father.

There are legitimate threats to the notion of family and they are not LGBTQ+ people. The fact is that being in a family right now is often financially impossible because of a spiralling cost of living and, more specifically, the extortionate cost of childcare. According to data from the Office for National Statistics, the median annual pay for full-time employees was £33,000; after tax and National Insurance are deducted, this leaves a person with £2,154 per month or £497 per week. The average monthly cost of childcare in the UK is £1,106.52 – or 51% of a post-tax salary. This means that even with two parents working, it is a struggle. After paying for housing, utilities, childcare and food, many families are in debt before they have even begun thinking about buying clothes, toys or supplies for their kids, let alone themselves.[32]

## And What You Can Do About It

→ Educate those around you about the different types of families that exist and how they form, including the existence of LGBTQ+ families. This might include mentioning different people's families in an appropriate context which usualizes LGBTQ+ relationships, talking candidly about how relationships form and fall apart and consuming media which showcases a wide number of families.

→ Use inclusive language that does not assume relationships or identities of people within families.

→ Raise awareness of the inequalities faced by LGBTQ+ people when starting their families and campaign for greater equality in access to treatments like IVF and IUI.

→ Actively seek out content in the family space – children's books, kids' TV and films, that feature LGBTQ+ families to share with the children in your life.

→ Be mindful of the fact that family does not necessarily refer to biological relationships. Many people in the LGBTQ+ community are estranged from their biological families and have found other ways to build community.

# Putting in the Work

## Freddy McConnell (he/him)

Freddy McConnell is a British journalist and transgender rights campaigner. As a trans man who gave birth, McConnell became a pivotal figure in the fight for legal recognition and equal rights for transgender parents when his experience was publicly documented in the film *Seahorse: The Dad Who Gave Birth*.

This groundbreaking documentary captured his experience of pregnancy and challenges the traditional notions of parenthood and gender. By sharing his story so openly, McConnell has brought significant attention to the unique challenges faced by transgender parents, promoting a broader understanding and acceptance of diverse family structures.

McConnell has been actively involved in legal battles to secure rights for trans parents and, notably, he challenged the UK's legal system to allow him to be recognized as his child's father or parent on the birth certificate rather than as the mother. Although he faced legal setbacks, his case has sparked important discussions about the need for legal reforms to ensure that transgender parents are accorded the same rights and recognition as cisgender parents, something which is still lacking.

McConnell's journalism further amplifies his advocacy. He writes extensively on transgender issues, healthcare access and legal rights, using his platform to educate and influence public opinion and policy.

## Lindz Amer (they/them)

Lindz Amer is a prominent LGBTQ+ advocate, writer and creator based in the US, best known for their groundbreaking web series *Queer Kid Stuff,* which has attracted millions of views online.

*Queer Kid Stuff* is designed to introduce topics around being LGBTQ+ and other aspects of diversity – such as family diversity, faith and race – to young children and their families in an age-appropriate and accessible manner. Using catchy songs and puppetry and featuring special guests from a range of backgrounds, the series was created by Amer in 2016 in light of the lack of resources and media available for LGBTQ+ families with young children aged three to seven.

Amer is an outspoken advocate for LGBTQ+ young people and their families and is the author of the book *Rainbow Parenting: Raising Queer Kids and Their Allies* and is also the host of the *Rainbow Parenting* podcast. Amer hopes that by giving parents and their children a vocabulary that helps them to express themselves, they might become more empathetic and accepting of different people in the world.

## Whitney and Megan Bacon-Evans (both she/her)

Megan and Whitney Bacon-Evans are campaigners and influencers based in the UK, who in 2020 launched a groundbreaking campaign fighting for IVF equality for LGBTQ+ couples after experiencing discrimination in the fertility treatment system, including higher costs and more restrictive eligibility criteria compared to heterosexual couples.

When they tried to start a family, their local NHS service required them to pay for twelve rounds of fertility treatment, including six IUIs in a private clinic, to 'prove' infertility before they – as a cisgender gay couple – were eligible for help. As well as a prominent press campaign, the couple gave evidence at the UK government's LGBTQ+ Commission's first inquiry, and their case was even discussed in the House of Lords.

In November 2021, the couple filed an application for judicial review, claiming discrimination under the Equality Act 2010 and Articles 8 and 14 of the European Convention on Human Rights. Their local integrated care board finally, in 2024, agreed to change their policies, expanding inclusion for LGBTQ+ couples, although it remains unclear what funding and resourcing will be applied to this expansion.

# CHAPTER 9
# Don't Stop Moving

I'd imagined spin classes very differently: toned, thin people in expensive matching Lycra, with not a hair out of place. Around me, in a studio just off Regent's Park in London, was a very different scene. Sweating on my stationary bike, I was surrounded by buzz cuts, facial piercings, tattoos, baggy T-shirts and an assortment of body shapes. The atmosphere was safe, warm and welcoming. It felt like home.

But then, this was no ordinary spin session. It had been organized by NDY Global in collaboration with famed queer club night Pxssy Palace. NDY Global is the brainchild of Ryan Lanji, founder of Hungama, the UK's first LGBTQ+ Bollywood club night, winner of Netflix's *The Big Flower Fight* and now LGBTQ+ well-being and fitness champion. After the session, I asked him how it all started.

'A few years ago, when I had a job as a towel boy at a gym, I was able to work with this amazing personal trainer. She taught me to harness and nurture my vessel – my whole body and mind,' he tells me. 'She taught me that the gym isn't about trends and jumping on trampolines, or bright colours and spandex outfits, but that it's about mastering a craft and understanding [working out] as a discipline.'

When the Covid-19 pandemic hit, Ryan saw the devastating

impact on queer and trans people's mental health, with queer and trans people of colour being particularly affected: 'I realized that kids were in their rooms in flatshares, without families because they had been exiled, and that they needed support.'

He set up free Zoom yoga classes that people could participate in wherever they were. NDY Global was able to provide free digital sessions seven days a week over the second and third UK lockdowns. They reached over 3,500 participants and uplifted our community by highlighting queer and trans stories and centring body, spirit and mind. After the lockdowns, they started offering more classes in person, in everything from boxing to Pilates.

NDY Global is forging new ways for queer people to be together, working in collaboration with iconic queer club nights. 'We are building a platform that offers fitness and wellbeing sessions that centre the needs and experiences of queer and trans people', Ryan tells me. 'Queer nightlife is great – but it's not enough – our mission is to help build a thriving "queer day life" alongside the provision of a curated digital space that operates as a queer events listings service and amplifies marginalized perspectives through storytelling.'

The benefits of having access to movement and exercise cannot be overstated. Getting enough exercise can help reduce the risk of major illnesses including heart disease, stroke, diabetes and cancer. Getting enough exercise reduces stress and rates of depression and improves mood. And it can lower the risk of an early death by up to 30%, according to the NHS, who call it a 'miracle cure'.[1] So, when LGBTQ+ people are excluded from opportunities to exercise, it places a restriction on our wellbeing (something we know is already under threat). In the UK, 56% of LGBTQ+ women, 55% of LGBTQ+ men and 64% of people outside of the binary gender were found in 2023 to not be active enough to maintain good health, compared to 33% of men in the general population, with significant ramifications for long-term wellbeing.[2]

## Physical Education

Despite having played sports for as long as I can remember and having spent a decade going to the gym, I was – and still am, a little bit – scared of fitness classes. Perhaps it was the residual trauma of being called a pervert whilst changing for PE lessons, or the shame I have about my clumsiness and how hard I find it to learn new movements.

I was on the netball and rounders teams at school, played rugby throughout my teenage years and went to the gym round the corner regularly. On the surface, I was quite sporty. But I never felt like part of the crew, especially after I came out. Once I had, my presence in the changing room was seen as inherently predatory. People would move away from me, convinced I must be getting off on seeing them undress, when mostly I was trying to avoid having my own body noticed. I had an ongoing joke with one of my PE teachers, who would marvel that I could get into a changing room, undressed and into my kit before the other class had even been let in, but I never quite worked out how to articulate that it wasn't a competition, it was the equivalent of running and hiding. My experience isn't uncommon.

Research shows that LGBTQ+ young people consistently shun physical education at school. The National School Climate Survey revealed that in 2018, 40% of LGBTQ+ young people continued to avoid changing rooms and physical education classes and a quarter avoided school athletic fields or facilities.[3] The same research found that just 5% of gender-diverse young people participated in sports that matched their gender identity, although this did increase to 42% if there was a gender-affirming school policy. It is no wonder, then, so many LGBTQ+ adults are less active, given we know that higher rates of physical activity in young people are correlated with higher physical activity rates in adulthood.

## We Can't Be What We Can't See

There is often a fear about sports fans and the culture around sport being somehow more dangerous for LGBTQ+ people; when I was organizing events for the LGBTQ+ society at university, we always avoided being near the sports society nights. Research by Scotland's Equality Network found that 79% of respondents thought that there was a problem with homophobia within sport and 62% had experienced it, and 80% of trans people had experienced or witnessed transphobia in a sports-related setting. Across the UK, a fifth of sports fans think anti-LGBTQ+ language is harmless if it is meant as banter.[4]

At the same time, one in ten LGBTQ+ people who attended a sporting event in 2023 experienced discrimination because of their gender or sexuality, an amount that almost doubles for LGBTQ+ people of colour.[5] Two-thirds of LGBTQ+ people don't feel that public sporting events are welcoming to them. Indeed, I probably would have gone to more football matches growing up if I had felt safer there as a woman and as an LGBTQ+ person, though by and large, with my dad being an avid West Ham season ticket holder, I probably would have been protected. Still, I shouldn't have to rely on my dad to feel safe going to a game.

With all this in mind, it's not surprising so few LGBTQ+ athletes are able to come out. Whilst there are several leading figures within sport who have come out as lesbian, gay or bisexual, this number is likely to pale in comparison to how many there are who feel unable to do the same. In 2022, the UK saw its first openly gay player come out in professional men's football in over thirty years – we cannot surely believe he is the only one? When Welsh rugby legend Gareth Thomas and diver Tom Daley publicly announced that they were LGBTQ+, both of them shared that they were initially dissuaded from going public with their sexuality by well-meaning but concerned parties.

Progress has been made since then, with the increase in popularity of women's football in particular driving greater visibility and acceptance. The 2022 Euros-winning Lionesses team boasted seven out LGBTQ+ players, and there were 199 out athletes at the 2024 Paris Olympics and forty-two out athletes at the Paralympics respectively – the highest number on record.[6]

## Not Welcome

In recent years, we've seen some outright bans come into place on trans people – and usually trans women – in sport, on the basis of them having a biological advantage because they are seen as male. What is interesting is that none of these bans uses a singular method to determine if a woman is considered trans. Some bans have used just a gender declaration, others use legal genders. Others require specific hormone levels – but these can vary greatly in range. Some look at other aspects, such as chromosomal testing. Now, I am not for one moment advocating for a world in which universal guidelines are created which ban trans athletes from sports – far from it – but I do think it is important that we recognize just how arbitrary many of these bans that do currently exist are.

Ahead of the 2024 Paris Olympics, former Olympic medallist Sharron Davies[7] wrote an article for the *Daily Mail* with the headline: 'Female athletes STILL face being conned out of medals by transgender competitors due to cowardice and misogyny'. All of this because the International Olympic Committee (IOC) has taken some effective steps in recent years to build inclusion for trans athletes.

## The IOC Does Something Good

Many of the bans operate from the consensus that trans athletes, particularly trans women, have a biological advantage, something which has largely been presumed rather than proven empirically. A recent in-depth review of all English-language scientific literature on trans women, commissioned by the IOC, revealed that factors such as lung size and joint angles – where cis and trans women can differ – are not indicative of athletic ability, nor do testosterone levels predict athletic performance.[8] This was the first time a study had explicitly looked at trained trans athletes; previous decisions had been based on the performance of cisgender men, not trans women. The recommendation of the IOC's Medical and Scientific Commission was clear: sporting federations should stop banning trans women from women's categories because the evidence to do so simply isn't there yet. And I want to be clear, the IOC has a poor history on trans inclusion, previously requiring trans people to undergo medically unnecessary treatments to suppress their hormones and even undertake genital surgery to play sports.

It was not until 2021 that the IOC created its Framework on Fairness, Inclusion and Non-Discrimination of the Basis of Gender Identity and Sex Variations – a guidance for sporting bodies. As part of this, the committee dropped several of these controversial policies.[9]

There were lots of incredibly sensible things in this framework, which, although not legally binding, were recommended to sporting bodies. The bodies were told that they should consider that 'determinations of disproportionate advantage be based on appropriate evidence, rather than assumed on the basis of an individual's transgender status and/or sex characteristics'. The framework emphasizes the prevention of harm to all athletes, whether that's by ensuring they are supported through any process of determining eligibility, to understanding that, in certain instances, such as a sport involving collision, injury risk is considered. But it also recognizes that a non-transgender athlete could have a higher muscle mass than a trans one, and encourages sports bodies 'to consider actual risk'.

One of the biggest conversations I have about trans people in sport is around the idea that trans women athletes have an inherent and specific advantage over other athletes. However, particularly at the elite level, we know there are always competitors with significant advantages over others, and they are lauded for it. Advantage – as the IOC recognized – is simply the thing which means ultimately one athlete is able to succeed over the other. The problem is a disproportionate advantage but, again, there are plenty of cisgender athletes with a disproportionate advantage over others but whom we praise, not condemn, because we don't associate their success with being transgender. Take Michael Phelps as an example – he was significantly taller than his competitors, with massive lung capacity, a two-metre arm span and a body that produced less lactic acid than his competitors. He wasn't banned from swimming because of it – he was supported – so why do we not penalize cisgender people's proven biological advantages and penalize trans people whose biological advantages are assumed (and are often not the case)?[10]

It was genuinely refreshing to read guidance which seems so considered and comes from a place of consideration and care for autonomy, health, privacy and scientific evidence. Unfortunately, many sporting bodies (and sometimes, governments) who are responsible for if and how this guidance is implemented have chosen to ignore it altogether.

## Fair Is Fair

If we want to talk meaningfully about women's sports and the inequalities experienced by women athletes, then we should be looking at the disproportionate nature of funding. In those US states which have passed anti-transgender sports bills under the guise of protecting women's sports and ensuring fairness (or have them pending), schools spent 64 million dollars more on men's sports than on women's sports[11] – approximately seventy cents on women's sports for every dollar on men's sports. Research using another database showed that across all fifty states in the 2018–19 athletic season, for every dollar spent on men's sports, around fifty-five cents was spent on women's sports, totalling 3.9 billion dollars more.[12]

One of the most startling aspects of sports bans is that they're not only affecting elite athletes – they're also affecting children playing sports, particularly at school. Laws banning transgender children from taking part in sport have been enacted in twenty-three US states, with variations on implementation. Some states do not clarify how sex might be ascertained and many are exceptionally vague; some include references to a physical examination or health inspection. Some laws, such as Florida's Fairness in Women's Sports Act introduced in 2021, state that genital inspections may be performed if there are concerns about whether a woman or girl is cisgender or not.[13] I feel incredibly uneasy about a law which requires women to be subjected to invasive genital examinations if they do not conform to a narrow ideal of womanhood. The fact this could be done to a child is even more disturbing.

In fact, it is sometimes even the idea of children playing sports in school that appears threatening. In 2021, a bill was entered in Louisiana that would require schools to only allow 'biological females' to play in sports. When Senator Beth Mizell, who introduced the bill, was asked if there was an example where there was a problem with trans students, Mizell replied, 'Not in Louisiana,' and that the bill was 'pre-emptive'.[14] In short, legislators are so keen to limit the freedoms of trans people that they have invented situations which are, by their own admission, not happening to justify it.

Similar bans were suggested in the UK by then Prime Minister Rishi Sunak, which would essentially have banned trans young people from participating in sport and PE lessons.

## Inclusive Fitness Spaces

'We've always had a policy that people can play for whichever team they identify with,' says Ella (they/them), who is non-binary and plays for the London Royals Hockey Club. 'We have a men's team, a women's team and a mixed team. So any gender can play in whichever team is most comfortable. We take it on a case-by-case basis.

There's lots of work that sports teams can do to push back to their governing bodies as well,' they tell me. 'One of the difficulties that can arise, especially when creating your own fitness space or sports club is how many governing bodies have adopted anti-trans stances, or are in seemingly indefinite consultation about whether trans people and especially trans women should be allowed to play.'

Recently, a friend started a local rounders group which, whilst not explicitly queer, is populated by a gaggle of queer and trans people. A natural progression for the group was to establish itself under Rounders England, to get support and insurance and to start working with other teams. The problem is that Rounders England had adopted rules which would exclude many of our community members because they are transgender.[15] For what it's worth, when the cis men have been on a team together, we have still beaten them.

London Royals have gone even further to help keep club members safe. They've established welfare officers to support players and worked to educate captains and other team members. Ella tells me, 'The team asks questions like, "What if someone says something that is biphobic or transphobic when we play other teams? How would we deal with that situation? Can we just walk off the pitch?" It could happen – it's sadly likely to happen – so we want to be as prepared as possible.'

One of the most joyous things about moving to Margate has been discovering so many community-led, movement-oriented LGBTQ+ spaces. One of my favourites is Queer Swim. It's a way for LGBTQ+ people from across all areas of life to come together and get into the sea (or not – we live in England; it's often quite chilly). By our own admission, it's less about swimming itself and more about community, and demystifying the fear of visibly queer and trans bodies being out on the beach. Lots of the benefits of movement spaces are actually less about the ways in which you contort your body and more about being with others, feeling accepted, being able to recognize what your body needs and supplying it. Some people just come to sit on the beach and breathe in the sea air, or join in the games we play on the sand in the summer months.

## Gender-neutral Facilities

Margate has scarcely any public toilets at all, a problem which is for a different soapbox, but it means we – and everyone else in the town – change on the beach. When I first moved, I was incredibly insecure and would attempt to try to hide my body under towels which were being whipped away by the wind. Quickly, I realized it was far more effective to whip your tits and bits out and get the job done and that – frankly – no one cared. A lovely side effect of being in LGBTQ+ spaces is that they help you stop seeing people's bodies as gendered at all. That's all bullshit society places on them.

'We should actively be trying to have more trans people in the gym,' Ryan of NDY Global tells me. 'We need a fitness industry that has gender-neutral locker rooms now – not just as a future aspiration for the next time they create a gym space. We need to keep our non-binary and trans people safe because we do not want to go back to the memories of being in swimming lessons or PE lessons.'

These spaces benefit not just trans and non-binary people, but people with children and those who have disabilities. When I was a kid, I was expected to get changed all on my own when my dad took us swimming, because I wasn't allowed to go into the men's changing room and vice versa. Likewise, friends of mine need support from carers in order to be able to get changed or go to the bathroom, and, whilst accessible changing rooms and toilets (in theory) exist, that isn't always the right accommodation.

For Ryan and me, creating intentional spaces specifically operated by and for the LGBTQ+ community is important, but we should be welcome to go to any fitness class, gym or sports team and be accepted.

Until that can happen, we cannot talk about sports and movement spaces as inclusive.

## And What You Can Do About It

→ Avoid policing people's bodies. In sport *and* in general – do not make comments about people's bodies.

→ Educate yourself, your staff and your members if you are running any kind of sporting club or movement space. It is essential that your staff are able to support LGBTQ+ people and are aware of the barriers they might face.

→ Ensure gender-neutral language. Exercise spaces and sports are so often unnecessarily gendered. If I ever hear someone say 'hey ladies' before telling me the next movement in a fitness class, I will scream.

→ Create gender-neutral options for bathrooms and advocate for them throughout any new developments.

→ Recognize that LGBTQ+ people are often financially disadvantaged or experience multiple marginalizations. Consider offering subsidized, free or sliding-scale tickets to classes to ensure that people are never deprived of movement.

→ Advocate for trans inclusion in sports. Especially if you are an athlete or prominent within your field, speaking up can encourage support for LGBTQ+ people and ensure they are safe when participating.

# Putting in the Work

## Schuyler Bailar (he/him)

Schuyler Bailar is a trans author, activist and swimmer and the first-ever openly transgender athlete to compete in any sport on a National Collegiate Athletics Association (NCAA) Division One team.

By the age of ten, he was already competing in the Junior Olympics, and by thirteen, he had qualified for national-level competitions. At the 2013 NCSA Junior National Championships he qualified for the US Open – the fastest US meet in a non-Olympic year. Bailar was faced with the challenge of coming out as a trans person and becoming a possible NCAA champion as a swimmer for the Harvard women's team. To his surprise, when he transitioned and chose to swim on the men's team, he was mostly supported by those around him. Bailar chose to come out publicly, and his story has since been shared internationally to millions of people through news outlets like *The Washington Post* and *60 Minutes*.

Now, Bailar is a prominent advocate for trans inclusion within sports, speaking frankly about his experiences as an athlete who is trans at a time of increasing hostility towards LGBTQ+ people. He has grown a substantial following online and feels passionate about being a representation for trans people within sports and, in particular, makes a point of showing his trans body as a swimmer.

## Emily Bridges (she/her)

Emily Bridges is a Welsh cyclist who was competing at the elite level until she came out as a trans woman. British Cycling implemented a policy amounting to a ban on transgender athletes competing as women and created a new 'open' category, whilst restricting the 'female' category to those assigned female at birth and transgender men yet to begin hormone therapy. She has been outspoken about the links between the exclusion of transgender women from sport and the impact this has on their perception as men and a threat to cisgender women. Bridges has stated she is prepared to go to the European Court of Human Rights to challenge the ban on trans people in sports.

Bridges has also participated in research led by Loughborough University to assess the fairness of trans women athletes with reduced testosterone levels competing with cisgender women and has spoken out about the exclusion of evidence-based research which supports the inclusion of transgender athletes.

## Ilya Parker (he/they)

Ilya Parker is the founder of Decolonizing Fitness, which initially began as a mobile personal training service with the aim of reshaping fitness culture to better support trans masculine and gender-expansive people, with a focus also on Black people in larger bodies. Since then, the project has developed into an online resource hub for coaches, gym owners, personal trainers and anyone who is involved in movement spaces to access in order to learn about supporting a diverse range of bodies.

Parker's work emphasizes the need for fitness spaces to be gender-affirming and trauma-informed, particularly for LGBTQ+ individuals, who may have experienced discrimination or dysphoria in traditional gyms or wellness programmes. The initiative also stresses the importance of bodily autonomy and self-determination in fitness. Their work has led to organizations across the globe overhauling their approaches to fitness, building inclusion for all.

# CHAPTER 10
# A Place of Refuge

## Do You Qualify for Protection?

'[W]e will not be able to sustain an asylum system if in effect simply being gay, or a woman, and fearful of discrimination in your country of origin is sufficient to qualify for protection.'[1]

Those were the words of Suella Braverman, then Home Secretary of the UK, in her address to a think tank in Washington DC in September 2023. Her comments were decried internationally and called out for undermining the UN Refugee Convention, which formally identified the term 'refugee' and outlined the international standards by which refugees should be treated. The UK is one of 149 countries that are party to either the 1951 Refugee Convention, its 1967 Protocol or both. In 2022, previous Home Secretary Priti Patel passed the Nationality and Borders Act, which the UN Refugee Agency and over 250 human rights organizations in the UK claimed also undermined the Refugee Convention. The Act created a two-tier system, criminalized those seeking safety in the UK and legitimized the 'housing' of refugees and asylum seekers in unsafe conditions – including a barge which was more akin to a prison ship.

It is no surprise, given that the UK government at the time had been accused of flouting the convention,[2] that they deemed it not 'fit for the modern age'. Braverman cited a study by the right-wing think tank the Centre for Policy Studies which stated that 780 million people might be eligible for refugee status under the convention.[3] Before even having a close look at the data, it's immediately clear this number – the equivalent to twice the population of the United States – is unlikely and a preposterous argument on which to base the rolling back of one of the most essential parts of international infrastructure. 'Might' is doing a lot of heavy lifting in Braverman's speech. Sure – 780 million people 'might' be considered refugees under the UN convention, but I would be much more concerned about what mass tragedy of presumably epic proportions would be required for that to happen.

Let's look at what we know. As of 2023, there were 117.3 million people who had been forcibly displaced, of which just 37.6 million people worldwide met the UNHCR definition of a refugee and only 6.4 million were asylum seekers. The vast majority are internally displaced – meaning they are still within the same country or region. This equates to barely 5% of the number Braverman mentioned. Even if, through a series of tragedies and almost unimaginably terrible situations that cause people to become refugees and asylum seekers, that number doubled or tripled, it would be nowhere near the amount cited. Remember, the figure above is a rundown of all refugees and asylum seekers worldwide – not a reflection of those who have the UK as a destination. As Rob McNeil of the Migration Observatory stated: '[Then home secretary] Suella Braverman has been using a report by the CPS think tank to support the claim that up to 780 million people are "notionally" able to become international refugees . . . I am "notionally" able to emigrate to the moon. Doesn't make it realistic.'[4]

One of the first acts of the Labour government was to scrap the Rwanda plan[5] and to announce the imminent closure of Bibby Stockholm, a floating barge that was 'housing' refugees and asylum seekers but which had been compared to a prison ship by human rights organizations.[6] Despite this, the Labour government has continued to undertake mass deportations of refugees and asylum seekers, aiming to deport more than their Conservative counter-parts.[7] The approach is different but it's fundamentally a turbocharged attack on refugees, one which came just weeks after riots spread across the UK targeting migrants, asylum seekers and people of colour.

## LGBTQ+ Rights Globally

Why is it so important to support LGBTQ+ refugees? Often, unlike other asylum seekers, they are not fleeing from war or famine but instead from societies that put them at risk – risk which is far more serious than Braverman's 'fearful of discrimination' criterion. This is not about being passed over for employment or enduring verbal abuse (although that's unacceptable wherever it occurs). In sixty-four countries, same sex acts between men are criminalized; the same is true for women of forty-one countries. In twelve of these there is the death penalty. It has been used in Iran, Nigeria, Saudi Arabia, Somalia and Yemen. Transgender people – erroneously perceived to be homosexual or otherwise deviant – are often caught up in these laws, though there are fourteen countries which also specifically criminalize the existence of trans people under laws surrounding 'cross-dressing', impersonation and 'disguise'.[8] These are just the judicial impacts, which is to say nothing of the threat imposed by one's community, friends or family for being LGBTQ+. When entrepreneur and activist Bandy Kiki came out as a lesbian on social media in 2017, a high-profile producer in Cameroon 'threat-ened to rape the spirit of lesbianism out of me if I ever set foot in my home country again.'[9]

The refugee and asylum process for the UK is gruelling and dehu-manizing and fails to treat people with dignity regardless of their reasons for fleeing. But for LGBTQ+ refugees, it can be even more so. One of the less discussed aspects of the Nationalities and Borders Act was that it introduced a higher standard of proof for refugees.

Which begs the question: how do you prove you are LGBTQ+, especially when being so makes you so unsafe you are forced to flee your home country?

## The Proof Paradox

It is almost impossible for LGBTQ+ refugees and asylum seekers to be in the closet or keep quiet or private about their identity, even if that is what they wish to do, because the Home Office forces people to 'prove' their identity. Although caseworkers are supposed to be open-minded, refugees and organizations that support them have reported that they usually operate from a position of disbelief and needing to be persuaded.[10]

As examples of evidence, LGBTQ+ asylum seekers and refugees may need to be active members of dating apps and provide screenshots of interactions. They are often asked about their involvement with LGBTQ+ groups and activities, which may not be available; not being acquainted with LGBTQ+ spaces and people, or even cultural reference points, is apparent cause for concern.

The introduction of the two-tier system – where people in group two are treated less favourably – is abhorrent.[11] Refugees are at risk of being placed into group two if they do not seek asylum 'without delay'. If you are fleeing a country that criminalizes homosexuality, you may not feel ready, able or comfortable to disclose your identity, let alone to government officials. You may not know that being LGBTQ+ might mean you have a basis for an asylum claim. And again, not all LGBTQ+ people realize they are LGBTQ+ until much later in life or until they have been embraced by the community. They may have been forced to leave for other reasons, but coming to terms with their LGBTQ+ identity might make returning home not an option. A system which not only insists people prove they are LGBTQ+ but penalizes those who do not do so immediately is a disgrace.

## Not Believed

In 2020, Sam, a sixty-eight-year-old gay man from Malaysia, attempted to claim asylum on the basis of his sexual orientation in the UK after being arrested in 2015.[12] He came to the UK on a travel visa and never left. His claim was denied eight times, largely because he did not have a boyfriend, something which, at sixty-eight, Sam didn't want. There are hundreds more stories like this – cases of lesbians denied asylum on the basis that they have children. One bisexual man felt compelled to show intimate photos of himself and another man to prove his sexuality, and still he wasn't believed.[13]

This happens in detention centres, too. Maiba, an asylum seeker from Zimbabwe, explained, 'Before I ended up in detention, I didn't feel the need to go outside and shout, "Yes, I'm a lesbian." Now everything I do, I have to prove something. If I don't put pictures of myself or my new haircut up on Facebook [before being sent to the detention centre], they will be saying I'm not open enough. That's how it is: "How much of a lesbian are you? Do you go to gay clubs? Do you hang around with other lesbians? How many lesbians can write a letter for you to say, 'Yes, I know her. She's a lesbian'? And of those lesbians, how many of those lesbians have been accepted by the Home Office or are British?"'[14]

## Hypocritical

There is something somewhat hypocritical in the rhetoric Braverman and the Conservative Party adopted: the UK is the place of choice for refugees, that we are somewhere people flock to because we are so benevolent, and our society is so great.

'I wouldn't choose to apply for asylum here,' Aryam Marafi (she/her), a Kuwaiti refugee, tells me. 'I applied because I was already living here because I was studying. My passport was expiring and if

I had to go back and renew my passport, I would need to get my father's permission. I could be honour-killed.'

She continued, 'And it's not exactly like it's easy for visibly Muslim women in here, let alone LGBTQ+ Muslim women, in the UK? Something people fail to understand is that being a refugee is not about choice, it's about being put into an impossible position by factors out of your control.'

I first met Aryam (she/her) at Trans Pride in 2023. We were marching together, with a mutual friend, under the banner of Imaan an LGBTQ+ Muslim organization. (I will explore religion and LGBTQ+ rights more in the next chapter.)

When we meet again for coffee for me to interview her for this book, she is dressed in a bright-purple hoodie and a lilac skirt, with a light-coloured hijab and black tights – 'Ace colours!' she proclaims when I compliment her outfit.

At seventeen, having endured years of abuse as a child, including sexual abuse at the hands of her family, Aryam felt compelled to escape. A scholarship to study medicine in London presented her with an opportunity to get away from her abusers and flee Kuwait. Despite this, her mother threatened to kidnap her, and her father to terminate the scholarship.

Eventually, Aryam made it to the UK and undertook to complete her studies. Even though her parents are thousands of miles away, Aryam tells me they found ways to harass her, with the Kuwaiti embassy even writing to her university asking for information about her. In 2021, at the age of twenty, Aryam was faced with a dilemma. Her passport was running out. In Kuwait, Aryam would need her father's signature to get any documents, and male guardianship laws would heavily restrict her freedoms and, indeed, legitimize the abuse.

'I would never have been accepted for asylum on the basis that I am a woman facing domestic violence and the laws don't protect me.' Aryam tells me how normalized violence against women is in Kuwait, including the fact that under Penal Code (adapted from laws introduced by the colonial French), murder of a wife, sister or daughter by a man who suspects they have committed adultery is treated as a 'misdemeanour'. There is no stipulation as to what would be considered evidence of this. And particularly, now that Aryam has spoken publicly about what she has experienced – as well as her asexual, aromantic and queer identity – she is at more risk of violence.

Knowing she could not go home without risking severe abuse or potentially even being killed, Aryam applied for asylum seeker status, which she was granted. 'Suella is implying that only some people are deserving of safety, only some people deserve to be welcomed into this country – other people can die abroad.'

'One of my friends at the march,' Aryam remembers, 'had only just come here as an asylum seeker – also from a Gulf Arab country and also escaping domestic violence, like me. It was really nice to see how happy and hopeful she was. She is queer and her family will kill her or she would suffer extreme violence if she was still there.'

She says it so matter-of-factly, as if we were talking about the weather. I guess violence against queer and trans people around the globe remains as commonplace as the weather.

There is a myth that LGBTQ+ people become refugees or seek asylum solely on the basis they would experience violence for their sexuality or gender. In reality, LGBTQ+ people are at risk of the same factors as those which force others to flee: conflict, domestic violence, terrorism, famine, war, political persecution, climate disaster and many more.

## Refugees in the UK and in Detention

Whilst we do not have data about how many LGBTQ+ people migrate due to anti-LGBTQ+ laws and attitudes, we do know that in 2022 only 2% of asylum claims in the UK included sexual orientation as part of the basis of the claim;[15] this does not mean that their claim is solely about protection from discrimination, just that this makes up part of it. Of these people, fewer than half will be approved.

Every year, thousands of asylum seekers are put in detention in the UK. We do not know how many of them are LGBTQ+ because the government does not record this information.

These are people coming to the UK because they are terrified and at risk of death, violence or incarceration. Our response? We essentially imprison them here. Britain is one of the few places that practise indefinite detention, meaning people have no idea if they will get out, let alone when. Gasha, an asylum seeker from Cameroon, told researchers about their experience in detention: 'I can't say I felt safe because I felt like I was in prison. When you don't feel like you've done anything wrong and you are kept in a place like that you don't feel safe at all.'[16]

It's important to emphasize that asylum seekers can be detained at any point in their claim process. Under the Detained Fast Track system – which was scrapped for being unlawful – LGBTQ+ people were detained because of being from so-called safe countries.[17] But even in countries where being queer or trans is not criminalized, LGBTQ+ people can be, and often are, at risk of violence from friends, family and community, including beatings, imprisonment and other abuse. The violence doesn't need to be from the state to threaten your life and livelihood. It is deeply concerning that the Home Office makes judgements about people's safety when they cannot provide it to some of the most vulnerable people in our society. Reports of asylum seekers being forcibly injected with sedatives and manhandled by the people operating the centres, treated as though they were objects, make disturbing reading.[18] Staff not only fail to act when it comes to discrimination against LGBTQ+ people by other detainees, but have been seen to partake in bullying and harassment themselves.

Of course, LGBTQ+ people should not be discriminated against in detention, but, to my mind, they shouldn't be held in detention at all. Nobody should. Detention centres are spoken of as an inevitability, but the truth is they are a choice – a choice to round people up and treat them appallingly, funded by your taxes.

There are viable alternatives available, ones the Home Office itself has piloted and which have been subject to independent evaluation.[19] The result of these pilots, which looked at community-based support for refugees and asylum seekers who otherwise would have been detained, shows that not only is support in the community better for their wellbeing, they still complied with Home Office directives.

It is possible for people in detention to receive bail, but this is rarely ever granted, often out of fear that they will abscond, despite research suggesting that 95% of people comply with government requirements; this likelihood also increases with help. Charities like Micro Rainbow, a specialist support for LGBTQ+ refugees and asylum seekers which provides safe accommodation and community support, help people on bail from detention. It costs the charity £30 per day to provide an LGBTQ+ migrant coming out of detention with housing, subsistence and support – a fraction of what the government are spending on their inhumane treatment of migrants.[20]

It also costs less than detaining people, which in 2022 cost £107 a day, or just under £40,000 a year per asylum seeker.[21] The only beneficiaries are the private companies, who rake in millions every year; imagine how much better it would be if we used that money to support people.[22] Every government talks about the economy and the need for cost-efficiency when it comes to cutting essential services, but when it comes to adopting a system which is more humane *and* cheaper to operate, they choose cruelty.

## Block 13, Kakuma

The refugee and asylum process in the UK is demonstrably villainous, but the situation here is far from unique. Kakuma is the world's largest refugee camp, with over 200,000 people living there.[23] The camp is situated in the north-western region of Turkana County, Kenya, not far from the borders of Uganda and Ethiopia, and refugees living there come from a range of countries – Burundi, Rwanda,

Somalia, Ethiopia and South Sudan. Kenyan policy prevents refugees and asylum seekers from leaving the camp: to be found outside it is illegal.

Around 500 people in the camp are known to be LGBTQ+ and many of them live in Block 13. Until 2020, Lucretia (she/her) was living in Uganda before being placed in an impossible predicament as a result of the country's anti-homosexuality laws: kill herself, leave the country or be killed or imprisoned. When Lucretia and I spoke, the Ugandan government were mulling over a new anti-homosexuality bill which not only increased the prison sentence for same sex conduct to ten years, but introduced the death penalty for 'aggravated homosexuality'. It also introduced laws against 'promoting homosexuality' – which might include advocating for the human rights of LGBTQ+ people, providing financial support or even renting a flat or hiring an LGBTQ+ person, resulting in a twenty-year prison sentence. Weeks after we spoke, the bill was signed into law, no doubt forcing more queer people to flee the country.

Even in Kakuma camp, LGBTQ+ refugees face extreme violence. Lucretia tells me of the death of her friend Trinidad, a proud trans man and leader in Kakuma. 'After getting several warnings that we will be battered and after several attacks, in March 2021, we were firebombed. Trinidad was burned alive and died as a result of his injuries just a month later. He was twenty-two years old.'[24, 25]

The camp is operated by the UNHCR, which partners with a range of organizations to support refugees, and there has been some engagement from them with the LGBTQ+ people in Kakuma. A statement released in 2021 stated that they remained 'deeply committed to the protection of lesbian, gay, bisexual, transgender, intersex and queer refugees and asylum seekers across the world, including Kenya',[26] and yet a report by the National Gay and Lesbian Human Rights Commission and Amnesty International found that serious human rights abuses, hate crime and violence including rape were perpetrated at the camp.[27]

The report also revealed that not only is violence occurring, it is actively enabled by the inaction of authorities and conducted with total impunity. Attacks came from all over – the police, other camp members and even aid workers. Of those surveyed in the report, thirty-one out of thirty-eight LGBTQ+ people had suffered violent attacks, threats or intimidation, data that aligns with a 2021 report by ORAM[28] and Rainbow Railroad in which 83% of LGBTQ+ people said they had been violently assaulted and 26% said they had been sexually assaulted. 'We cannot go to the police,' Lucretia tells me. 'These officers subject us to conversion therapies. They subject us to intimidations, illegal detention, threats, all kinds of things. They will strip you naked if they do not know your gender. We feel like the UNHCR are sending us to the people we need to be protected from.'

One of the most startling things Lucretia told me was that the response of the UNHCR was to encourage a dialogue and negotiate peace with the people who were brutalizing them. 'We have been making engagements with the UNHCR to request a solution, a durable solution. The only solution that is given to us is to sit down and negotiate peace with the people who are beating us, who are threatening to kill us.'

A 'durable solution' has a particular definition in the context of refugees, and the UNHCR provides three durable solutions as part of its core mandate: voluntary repatriation, local integration and resettlement.[29] Local integration cannot happen in Kenya for LGBTQ+ migrants, especially in the context of the Kenyan government looking at increasing anti-LGBTQ+ laws. In 2018, the UNHCR, supported by the Department of Refugee Services, did move some LGBTQ+ refugees to Nairobi, the capital of Kenya, because they were deemed to be at too much risk in the camp.[30] But in 2019, the Kenyan authorities decided that seventy-six refugees, including LGBTQ+ refugees, could be sent back to Kakuma – back to danger.[31] The UNHCR explained, 'The policy of government is that refugees should normally live in camps, and those who don't should have the proper documentation, as well as avoid living in large groups for the host community's and their own safety.' If the

UNHCR consider rape, firebombing and violent beatings normal, I have serious concerns.

'Whilst we wait for the UNHCR to act, individuals can stand in solidarity with us,' Lucretia says. Private sponsorship for resettlement is something individuals or groups can do to support refugees as they come to a new country; this has been how most of the refugees at Kakuma have been able to leave Kenya. 'Getting three or four people privately sponsored by a group of people, by an organization, by a church would be heaven.'

'People can also write to their governments, the Kenyan embassies in their country and to their embassies in Nairobi. Donations are also key to ensuring the community can stay well and nourished, as many of the refugees are unable to work in the camp or associate with others for fear of being killed or beaten.'

A year after I interviewed Lucretia, I got the most joyous news: she had been relocated with her boyfriend from Kenya to Canada in March 2024, supported by the Canadian government through Amnesty International and Protect Defenders.

'I am safe, protected and free,' Lucretia tells me. 'I am back to university doing a degree in political science. I feel so empowered and good that soon, I am going to be able to constructively support our siblings in Africa.'

The intervention came as a result of tireless campaigning not only by those living in Block 13, but also due to a campaign held in conjunction with Queers of Joy – a trans and gender non-conforming night – which brought attention to the LGBTQ+ people fighting for survival in the camp. Despite being thousands of miles apart, the community was able to unite for good and create transformational change.

Many have not been as fortunate as Lucretia. There is always more to do and, as attacks on migrants and LGBTQ+ people both continue to rise, this work is more important than ever. But I cannot help but feel pride, and hope that change is possible and that community and solidarity will get us there.

## And What You Can Do About It

→ There are many groups and organizations working to support LGBTQ+ refugees and asylum seekers across the UK and the world. These include Lesbians and Gays Support the Migrants, Rainbow Migration and African Rainbow Family. Donate to, fundraise for and take part in actions organized by these organizations.

→ Challenge harmful rhetoric about migrants and migration, not just when in relation to LGBTQ+ people. Write to your MP to oppose bills that seek to criminalize migrants and particularly refugees and asylum seekers in the UK. Also write to the embassies of countries that are treating LGBTQ+ migrants appallingly.

→ It's a big ask, but private sponsorship is one way in which some refugees are able to get out of their situation. Individuals, or in some instances groups (each region has slightly different policies), can sponsor a refugee to come to the UK and help them start a new life. Sponsors provide financial support, housing support and community.

# Putting in the Work

## Moud Goba (she/her)

Moud Goba is a prominent LGBTQ+ and human rights activist originally from Harare, Zimbabwe, now based in the UK, where she is the national director of Micro Rainbow and a trustee of UK Black Pride, of which she is also a founding member.

In 2001, Goba came to the UK at the age of twenty to escape lesbophobic persecution in Zimbabwe. She went on to seek asylum in the UK in 2008 and then was granted refugee status in 2010 after initially being refused earlier the same year, the delay caused by her lacking proof of her sexuality that would satisfy the Home Office. Goba has gone on to spend decades advocating on behalf of LGBTQ+ asylum seekers and refugees, including over ten years working for Micro Rainbow, an organization which provides LGBTQ+ asylum seekers and refugees with access to employment, volunteering, training and education.

## Aderonke Apata (She/her)

Aderonke Apata is a prominent LGBTQ+ rights activist, a barrister and the founder of African Rainbow Family, known for her extraordinary efforts in supporting LGBTQ+ asylum seekers. As a lesbian woman in Nigeria, she faced severe discrimination and threats to her life, prompting her to come to the UK, where she then sought asylum.

Apata was detained in Yarl's Wood immigration removal centre in Bedfordshire, which was used mainly for women, from the end of 2011 until the beginning of 2013, including a week spent in solitary confinement in 2012. Apata supported other women living in the barbaric conditions of Yarl's Wood with their legal documentation, which was written in difficult-to-understand legal jargon and not made available in people's own languages.

At the age of fifty – after thirteen years of fighting the Home Office – Apata was granted asylum in the UK. She founded the organization African Rainbow Family in 2014, which provides support to LGBTQ+ refugees and asylum seekers from African countries. The organization offers vital services such as legal advice, mental health support and advocacy, helping individuals navigate the complex asylum process and integrate into their new communities.

## Aloysius Ssali (he/him)

Aloysius Ssali is the founder of Say It Loud Club, an organization which supports LGBTQ+ refugees and asylum seekers through services like legal assistance, healthcare support and helping individuals navigate hostile environments.

Say It Loud Club was first set up by Ssali in 1994 whilst he was a student in Uganda, a country which heavily persecutes LGBTQ+ people. The group began with just six students, but grew over the course of a decade, and by 2003, they were known to authorities as an LGBTQ+ organization. Members were arrested, tortured or disappeared. Ssali had become well known enough to be a target and decided to come to the UK to continue with his education. When Ssali returned to Uganda in 2005, he was captured and tortured for being a gay man. With six months still left on his visa, he fled to the UK.

Ssali decided to found Say It Loud Club in the UK in 2010 and has gone on to help hundreds of LGBTQ+ refugees gain the right to live freely in the UK. For many years, Ssali ran the organization out of his own pocket whilst working as a nurse, but in 2018, with the support of Help Refugees, he was able to work full time to help LGBTQ+ refugees and asylum seekers for the next year.

# CHAPTER 11
# For God's Sake

## It's a Sin

'My feeling towards the church now is primarily fury,' Parker (they/them) tells me. 'I spent my childhood in the Free Presbyterian Church of Scotland, which was as if a bunch of dour-faced Puritans had stepped through a portal from 1560.' The Free Presbyterian Church is a sect of Christianity which is committed to the whole Bible and the gospel of Jesus Christ, whom they believe to be the Saviour. Although this sect originated in Scotland, it has spread far further.

Every Sunday, Parker's family would drive the two hours to London from Kent for sermons. They would spend the whole day at church – morning service, then studying the Bible or approved Christian literature or learning the Catechism, before evening service for a further two to three hours. Midweek, they would gather at another local family's house for a prayer meeting, which was another two-hour session or, as Parker puts it, 'An ordeal of listening to how terrible we were as people, how scary the world was and how everything inside was wrong and sinful in every possible way.' They were homeschooled to prevent them from learning about the world and did not have access to a computer until into their teens.

'The regularity and number of meetings felt like a lot,' Parker says, 'but it doesn't compare to the constant – more intangible – presence

of the Free Presbyterian's version of Christianity through my childhood and adolescence. We were always told that our thoughts were
very sinful, as well as our deeds, and if you followed the will of your
heart, that was your own wicked nature trying to turn you away
from the right path. If something ever felt natural to you, it was
probably – definitely – a sin.'

Parker is non-binary but was assigned female at birth and was
viewed as a girl and woman in the church, where there were strict
rules about the ways women could dress. 'It felt to me that the
church despised women, even though they dressed it up with
"different but equal" rhetoric,' Parker tells me. 'The message that I
got from this was that a female-presenting body was something to
be ashamed of. And worse than that, it was something dangerous.
Eve tempted Adam, Delilah betrayed Samson, and Tamar seduced
her father-in-law under false pretences. For every sermon that
praised the virtue of Mary and the bravery of Esther, there were a
dozen more that painted women as dangerous temptresses who
existed to lure God-fearing men into sin. Any women who weren't
condemned succeeded in spite of their femininity, not because
of it.'

And what about sexuality? 'For a very long time, I was convinced
that I wasn't asexual, I was just a damn good Christian.'

Parker discovered asexuality in the way lots of us learn about our
identities – fan fiction. Specifically, in Parker's case, an author's note
of a Joker/Scarecrow slash fiction. 'There's no guarantee that coming
to terms with that part of my identity would have been any less traumatic if I hadn't been in the church, but I still can't help wondering
what my coming-out journey would have looked like if I'd had the
vocabulary to understand what I was feeling.'

'The church really only spoke about gay men and lesbian
women, and then, of course, it was only in a "What's happening
to this once God-fearing land? Won't somebody think of the
children?" kind of way. So, neither of my labels – non-binary
or asexual – felt like they were an option. Any wrongness or

discomfort I felt could only be down to sin, so it was something to be wrestled with and mourned over, but not explored or even thought about too much.'

The impact of their upbringing and time in the church is colossal, even eight years after leaving. They had a mental breakdown and still have recurring nightmares about going back to their childhood home and being forced to attend church again.

'At the moment, I can't see any scenario where I would willingly attend a Christian church ever again. I went to a friend's wedding earlier this year, and even that made me uncomfortable.'

I can understand Parker's discomfort. My late granny was a prominent figure in our local Church of England church, where she was head of the Mothers' Union for a number of years. One of my resounding memories is of her worrying about the flowers whilst recovering from septicaemia and narrowly escaping death. Church was a hugely important part of Granny's life to the extent that there were almost as many members of the clergy as there were family at her funeral.

Whilst I have never believed in God, I still attended church with Granny, Mum and my brother well into my teens, albeit patchily. And I enjoyed it – the singing and the community and the sense of care – even if the sermons went on a little too long on more than one occasion. Although my attendance had always been sporadic, church did always feel like a safe space for me to be and to exist in. But, when I realized I was gay and went through the process of coming out, that was no longer the case. When I came out as a lesbian, I was told repeatedly that I deserved to rot in hellfire and deserved eternal damnation from people in the local community and online alike. Oddly enough, this never actually happened in church – I suspect Granny's position in the community shielded me somewhat. If I had ever told her what had been said, I suspect she would have had their guts for garters.

## Faith Wars

One of the reasons writing a chapter on LGBTQ+ people and religion is tricky is the sheer number of different religions, denominations and practices. Generalizations about different faith groups don't necessarily reflect the experiences of people inside those religions or individual experiences. Often, LGBTQ+ people and people with faith are talked about as different groups, but of course there is significant overlap. In the US, for example, research found that nearly half of LGBTQ+ adults are religious, with many coming from a Christian denomination.[1] We don't have quantitative data for this around the world, but there are likely to be significant variations.

Faith and queerness will always be intertwined for me, because I discovered lesbians existed from *The Vicar of Dibley*, a British sitcom. The vicar, Geraldine, and her ditzy best friend, Alice, are debating who they would go to bed with if all the men had died because they found out football was poisonous (which, it should be emphasized, is said in the show as a sarcastic joke). Alice plumps for Queen Elizabeth, whilst Geraldine chooses model Rachel Hunter, who, due to a series of unlikely events, does end up in her underwear at the vicarage, leading to the rest of the villagers assuming that the vicar is secretly a lesbian.

The TV show handles the storyline beautifully. 'I would like to say here and now that you do not have a gay vicar,' Geraldine tells the parish council, before adding, 'More's the pity. In my experience, gay priests are usually splendid people. They know what it's like to experience prejudice and so know how important it is to treat people decently.'

That episode first aired at Christmas 2004 (although I first watched it some years later in a summer holiday when my younger brother and I binge-watched the box sets). This compassion and understanding of LGBTQ+ people from a member of the clergy – albeit a fictional one – feels as fresh and needed today as it must have done over twenty years ago, particularly given the consistent use of faith as justification for anti-LGBTQ+ sentiment.

Of all the topics in this book, religion is the aspect I have found most difficult to write about. Religion has been a driving force, or at least has been claimed as a motivation, for some horrendous homophobic atrocities in the world, both historically and right now.

## Weaponizing Religion

In the US, the Christian right wing wields extraordinary power and has been instrumental in overturning progressive legislation, such as the Roe v Wade abortion protections, and targeting trans people through laws which restrict their access to healthcare. Many of the evangelical Christian right and the TERFs can be found not just espousing the same ideals, but collaborating. This alliance has been recognized since the 1990s, although has seemingly increased in prominence in recent years.[2] In Birmingham, Muslim parents withdrew their children from school over lessons which included references to the existence of same sex parents, claiming they were being brainwashed.[3] This was followed by high-profile protests driven by the wider local Muslim community.[4] In 2014, a Belfast bakery famously refused to make a cake for a gay wedding on religious grounds, a decision which was upheld by the Supreme Court in 2018.[5] More amusingly, Turning Point UK, a far-right group that claims 'faith' as one of its three key pillars (alongside 'family' and 'freedom'), attempted to picket a non-existent drag queen story time event in south London in 2023. The listings they were using turned out to be out of date.[6] A 2023 report by the UN found that recently there had been a significant and unprecedented pushback 'by conservative political ideologies and religious fundamentalists in advocating for the criminalization of gender recognition in numerous states.'[7] What was notable about this report is that it emphasized these groups rarely positioned themselves as explicitly religious organizations, but instead as human rights groups working to protect family values and or religious freedoms.

The clear difficulty comes when different protected characteristics under the Equality Act – religious beliefs and being LGBTQ+ – are set in opposition and repeatedly clash. At the heart of this discussion is the fact that for religious people who do not accept LGBTQ+ people (and, of course, plenty of religious people are LGBTQ+ themselves, or are very accepting and supportive), our existence is wrong and offensive. We must be kept from their children, lest we 'infect' them; we do not deserve the same rights – of marriage, or to have children, for example – as straight people. Our 'non-traditional' gender identities are not 'real' or valid. To my mind, though, religion is not an excuse for bigotry. To take the example with which we began this book: if your religion tells you that gay marriage is wrong, don't marry someone of the same gender as you – but when you attempt to impress the rules of that religion on other people, we have an issue.

Let's be clear, LGBTQ+ people and religious freedoms are not polar ends of the spectrum – having one does not inherently cancel the other one out. But, there are many religious people who perceive the existence of LGBTQ+ people – and our increase in rights – as a direct threat to them.

As the Christian Action, Research and Education group stated, '[Under the Equality Act] in theory, all of the protected characteristics should be treated as equally important and all rights protected, but in practice these different rights often push in diametrically opposing directions. This is particularly problematic if one protected characteristic repeatedly clashes with and quashes another protected characteristic. For example, religious discrimination has been given lower priority than discrimination on the grounds of sexual orientation.'[8]

But by being themselves, LGBTQ+ people are *not* quashing religious freedom. The clash seems to be going in only one direction. Christians, the last time I checked, are not an endangered species, and yet, the mere existence of LGBTQ+ people is positioned as a threat to their existence. In 2017, the chief of the Christian Legal Centre described the LGBTQ+ movement as 'totalitarian', saying, 'They cannot tolerate any whiff of dissent. They demand not just tolerance, but unanimous approval and celebration. Anything less is met with name-calling, vilification and punishment. This lobby is deeply illiberal and unkind.'[9]

But why shouldn't we be celebrated? Why should we settle for 'tolerance'? Here, any attempt by LGBTQ+ people to argue that religious freedom does not include the right to contest LGBTQ+ people's existence or human rights is met with the argument that we are dictators, unwilling to enter into a discussion or dialogue, when all we are asking for is the bare minimum of respect.

## What Do Religions Really Say About LGBTQ+ People?

Defining how religions consider LGBTQ+ people is an impossible task. Which religions? Practised by whom? When? Where? Even in my home town, the experience on Sunday varied massively, depending on not just the church, or the denomination even, but which vicar was in charge, and trying to encompass the experiences of people around the globe would be even harder. Some religions have a central governing body or specific individuals or scriptures, others do not have these, and this accounts for a least some of the variations.

What I do know is this: LGBTQ+ people of faith exist and have always existed, as far back as records go. There are also people who believe in the importance of LGBTQ+ equality – as a matter of both law and religious belief – in every faith, though they are sometimes less well represented than those who oppose LGBTQ+ rights.

I recently encountered two older gay men who told me – unequivocally – that the rise in homophobia in Britain was because of 'the number of Muslims we let in'. Whilst such a comment was fuelled by anti-immigrant and racist sentiments, this was not the first time I had heard such a thing said. And whilst, yes, there are anti-LGBTQ+ Muslim people, it is wrong to assume that people are prejudiced simply on the basis of their faith, or to assume that one faith is inherently more tolerant than another, because it simply isn't true. What's more, there is huge variation in the acceptance and celebration of LGBTQ+ people within different religions. Here's a rundown of some key points on how the six major world religions view LGBTQ+ people.

## Christianity

The leaders of the global Anglican Communion have taken a stand against homophobia and violence,[10] committing themselves to provide pastoral care and support regardless of sexual orientation, whilst the National Church of Iceland,[11] as well as the Episcopal Churches of the United States[12] and Scotland,[13] have made it possible for same sex couples to marry within their religious institutions. The Church of England voted to allow priests to bless the civil marriages of same sex couples, but not to allow them to marry in churches, as they believe marriage is between a man and a woman.

Meanwhile, in the Catholic faith, whilst the Pope has made clear that the church is open to everyone, it is still a sin to be gay.[14]

## Judaism

Of the four major Jewish denominations, three openly support the decriminalization of same sex relationships,[15] and of those in the Orthodox tradition – which is generally less inclusive of LGBTQ+ people – over 150 leaders have come forward with their support.[16] Several Jewish denominations also embrace transgender people, including the ordaining of transgender rabbis and the creation of specific prayers that are inclusive.[17] Since the 1960s, the Reform movement has taken significant steps to support the LGBTQ+ community, and in 2015, the Union for Reform Judaism adopted a historic resolution affirming the full equality and inclusion of transgender and gender non-conforming people. Conservative Judaism has held somewhat mixed opinions, meanwhile, endorsing two contradictory opinions: one upholding the traditional prohibition on homosexual relationships and the other allowing the ordination of gays and lesbians as rabbis and cantors.[18]

## Islam

Islam is a religion that does not have a central governing body and, as such, there are no clear policies regarding the inclusion of LGBTQ+ people. The variation of inclusion for LGBTQ+ people who are Muslim is huge, and whilst some Islamic organizations and mosques are inclusive, some are deeply exclusionary to LGBTQ+ people. Notably, the inclusion of transgender people is more recognized and accepted in Islamic cultures, and gender reassignment surgery was declared acceptable under Islamic Law in 1988.[19] This does not mean trans Muslims are embraced, and many still face exclusion and rejection. There are several leading Muslim groups working to build inclusion within Islam, for example, Al-Fatiha Foundation, which argues that criminalizing homosexuality is fundamentally incompatible[20] with the teachings of the Prophet Mohammad. There are several LGBTQ+ imams – people who lead worship – who play significant roles in local communities, forging ways forward for LGBTQ+ people.[21]

## Hinduism

The Hindu American Foundation is clear that Hinduism does not provide a fundamental spiritual reason to reject or exclude LGBTQ+

individuals and that they have 'inherent spiritual equality'. Traditional Hindu texts and epics, such as the Mahabharata, depict characters with diverse sexual orientations and gender identities, including Shikhandi and Brihannala, who are treated with respect and judged by their abilities rather than their identity. Furthermore, the Vedas refer to a third sex,[22] whose members are generally embraced or otherwise considered to have divine powers. Many Hindu deities have a level of fluidity in their gender or expression. Some Hindu priests in the US and other countries have started performing same sex marriage ceremonies, incorporating traditional rituals to bless these unions. The decriminalization of homosexuality in India in 2018 marked a significant step towards broader acceptance and legal recognition of LGBTQ+ rights in Hindu-majority regions; however, conservative values still remain.

## Sikhism

In Sikhism, the Guru Granth Sahib – the primary religious text – does not mention homosexuality at all. However, homosexuality has been condemned by some Sikh priests as harmful in part because the Sikh Rehit Maryada focuses on the importance of a family life-style, and since same sex couples cannot reproduce, it ought to be condemned. In 2005, the Sikh religious leadership of the Akal Takht at the Golden Temple in Amritsar in Punjab restated the position that same sex marriage was unacceptable; however, there are a number of Sikhs who disagree with this interpretation of what it means to be Sikh. Punjabi culture – which the majority of Sikhs share – can be conservative, with prevalent homophobia and rigid gender norms, and this impacts people's experiences of faith. Organizations like Sarbat provide support and community for LGBTQ+ Sikhs worldwide, promoting understanding and accept-ance within Sikh spaces.[23]

## Buddhism

There is no mention of sexual orientation by the Siddhartha Gautama outside of restrictions placed upon monks and nuns from having sexual relationships with anyone. One of the five precepts followed by Buddhists includes refraining from using sexual behaviour in ways that are harmful to others and to express sexuality in ways that are beneficial and bring joy. The focus on personal enlightenment leads to opportunities open to interpretation.

## Queer *and* Religious

Whether any religion really is inherently anti-LGBTQ+ is a matter for discussion, but the justification of homophobia and transphobia based on religious belief neglects to consider the large number of queer people who have faith.

Just as there are people who struggle with their relationships with faith, there are those for whom their religion or faith is as essential to their wellbeing and the way in which they move through the world as the fact that they are LGBTQ+. The two things are not always easily separated.

Remarkably, there is a lack of detailed research into LGBTQ+ people with faith backgrounds, given the number of people in the community with this experience. I wonder if this lack of representation results in the perception of LGBTQ+ people and religious people as separate groups diametrically opposed to one another when, in fact, the rise in anti-LGBTQ+ hate crime within the UK is correlated with the rise of hate crime on the basis of religion.[24]

What information we do have is telling. Research conducted in 2018 revealed that a third of lesbian, gay and bisexual people and a quarter of trans people were not out to anyone in their faith community about their identity. Just 39% said they felt their faith community was welcoming of lesbian, gay and bisexual people, a figure that dropped to 25% for trans people. That said, it's important to point out that there *are* inclusive faith spaces to be found, and more than a third of LGBTQ+ people had access to LGBTQ+ inclusive faith groups, although this number decreased in rural areas.[25] A study conducted by Switchboard found that 80% of participants said they had experienced LGBTQ+ prejudice in a faith setting and 36% felt that LGBTQI+ prejudice in their faith communities constituted a hate crime.[26]

Faith is more than what a person believes in or what rules they abide by; it also has deep cultural and community significance. If LGBTQ+ people feel unsafe in places of worship, for example, not only do they become excluded from practising their faith with others, but they are also at risk of being alienated and separated from their community.

Coming out can be a more complex decision for those from religious backgrounds, forced to weigh up the cost of potentially losing access to that wider community. It is unsurprising that in the UK, LGBTQ+ people who have a religious or culturally conservative background are 30% less likely to be out to their parents, with the primary reasons cited being fear of being a disappointment or making their parents sad or angry.[27] One in ten people stated they feared being abused and one in twenty felt they might be forced to leave their home. 'I was physically hit by my father and both parents told me I was illegal and that being gay was wrong,' one Christian gay man shared with researchers. This isolation leads to devastating impacts; LGBTQ+ people with parents from religious or culturally conservative backgrounds are twice as likely to feel suicidal as the result of negative experiences of coming out to their families.

## Context is Everything

'I think it's really strange when I see Muslims being so aggressively transphobic, biphobic, homophobic,' Aryam (she/her), a twenty-three-year-old, asexual, aromantic, queer medicine student tells me, 'when historically we have trans people and gender-variant people. We have the *mukhannathun*, which refers to gender-variant people in Islam – they were assigned male at birth but they acted in a feminine way and they were accepted as women in society. The Prophet, peace be upon him, actually allowed them to enter women's spaces and see women unveiled. So there's evidence of trans acceptance even at the time of the reading of the Quran.'

Aryam also tells me that one of the chapters of the Quran – Chapter 24, Verse 31 – which talks about the veiling of women, explicitly mentions queer men and the fact women may be unveiled in front of men who do not desire women or have no desire at all.

I ask Aryam if she feels that part of the difficulty with religion is that many practices and texts were created at times when the world looked very different and these ideas have been embedded as supposed traditions. 'It's always interesting how, when people do talk about religion, they talk about the things that support their prejudice without the context of the time or just by completely ignoring important verses that disqualify that prejudice.'

It is not only in Islamic texts that this happens. Leviticus 18:22 is often used to argue that queer sex is an abomination, whilst other parts, which explicitly prohibit the wearing of mixed fabrics or the planting of seeds, for example, are ignored. By that token, everyone who's ever had a potter around in the garden might be considered a sinner. Other verses that are regularly used to justify homophobia rarely refer to homosexuality outright, but instead refer to and conflate homosexuality with rape and attempted rape, prostitution, paedophilia and cultish behaviour.

And it's not only the culture of the time in which these texts were written that influences their contexts. It's also how they are rewritten and reprinted. It would probably surprise most people to know that prior to 1946, no Bibles contained the word 'homosexual'; it's a contested translation of the words *arsenokotai* and *malakoi*.[28] In fairness, these words are difficult to translate into modern English. But *arsenokoitai* is about more than queerness, it has more to do with exploitation and abuse of another person in order to generate power, with *malakoi* previously having been translated as 'soft' or 'effeminate'.[29]

## Conversion Therapy and Failed Promises

The right to religious freedom being given more importance than the safety and wellbeing of LGBTQ+ people is reflected in some religious groups' support of conversion therapy, or conversionary practices. These include anything designed to change a person's sexuality, gender or gender expression. It is often described as a kind of torture by those who have experienced it and, indeed, the International Rehabilitation Council for Torture Victims agrees that conversion therapy *is* torture. It's also condemned by the World Health Organization, World Psychiatric Association, United Nations and many other groups.

Sadly, however, conversion therapy is something that 7% of LGBTQ+ people have been offered or undergone, rising to 10% for asexual people and 13% for transgender people.[30] This practice does happen in a range of contexts, but over half of the respondents to the UK government's National LGBT Survey said that it was religious and faith-based groups who'd subjected them to it.[31]

Several religious organizations have argued that banning conversion therapy is unnecessary – as LGBTQ+ people are protected under existing laws – but demonstrably this is not the case. The Christian Institute has begun mounting a legal challenge in Scotland on the basis that any such ban would restrict religious freedom and could criminalise the ordinary work of churches.[32]

The so-called cures can include anything from the laying on of hands and enforced prayer to even prolonged starvation. Sometimes, LGBTQ+ people enter into this practice because they feel they have no choice or because they believe their faith demands it of them; these people are often deemed as consenting. However, the Cooper Report, produced by the 'Ban Conversion Therapy' Legal Forum, identified existing legal frameworks which show it is impossible for people to consent to conversion therapy, in a similar way that people cannot legally consent to practices like forced marriage or female genital mutilation.[33] 'Allowing conversion practices to take place is out of step with the position of the law.'

The suicide of Ohio teenager Leelah Alcorn in 2014 was a pivotal moment in bringing the conversation about conversion therapy into the mainstream.[34] Leelah was transgender and came out at the age of fourteen to her parents. At sixteen, she asked to transition. Instead, she was sent to conversion therapy by her devout Christian parents. Leelah posted her suicide note online before taking her own life. In it, she wrote candidly about the impact of these practices. The post went viral and petitions were started to create 'Leelah's Law' – a ban on conversion therapy in the United States. Whilst that never came to pass, Cincinnati criminalized the practice, the second city in the US to do so after Washington DC.[35] 'She challenged us to make her death matter,' one council member stated, 'and we're doing just that.'[36]

Leelah's experience is far from unique. The devastating impacts of conversion practices are huge, with people experiencing the practice twice as likely to have suicidal thoughts and far more likely to attempt suicide, too. 'If you look at survivors' groups for people who have been through conversion and reparative therapy,' one chief executive of a local Mind group stated, 'you see an increase in levels of depression, panic disorders, anxiety, suicidal ideation, increased suicide attempts, increased substance misuse, increased self-harm.'[37]

The last Conservative government committed to banning conversion therapy in 2018,[38] but six years later, by the time they left power, a ban still had not been implemented. In 2022, the government decided to drop this commitment, leading to mass public outcry, which resulted in them bringing it back but failing to include a ban on conversion therapy for trans people.[39] Under the new proposals – which have still not been implemented – the government would allow adults to consent to counselling that would help them 'live a life they felt is more in line with their personal beliefs'.

The UK's Equality and Human Rights Commission published a report stating that a ban on conversion therapy for trans people could follow but only once more evidence-based proposals were available.[40] It also stated that 'legislation to ban conversion therapy attempting to change a person to or from being transgender should follow, once more detailed and evidence-based proposals are available which can be properly scrutinized'.[41]

For an organization supposedly designed to protect and uplift human rights, not outrightly condemning conversion therapy is surprising and worrying. This is another instance where UK institutions fall out of step with other leading global organizations on their approaches to trans rights. Canada, New Zealand, France, Malta, Brazil, Uruguay and Germany, as well as specific states and territories of Australia, have all banned the practice. For years, various conversion therapy leaders have attempted to meet with the UK government. They were always knocked back, until 2021, when Kemi Badenoch, at that time the Minister for Equalities, invited one group – which claims to cure 'unwanted same sex attraction and gender confusion' – to meet.[42] The meeting was described as 'productive' by Badenoch, although was criticized heavily by others in her party. 'The government's values do not align with those of the Core Issues Trust,' a spokesperson for the government's Equality Hub stated. 'We believe that conversion therapy is an abhorrent practice and will shortly publish our plans to ban it in this country.' No such guidance ever materialized under the Conservative government, though Labour have announced in their King's Speech that the practice will be banned. After waiting nearly six years and five prime ministers since a ban was first promised, however, it is hard to feel optimistic.

## A Different Way

It's crucial we don't paint all religious organizations and leaders with the same homophobic and transphobic brush. There are a huge number of groups and individuals doing amazing work to ensure that queer people are welcome and supported by their faiths. Even in the realm of conversion therapy, in 2020, over 370 religious leaders from around the world called for a ban on conversion practices.[43] Among those involved were ten archbishops, sixty-three bishops, eighteen deans, sixty-six rabbis and other leaders from Sikh, Muslim, Buddhist and Hindu religions.

I had my first experience of an inclusive church through my first girlfriend, aged fifteen. She went to a city-centre 'youth church'. Whilst the congregation were intergenerational, their focus was on bringing young people into the church and into Christianity, along with supporting them in the community. The church I went to when I was growing up had a congregation with an average age of about forty-five, so it was a shock to walk into a huge medieval church and to be surrounded by younger people. Not only was there a vicar, but there was also a youth worker. Some services ran in a way I was more used to – prayer, singing, sermons – but there were also several services a week that involved games, discussion, pizza, and I honestly felt more like I'd gone to a kid's club. And yet, when I went into the church for the first time for an evening service with my girlfriend, I was on edge. It was clear that we were queer, and it soon became very obvious to me that this was a quite heavily evangelical church – their focus was on preaching the gospel and bringing people into the religion. Evangelism and LGBTQ+ inclusion are spoken about often as opposite ends of the spectrum because there are a number of evangelical individuals and churches that are anti-LGBTQ+ and, in general, evangelical Christians tend to be more conservative. The church my girlfriend went to managed somehow to be both accepting and evangelical: they were preaching Jesus and Bible verses, not hate. A lot of what they spoke of were things intertwined with what I understood (as a baby gay) to be integral parts of being queer: community, love, acceptance, hope, compassion. All that said, I never fully became comfortable there, or in any religious space, really.

Across the world, there are people creating explicitly inclusive practices for LGBTQ+ people, not because religious texts were intentionally exclusionary but because language and attitudes have evolved over time, or the languages in which the texts were originally written have specific gender systems. What's been delightful whilst researching this chapter is to have discovered quite how many incredible individuals and organizations there are doing this work. I've been able to find a template for a ritual for a Jewish wedding service written by a queer non-binary rabbi, prayer spaces specifically led by and for trans Muslim people, and naming ceremonies for trans people across every world religion. There are hundreds of places of worship around the world which specifically welcome LGBTQ+ people into their congregations. There are networking and friendship groups for queer Jewish people, Muslims, Sikhs, Buddhists, Hindus, Christians and more.

Wherever you look, there are LGBTQ+ people forging their own paths – we're fab like that.

## A Double-edged Sword

As a community, though, we must do better to support LGBTQ+ people with a faith. Many LGBTQ+ people with a faith background feel excluded not only from religious spaces but also from the LGBTQ+ community itself. Sometimes, this arises from the fact that many queer people have had negative experiences with religion and so wish to distance themselves from it. It can also arise from the pressure to be out, which may well not be safe for everyone. 'I wish non-Muslims understood this,' bisexual and genderqueer activist and writer Hafsa Qureshi (any pronouns) explains. 'There is so much pressure from the queer community to be out and proud, without stopping to think about how that isn't feasible for some of us.'[44] The last thing we ever ought to do as a community is endanger others, or demand they articulate or perform their identity in a specific way to be seen as legitimate. In fact, we regularly rally against this. Why then, when it comes to those with a faith, do we demand so much?

For this chapter, I interviewed religious LGBTQ+ people. I was struck repeatedly by the parallels between their experience of faith and my experience of queerness. I do not understand why some people have a faith and why they believe in a god or gods. It's not an experience I have ever had, not once in my life. But I can recognize they do, the authenticity of that experience, and respect it. I do not understand all the cogs that are turning to make it so.

But do you know what? I don't need to.

In the same way that someone doesn't need to understand why I am attracted to women to respect me, I don't need to understand what makes someone believe or adhere to specific ideals to respect them. Many religious people I spoke to shared their insights about decisions they had made to adhere to parts of a practice, or to queer it. There's something beautifully radical about that.

And I wonder if some of my passion for what I do – for supporting my LGBTQ+ community and for the idea of collective care – comes from the values I was taught as a result of my Church of England upbringing. I've never believed in God or been particularly interested in Jesus, at least not as the son of a god I don't believe exists. What I cared about then and care about now are people, community and compassion – standing up against injustice and saying no, even if it puts you in harm's way.

Despite the differences among religions and faiths and despite the rhetoric that flies around about different religious groups, most religions seem to be rooted in these same ideas. There's also a desire to explain, or perhaps a belief in, how the world works, how things came to be. There's a questioning of the way things are, an analysis of the world and your place in it.

Is that not the queerest thing ever?

# And What You Can Do About It

→ Challenge the idea that religious people are inherently more anti-LGBTQ+ than anyone else, and vice versa, recognize that many people in the LGBTQ+ community have a faith background. If you run a community group, consider if there are any accommodations which might be needed (for example, an opportunity to break fast during Ramadan at an event).

→ Challenge anti-LGBTQ+ sentiment in religious spaces and the notion that there are no LGBTQ+ people present in religious spaces. Research people within your faith, or within faiths more broadly, who have an LGBTQ+ identity or are prominent allies. Equip yourself with knowledge of what the common arguments are for excluding LGBTQ+ people within your religion and have alternative inclusive perspectives to hand, remembering that much of scripture is open to interpretation and that translations vary considerably.

→ Some useful responses to 'in our text/scripture it says that homosexuality is a sin':
  → Where does it say that?
  → Does the text actually say that? What does it say? Is that the original text, or a translation or interpretation?
  → What other aspects does it mention that we ignore?

→ Some useful responses to 'it is unnatural':
  → If God created everyone, then God created LGBTQ+ people, too.
  → It is unnatural to you but not to me.
  → So are water bottles. And central heating. And computers. It doesn't mean it's wrong.

→ Some useful responses to 'but if you can't have children, it is not natural':

➔    Many people who are not LGBTQ+ cannot have children –
      are they also unnatural?
➔    The focus is making sure children have parents who love
      them. That is very natural.

➔  Some useful responses to 'we don't have LGBTQ+ people in our
   culture':
      ➔    There are LGBTQ+ people across every single culture,
            faith and continent. Just because something is not
            spoken about does not mean it is untrue.

# Putting in the Work

## Asifa Lahore (she/her)

Asifa Lahore is a groundbreaking figure in the UK's LGBTQ+ scene and is celebrated as the country's first out Muslim drag queen. Lahore's Muslim identity plays a central role in her advocacy and artistic expression as she navigates the complexities and challenges that come with being both Muslim and LGBTQ+.

After a decade on the UK club scene, Lahore began experimenting with drag and became a common fixture, although she did have to argue with judging panels who found her explicit Muslim identity and incorporation of garments like the burqa in her drag problematic.

Lahore first came into the national spotlight in 2014 after she was barred by the Birmingham Central Mosque from discussing Islam and homosexuality on the BBC show *Free Speech*, something which caused uproar in the British press. Lahore went on to be featured in Channel 4's groundbreaking documentary *Muslim Drag Queens* in 2015, and in the same year, she received the *Attitude* magazine Pride Award for activism and increasing the visibility of the 'Gaysian' community.

Lahore is also an advocate in the space of disability rights as a person who is blind. She is passionate about creating accessible, intersectional spaces that welcome people from all walks of life, informed by her experience of holding multiple identities.

## Reverend Jide Macaulay (he/they)

Reverend Jide Macaulay is a prominent LGBTQ+ activist and the founder of House of Rainbow, an inclusive religious organization that supports LGBTQ+ people of colour with their faith. Born to a British–Nigerian family living in London, Macaulay grew up in a Christian Nigerian household, and his father was involved in creating churches across Nigeria. In 1994, Macaulay divorced his wife and found himself ostracized for being gay by his church, and later moved to join a Pentecostal church in 1996. Two years later, he began working as a minister.

In 2000, Macaulay took part in a piece where he shared his story about being a gay Christian man. As a result of this, the Pentecostal church he had been involved in subjected him to abuse including conversion therapy, which he submitted to at the time.

House of Rainbow was initially started by Macaulay in 2006 as a gathering of LGBTQ+ Christians in Lagos, which the media began to describe as 'Nigeria's first gay church'. The media attention resulted in intimidation and death threats, prompting Macaulay to return to the UK, where he founded House of Rainbow anew as a global organization based in London. Today, House of Rainbow supports sister organizations in twenty-two countries in Africa and the Caribbean and has become a leading global advocate for LGBTIQ+ people of faith.

Macaulay is also HIV-positive and speaks about this, advocating for the rights of people living with HIV both in the UK and across Africa. When he was first diagnosed in 2003, he felt God was punishing him for his identity. Now, he speaks openly about being HIV-positive and leverages his position within the community as a Black African Christian to support others experiencing similar challenges.

## Matt Mahmood-Ogston (he/him)

Matt Mahmood-Ogston is the founder of the Naz and Matt Foundation, which works to provide comprehensive support to LGBTQ+ individuals and their parents who come from religious or culturally conservative backgrounds. Mahmood-Ogston set up the foundation in 2014, after the suicide of his fiancé and partner of thirteen years, Naz, who died just two days after his deeply religious family confronted him about his sexuality.

Since then, Matt's organization has gone on to support hundreds of LGBTQ+ people who have experienced controlling, coercive, threatening or violent behaviour because of the response to their LGBTQ+ identity from their religious community. Notably, the organization also works with those who have perpetuated the harm, such as parents, to help resolve challenges they face navigating religion, culture and LGBTQ+ identity. Mahmood-Ogston is also one of the creators of Out and Proud Parents Day, created in 2019, to encourage parents to come out on social media with their acceptance of their child (of any age). The project aims to include all parents, but parents from religious or culturally conservative backgrounds are particularly encouraged to take part.

# CHAPTER 12
# Age-old Problems

## Lost Generations?

Ageing is a privilege for everyone, but even more so for LGBTQ+ people, who die on average much younger than our peers, particularly since the AIDS crisis led to the deaths of many queer and trans people. The latest research shows that bisexual women die on average 37% sooner than their straight peers, and lesbians 20% sooner.[1] Trans people, too, have significantly higher mortality rates than cisgender people.[2] There is less up-to-date research on queer men, but the evidence available shows, again, higher mortality risks, though these are often linked to HIV.[3] That is not to say that LGBTQ+ elders don't exist, of course. But whether due to the AIDS crisis, violence, depression, exclusion, denial of healthcare, suicide or homicide, there are simply fewer older LGBTQ+ people than there ought to be alive, fewer than there might be if society were different.

I have always wondered what my life would have looked like had my mum's gay cousin, Arthur, not contracted HIV, what it would have been like to have had a family member – another writer, too – who I could have confided in and felt a sense of belonging with. I have no doubt there are things I could have learned from him, and maybe even things he could have learned from me. Alas, it was not to be.

There are often limited opportunities for LGBTQ+ people of different generations to interact. Of course, the generational divide isn't exclusive to the LGBTQ+ community, but it feels particularly pertinent given the significant political and social shifts in the last century. In a very short space of time in the UK – and across many other countries, though not all – we have gone from the imprisoning, 'treating', vilifying and vast public hatred of LGBTQ+ people, who were forced to keep almost every aspect of their lives secret for protection, to a lot more acceptance. As we have seen in preceding chapters, things are far from equal, but we are reaching a point where for the first time in a long time, LGBTQ+ people in the UK are able finally to exist with less *extreme* persecution than in the past, and with greater understanding. But, as with so many of the other issues I've covered, when it comes to ageing, we see that many LGBTQ+ people have important needs that are not being met by society.

## Risk of Isolation

In the UK at least, it is often culturally assumed that your children will look after you in old age, but what if – like many LGBTQ+ people – you don't have them? Research has shown that just 49% of lesbian and bisexual women and 28% of gay and bisexual men had children, compared to 88% of straight men and 87% of straight women.[4] LGB people are also reported to see members of their biological family less than half as often as heterosexual people. The same report identified LGB people over the age of fifty-five, finding that 40% of gay and bisexual men were single, compared to 15% of heterosexual men.

Even when it comes to peers – friends or chosen family rather than blood relations – there can be difficulties. Francesca (they/them) could hardly be described as old, but they told me, 'I feel the entire gay scene is aimed at those in their twenties. I don't feel the gay community in my city caters for older gay people at all. I'm a forty-eight-year-old lesbian and my best friend is a forty-five-year-old gay man. Neither of us feels we're welcome in the gay bars and clubs.'

So LGBTQ+ people are more likely than heterosexual people to be isolated as they age and more likely, therefore, to need provision and support from strangers.

## Such a Tonic

I meet Geoff Pine (he/him), seventy-eight, on an exceptionally sunny September lunchtime. We're in the John Lewis cafe on Oxford Street – a favourite writing haunt of mine because no one cares if you sit there for hours and because you can watch the people swarming the streets like ants below.

Geoff spent thirty years with his partner, Jamie, an opera singer turned agent to some of the biggest names in the dance and musical world. In the mid-1990s, the couple received the devastating news that Jamie had a heart condition and it was terminal – he had two years to live. 'Being Scottish, and stubborn, he actually survived seven,' Geoff chuckles. As Geoff was working full time, carers were arranged to come into their house and care for Jamie.

Things were fine until they weren't.

'Jamie became very, very depressed – more depressed than usual,' Geoff remembers. 'He knew he was dying, he was accepting of that. But I couldn't get him to eat, couldn't get him to engage. Eventually, I asked him what was the matter. And he said, "I don't like the woman who comes in the morning to look after me, because when she visits, she kneels at the bottom of the bed and prays for my condemned gay soul."'

Geoff was able to intervene and the situation was addressed, but it got him thinking. 'There are lots of people of my generation, who remember when being gay was not legal, when there was HIV stigma – who might not have felt able to speak up. And I kept thinking, "Where do you go? What if you have no people to advocate for you?"'

The experience led Geoff to found Tonic Housing, the UK's first-ever organization specifically designed to create LGBTQ+ affirming retirement communities. When the team first began researching for the project, they made enquiries to care homes looking for information about their LGBTQ+ residents. The response was frightening: apparently, there were none. Clearly this was data that was not being collected.

They travelled to Berlin to look at a centre there, then to Philadelphia, New York and Los Angeles to find out how each place worked, and what the people who lived there were like, what their needs were. 'They were all quite different,' Geoff tells me. 'Then again, so are people. We knew we had to find out what people wanted from us, we could not just assume.' Geoff recounted meeting people who had been told it would be dangerous for LGBTQ+ people to come out, because of the prejudices of not only the staff, but the fellow residents. There is sometimes the idea that it is only in low-standard care homes where abuse happens, but the charity Compassion in Care found that of the reported abuse faced by LGBTQ+ in residential care settings, 99% took place in care homes that were rated by the Care Quality Commission as good or outstanding.[5]

Unable to either access or find much information about the experience of LGBTQ+ care home residents, Tonic teamed up with Opening Doors London, a charity providing services for queer people over the age of fifty, and Stonewall to commission their own research.[6] They found that of those surveyed, 89% wanted to receive care from an LGBTQ+ specific, or LGBTQ+ accredited provider and 79% wanted to live in an LGBTQ+ specific or LGBTQ+ accredited retirement community. The report concluded that queer people wanted housing, care and support services that are safe, recognize their lives and histories, and treat them with dignity and respect.

The concerns LGBTQ+ people have about housing, health and community don't evaporate when they get older. If anything, they seem to become even more significant. The biggest reason the respondents gave for potentially moving into supported accommodation was accessibility, with a third saying their current living space was not accessible. Many had fears that whilst they may be able to access their homes now, as they age or their health deteriorates, they may not be able to. They mentioned the way the built environment of residential homes could exacerbate those fears: 'The main thing is you want to feel safe and secure,' one bisexual man in his fifties shared, 'Even if you have your own flat you have to share entrances and hallways . . . I always worry if new neighbours are moving in.'

When asked what housing providers needed to consider, one respondent wrote: 'In addition to LGBT+ housing, I would welcome LGBT+ affirming healthcare, dementia support and hospice. And palliative care. And gay bingo.' Gay bingo might seem like a small addendum, particularly alongside things like palliative and hospice care, but we all deserve full and enriched lives, and sometimes that looks like gay bingo.

Tonic has been operating now for several years and the project continues to grow. The next step is to explore how people can benefit from what Tonic has learned and from their services if they are unable to afford to live in the community themselves.

## Late Bloomers

Conversations about coming out are often associated with youth. But, in fact, plenty of people come out later in life, and doing so brings its own set of challenges.

'I came out publicly on my own terms at fifty,' Raga (she/her), the founder of OutSpoken whom we met earlier in the book, tells me. 'I'd actually been outed many times before that, but I came out publicly at fifty, which is when I accepted my sexuality.'

Although we often talk about coming out as a singular event, life is rarely so straightforward (pun intended). For Raga, growing up in the 1970s in India as part of a Roman Catholic family, there was almost no representation of LGBTQ+ people at all. The language she spoke, Konkani, had no word for lesbian.

'If I had to come out to my mother and I said to her, "I think I am gay," she wouldn't have known what that meant.' Raga discovered, many years later, that her mother thought she was going to change her gender, to become what is known as a hijra.

Raga enjoyed a long career in the creative industries, raised her twins and went on to live in New Zealand before moving to the UK. Although she now lives in London, she considers all three countries her home.

Coming out was a positive experience for Raga, but also a risky one. 'The outcome was surprisingly very positive. Of course, I experienced the usual death threats, rape threats, threats that if I tried to come to India I'd have acid poured on my face. But the people who rejected me, actually embraced me, including my own family.'

I ask Raga why, against a background of such normalized violence, she came out at all.

'What prompted me was my children and my partner because I could see that I lead just not one life, or two lives, but so many. I was a woman – a woman of colour – I was married to a man, worked in different countries, and now I'm married to a woman and I have children.' For Raga, accepting her sexuality and publicly announcing it was about accepting more than just her identity, but the richness of her experiences. More than that, it enabled her to lessen the ways in which she was splicing herself into disparate people, which was exhausting. 'I was having to become a different human, a different personality, depending on which country I was in and which people I was speaking to. What is their age? Is it an Indian person? Or a Middle Eastern person? Or someone in the UK? New Zealand?'

Despite being out, Raga still faces barriers. She and her partner never engage in public displays of affection, and yet, despite this, have still faced hate crimes. 'We were assaulted, Nicola and I, on the South Bank in London on a very crowded evening.'

I ask Raga what she would tell her younger self, or another person going through a similar experience. Her answer is incredibly to the point: 'It's never too late. I'm fifty-three now and I'm setting up a business where everyone is telling me, "Sorry, it's not going to work". But I have done so many things that seemed impossible. My only regret is that I waited so long to say this. I feel like, why did I wait? Till fifty? I'm the kind of person who goes all out and battles. I don't put up with shit, but I did for so long.'

Still, Raga worries about the future, about what might happen to her and her peers as they get older. Statistically, older LGBTQ+ people find themselves going back into the closet, particularly if they find themselves in a care setting.

'I worry that if ever in the future my partner or I needed care, what would happen? Especially as a lesbian of Indian origin, I think I would really struggle being in a care home because I also know that people from India who are nurses and doctors are not sensitized to this. So, either they are open and they learn here, or they are closed, and they behave in a certain way. When you're in care under them, you are vulnerable. So that's a big worry.'

I think often of the amount of knowledge that has been lost and that we are still at risk of losing if we fail to acknowledge the existence and needs of older LGBTQ+ people. It is easy to look at historical movements that drove social change and to view them as something that materialized out of thin air, but this is simply not true. Many of the people involved in campaigning in feminist movements in the 1970s were key players in driving forward LGBTQ+ equality in the 1980s. People working for anti-fascist organizations and anti-racist organizations were the people working to drive forward change.

If this book has demonstrated anything, I hope that it is that there is much work to be done to create a world where LGBTQ+ people can survive and thrive, and that there are many approaches that might be taken. There are lessons to be learned, but we can't learn about them if these stories are lost. Lots has been done, but there is lots still to do.

## And What You Can Do About It

→ Actively include older LGBTQ+ people in social gatherings and community events. Invite them to participate in events, be part of panels, come to the pub quiz. Alternatively, meet them where they are at: offer to pop round and spend some time together. Building connections doesn't have to be complicated, and I tend to find people have more in common than they think with older people.

→ Be mindful that older LGBTQ+ people are less likely to have family around them and supporting them and so are at greater risk of becoming lonely. Never assume that an older LGBTQ+ person needs help, but you can always offer it. There's a gentleman local to me in his eighties who I always visit for a chat, to help with his groceries and walk his dog just in case, and likewise, he checks in on me. Building connections and supporting people doesn't have to be complicated, it just has to be compassionate and intentioned.

→ If you come into contact with services or care providers for older people, always ask them how they support LGBTQ+ people in their care. If you work in an industry or organization that supports older people, advocate for the inclusion of LGBTQ+ people publicly. If you have never had LGBTQ+ clients, that tells me they do not feel safe enough to disclose because, statistically, there will be LGBTQ+ people in every care home in the country.

# Putting in the Work

## Cat Burton (she/her)

Cat Burton is a retired British Airways captain, diversity advocate and current chair of the Gender Identity Research and Education Society. Although she knew she was a girl at the age of fourteen, Cat felt unable to express her true self growing up in the 1950s and 1960s. She felt for a long time that it would be impossible to transition whilst working in the aviation industry, an attitude which only shifted after meeting two other trans pilots who had been supported in the industry.

After decades working at British Airways, at the age of fifty-eight, she decided it was time to transition and, after being medically grounded for a few months, returned to work now presenting as a woman. In 2017, she finally retired and is now an independent aviation and diversity consultant and a flying instructor at Cardiff International Airport. Cat has been outspoken about the need for inclusive resources for older LGBTQ+ people and particularly trans people, who have specific needs which some individuals and organizations are not knowledgeable enough to deal with.

## Jennie Kermode (she/her)

Jennie Kermode is a trans journalist, author, critic, advocate, former chair of Trans Media Watch – a charity promoting positive media representations of the transgender community – and author of *Growing Older as a Trans and/or Non-Binary Person: A Support Guide*.

Throughout her career, Kermode has worked to ensure trans people are represented in ways that not only are not harmful or perpetuate negative stereotypes, but which are actively positive.

Her latest book draws upon the experiences of older trans people and people transitioning later in life, exploring fundamental challenges they face which are often overlooked, whether that be inclusive care homes, inheritance or funeral planning. Kermode also advocates for professionals to do a better job at supporting transgender people both at the institutional and individual levels.

# Epilogue: Hope

Being queer is the greatest joy of my life. A decade ago, those were words I never expected to write. Hell, in this current world, it still feels like a bold statement because of the political, media and social landscapes that make it feel damn near impossible, at times.

It is a privilege to be a part of a community which embraces difference, loves fiercely and continually challenges the status quo. That doesn't mean it is easy to exist outside of what society has determined to be 'normal' or 'acceptable', and this book has been my attempt at illustrating just some of the difficulties we continue to face as LGBTQ+ people, not because of our identities but because of other people's intolerance, ignorance and outright hatred.

There are still those who think that members of our community are bad, sinful, broken, a threat, something that needs to be eradicated or kept away from other people. As though we might be contagious. These people, sadly, are everywhere: from the person standing on a street corner to the leaders of whole nations.

I was angry for so long at those who made it their mission in life to destroy the hard-won rights of LGBTQ+ people, who were so often fuelled by their own hatred and limited views of the world that they insisted on imposing them on others. These days, I tend to pity them instead.

Whilst some of the most threatening, pernicious voices have

power, influence, money and the apparatus of the state – they still haven't eradicated us. Their efforts have been fruitless. I've written throughout this book about history repeating itself and the risks of assuming that social progress is linear, something that feels ever more prescient as we witness a global rise in fascism once more. But there is also the much-underlooked fact that the continued fight against us reminds us we have always been here, disrupting systems just with our presence. We are everywhere and always have been.

What scares so many people who despise us, who would rather we shrank into the background – even those who don't mind us but would prefer if we were less loud, less blatant – is that there is no world that is divorced from the influence, power and strength of LGBTQ+ people. And if there were? I wouldn't want to live in that place – devoid of our impact on art, music, fashion, technology, science, medicine, literature and so much more.

Whether you make us illegal, remove our access to support, debate our existences, threaten our lives or indeed kill us – we prevail. Always. We're stubborn like that. A dandelion that sprouts between the narrow confines of concrete paving slabs is still a flower in bloom, just one someone has decided is doing it incorrectly, so we call it a weed and try to get rid of it. I take great comfort in this fact, especially on the hard days.

Growing up queer, there were a lot of hard days. I was lucky. I eventually found people who cherish me, who hold me and see me for who I am and who love me. I am acutely aware there are so many people who will never be able to be recognized as LGBTQ+ because of the danger that would place them in. I am a loud, proud person but I know that is not possible for everyone. Whoever you are, wherever you are, I see you. And we've got you. Progress is much more of a relay race than people imagine, and we are always passing the baton to those who are able to do the most in that moment.

I am shocked when people say they don't know anyone who is LGBTQ+. Of course they do.

Even if you are straight and cisgender and think you have nothing to do with us, I promise you have friends, family or acquaintances who are part of the community. But they won't tell if you if they don't feel safe.

LGBTQ+ people are not 'other'. We're the people who teach your children to do times tables, who clean your streets, who offer you a seat on the bus. We're the people who scan your shopping or make your favourite TV show or take your blood pressure. I'm fond of saying, 'LGBTQ+ people – almost the same thing as people'.

We are messy and complicated and brilliant because that is what it means to be a person. We are people and we are not demanding too much by expecting to be treated as such. We do not have to be perfect or conformist to be worthy.

I wrote this book with the aim of engaging what I called the 'compassionate middle'. I could see a growing divide between the depictions of LGBTQ+ people in the press and by politicians, and the people I encountered on the ground, most of whom were at least partly supportive. They might have had uncertainties, questions and/or concerns, but they were not vehemently against the rights of LGBTQ+ people, on the whole. Sometimes they had just never had the opportunity to have a conversation where they got things wrong and were able to be to be a bit rude and use the wrong language and say the wrong thing, not because they were scared we would come down on them but because they didn't want to be rude or hurtful.

I realized that was a good place to start – because it showed that somewhere, they cared enough to recognize the person in front of them had feelings. Seeing us as people was a start.

Even though there are more out LGBTQ+ people than ever before, we are still a minority. It is still profoundly unsafe to be LGBTQ+ in parts of the world, and, as this book has demonstrated, the UK has become increasingly hostile in recent years, in part because of the complacency that set in after same sex marriage equality came to pass.

Within the community, there is still a hell of a lot to do. As queer people, we've got to tackle the rampant transphobia that's inveigled its way into our media, politics, laws and attitudes with alarming rapidity, if not for our trans siblings then because it will be our heads on the chopping block next. We've got to realize we can commit to both learning and unlearning whilst also holding grace for those who know less, who might be newer to the community, might not have had access to knowledge. We've got to continue to build solidarity with other movements and communities because, as should be apparent by now, nothing affects just LGBTQ+ people. We must fight, but we don't have to fight alone. We need those outside of the community to publicly and loudly ally themselves with us. It is not enough to say you support us if you don't match those words with actions when those who strive to remove our rights are raucous, organized and well-resourced.

Quiet, interpersonal acts of support are important and life-saving but they are insufficient. We need the people who turn up to our bars or our Pride marches, who value diversity, who like what we make – frankly, people who value human rights – to start proving it. You've made it to the end of this book, which is a good start, but getting started or increasing your efforts to support LGBTQ+ people in tangible ways is important, too.

The persecution of LGBTQ+ people is aligned with racism, ableism, misogyny and other structural violence. We have repeatedly seen how the pursuit of anti-LGBTQ+ laws and practices serves as a diversionary tactic, drawing people into debates rather than tackling important matters like poverty, underfunded education and paltry access to healthcare.

A world that supports LGBTQ+ people and values our existence is a world that fundamentally cares about people. It shouldn't be idealistic nor should it be radical to be compassionate, to value difference, to have empathy. It should be an alarming indictment of any society that there is anyone, let alone children, who thinks it is better to be dead than to have to live as an LGBTQ+ person. And who is to say it couldn't be you next? After all, the world always needs scapegoats.

I find it difficult to balance the exquisite magic of being queer with the darkness of the challenges we face. I am still angry a lot of the time – in fact, I'm still regularly outraged. It hurts to see people in my community in pain, to see them needlessly suffer because of other people's ignorance or cruelty or both. It is indescribably awful going to lay flowers at the graves of friends younger than you when their deaths were preventable, in a country that claims to be world-class in supporting LGBTQ+ rights. Especially when what they needed was not asking the earth: less cruelty, less ignorance, more care.

I originally worried that writing this book might scare LGBTQ+ people who were less confident in themselves but I came to realize that nothing I write can be as scary as the reality. But I wanted to end this book with this: to be part of the LGBTQ+ community is a privilege, one that has afforded me love, solidarity and care. To be queer is to be held and supported and nourished by other wonderful people from every walk of life. It has given me a unique vantage point through which to see the world and a ready desire to shrug off any societal expectations placed upon me. It is freedom, it is joy and it is hope.

Some say rage and anger corrode, but they just seemed to galvanize me, to make me love harder, to want to learn more. It's something no one can ever take from me. It's how I'm not numb to all of this.

My inner cynic tells me things can get worse, but they can get better, too. I have to have that hope.

We've got work to do.

# Acknowledgements

Thanks must go to my agent Anna Pallai who always made me feel like anything was possible and that I was a capable human being. Your patience, wisdom and support is unmatched; I would never want to publish my first book with anyone but you.

Thank you to my editor Jodie Lancet-Grant for pushing me to be bolder and braver and for making this book what it is. Thank you also for your dedication to putting LGBTQ+ books into the mainstream. Thank you to Katy Denny and Jack Alexander for helping get this book into shape. Thank you to Annie Rose and Maya Conway for all of your support marketing this book and getting it into the hands of readers. It is in no way easy to sell books, especially about communities that have been maligned and marginalized and you are both wizards.

We are not a family that talks loudly about how much we love each other – though we do, deeply. We do it in how we show up for one another. Thank you to my dad, Chris, who will always be my first editor, sense-checker and person who I rely on to tell me if I have written absolute nonsense. Thank you to my mum, Gill, for teaching me how to be a person, for engendering a passion for social issues, and for reading to me every day as a kid. I feel exceptionally fortunate to have been raised by people who loved learning and understood the power of asking questions, gaining knowledge and thinking big. Both my parents have been an immense support both practically and personally throughout my life. I know it has not always been easy to be my parent, and lots of people would have baulked.

Thank you to my brother Morgan for supporting me with my referencing, making sure my calculations were correct and keeping me company in the small hours. Thank you to my godmother Fi for your constant support, encouragement and letting me crash at yours.

Thank you to Wednesday for your insights, wisdom and pictures of small creatures at four in the morning when I thought the world was ending. Thank you to Natasha, for helping me know even as a teenager it was possible to be myself and thrive. To Josephine for basically appearing out of nowhere in the last year of writing to get me through. To Donna for keeping me going all of these years and always quietly showing up for me. To Jamie for teaching me to be more brazen and more brave. And to Shahroo for supporting me through everything. Thank you to Rosie for your constant belief and reassurance.

Thank you to the Hot & Hilarious crew for making me feel infinitely less alone in the universe.

Thank you to Margate, who took me in with open arms, held my hand and kept me going no matter what. Thank you especially to Fran & Aly at the Margate Bookshop for consoling, entertaining & supporting me. And, let's be honest, not being totally freaked out when a purple-haired girl started turning up every day for a chat.

This book – and so much of the joy I have found – would not have been possible without the support of my Granny, Doreen. She died unexpectedly when this book was only an idea, but she taught me everything about community, compassion and keeping going in spite of the hard things. She's the kind of woman who did a Radio 4 phone-in with John Major and embarrassed him so substantially he reversed his policy the next day. You would have loved her.

And finally, thank you to the hundreds of LGBTQ+ people in the UK and around the world who took the time to share their stories and insights with me during the course of this book being written. I do not take for granted for a second how significant that was for so many of you. I hope to have done you justice.

# Bibliography

Alqasim, Elias, ed. *This Arab Is Queer.*

Atherton Lin, Jamie. *Gay Bar.*

Baker, Paul. *Outrageous!: The Story of Section 28 and Britain's Battle for LGBT Education.*

Brown, Leighton, and Matthew Riemer. *We Are Everywhere: Protest, Power, and Pride in the History of Queer Liberation: A Visual Guide to the History of Queer Liberation, So Far.*

Burns, Christine. *Trans Britain: Our Journey from the Shadows.*

Choudrey, Sabah. *Supporting Trans People of Colour: How to Make Your Practice Inclusive.*

Clark, Kelly Hayes, and Mariame Kaba. *Let This Radicalize You: Organizing and the Revolution of Reciprocal Care.*

Connelly, Kevin Guyan. *Queer Data: Using Gender, Sex and Sexuality Data for Action.*

Davies, Stephanie. *Queer and Trans People of Colour in the UK: Possibilities for Intersectional Richness.*

Downs, Alan. *The Velvet Rage: Overcoming the Pain of Growing Up Gay in a Straight Man's World.*

Fahs, Breanne. *Burn It Down!.*

Faye, Shon. *The Transgender Issue: An Argument for Justice.*

Flynn, Paul. *Good as You* (2018).

Frazer-Carroll, Micha. *Mad World: The Politics of Mental Health.*

Gevisser, Mark. *The Pink Line: Journeys Across the World's Queer Frontiers.*

Gupta, Sunil. *We Were Here: Sexuality, Photography, and Cultural Difference: Selected Essays.*

Jaques, Juliet. *Front Lines: Trans Journalism 2007-2021.*

Jeffs, Lotte, and Stuart Oakley. *The Queer Parent.*

Kuntsman, Adi, and Sayan Bhattacharyya, editors. *Queer Asia: Decolonising and Reimagining Sexuality and Gender.*

Lee, Catherine. *Pretended: Schools and Section 28: Historical, Cultural and Personal Perspectives.*

Martel, Frédéric. *Global Gay: How Gay Culture Is Changing the World.*

Miss Major and Toshio Meronek. *Miss Major Speaks: Conversations with a Black Trans Revolutionary.*

Nash, Catherine Jean, and Kath Browne. *Heteroactivism: Resisting Lesbian, Gay, Bisexual and Trans Rights and Equalities.*

Nicholas, Harry. *A Trans Man Walks Into A Gay Bar.*

Nixon, Liam Warfield, and Walter Crasshole. *Queercore: How to Punk a Revolution: An Oral History.*

Pechey, Ben. *The Book of Non-Binary Joy: Embracing the Power of You.*

Schulman, Sarah. *Let the Record Show: A Political History of ACT UP New York, 1987–1993.*

Sharman, Zena. *Care We Dream Of: Liberatory and Transformative Approaches to LGBTQ+ Health.*

Sharman, Zena. *The Remedy: Queer and Trans Voices on Health and Health Care.*

Shearing, Lois. *Bi the Way: The Bisexual Guide to Life.*

Shearing, Lois, and Vaneet Mehta, editors. *It Ain't Over Til the Bisexual Speaks: An Anthology of Bisexual Voices.*

Stryker, Susan. *Transgender History.*

Taylor, Yvette. *Working-Class Queers: Time, Place and Politics.*

Todd, Matthew. *Straight Jacket: Overcoming Society's Legacy of Gay Shame.*

Vincent, Ben. *Transgender Health: A Practitioner's Guide to Binary and Non-Binary Trans Patient Care.*

# Endnotes

## Introduction: Outraged

1  https://journals.sagepub.com/doi/abs/10.1177/0196859904267232
2  https://actupny.org/documents/research.html
3  https://translegislation.com/learn
4  https://www.gendergp.com/transgender-suicide-rate-youth-explodes-in-uk/
5  https://rainbowmap.ilga-europe.org/
6  https://www.ilga-europe.org/files/uploads/2022/04/rainbow-map-2015.pdf
7  https://www.stonewall.org.uk/about-us/news/new-data-rise-hate-crime-against-lgbtq-people-continues-stonewall-slams-uk-gov-?ref=wearequeeraf.com
8  https://www.ohchr.org/en/press-releases/2023/04/uk-un-expert-assess-human-rights-lgbt-persons
9  https://www.cps.gov.uk/cps/news/racial-and-religious-based-offences-drive-increase-hate-crime-cases
10  https://www.npcc.police.uk/our-work/violence-against-women-and-girls/
11  https://www.legislation.gov.uk/ukpga/2022/32/contents
12  https://www.theguardian.com/uk-news/2023/may/12/police-apologise-after-detaining-royal-superfan-for-13-hours-coronation-just-stop-oil#:~:text=Police%20have%20been%20forced%20to,protesters%20at%20King%20Charles's%20coronation.
13  https://abcnews.go.com/US/genocidal-transgender-people-begin-flee-states-anti-lgbtq/story?id=99909913
14  https://newrepublic.com/post/172444/florida-passes-bill-allowing-trans-kids-taken-families; https://www.aclu.org/legislative-attacks-on-lgbtq-rights-2024

15  https://www.bbc.com/news/world-europe-63029909
16  https://www.bbc.co.uk/news/world-africa-65034343
17  https://www.lgbtqnation.com/2024/02/ghanas-parliament-votes-unanimously-to-criminalize-lgbtq-identities-allyship/
18  https://www.statista.com/statistics/1270166/lgbt-identification-world-wide/
19  https://www.hrw.org/news/2022/09/06/how-targeting-lgbtq-rights-are-part-authoritarian-playbook; https://www.thetaskforce.org/programs/queering-equity/queering-reproductive-justice/
20  https://www.ilga-europe.org/press-release/deadliest-rise-anti-lgbti-violence-decade/

### Chapter I. The Marriage Equality Myth

1  https://www.legislation.gov.uk/ukpga/2013/30/contents/enacted
2  https://www.legislation.gov.uk/ukpga/1988/9/section/28/enacted
3  https://www.legislation.gov.uk/ukpga/2004/33/contents
4  https://publications.parliament.uk/pa/cm200304/cmhansrd/vo041012/debtext/41012-11.htm
5  https://www.thebritishacademy.ac.uk/blog/aids-epidemic-lasting-impact-gay-men/; https://www.bbc.co.uk/iplayer/episode/m001xpr2/big-gay-wedding-with-tom-allen
6  https://hls.harvard.edu/today/how-same-sex-marriage-came-to-be/
7  https://assets.publishing.service.gov.uk/media/5a7acbd640f0b66e-ab99cb42/impact-assessment_1_.pdf
8  https://www.thepinknews.com/2010/09/29/sir-ian-mckellen-gay-marriage-has-to-be-on-stonewalls-agenda/
9  https://www.thepinknews.com/2010/10/27/stonewall-says-it-will-campaign-for-gay-marriage/
10  https://www.theguardian.com/politics/2012/dec/15/nigel-farage-ukip-anti-gay-groups
11  https://www.petertatchell.net/lgbt_rights/partnerships/equal-love-campaign-launched/
12  https://www.independent.co.uk/news/uk/home-news/voices-of-dissent-gay-marriage-opponents-attack-8406636.html
13  https://www.theguardian.com/society/2013/feb/05/gay-marriage-vote-cameron-adrift#:~:text=Parliament%20took%20a%20historic%20step,heart%20of%20the%20Conservative%20party;

https://www.independent.co.uk/news/uk/politics/tories-warn-cameron-that-gay-marriage-will-split-party-in-two-8397629.html

14 https://blogs.lse.ac.uk/politicsandpolicy/austerity-past-present-and-future/

15 https://bills.parliament.uk/bills/1135

16 https://www.today.com/popculture/elton-john-admits-cried-listening-yellow-brick-road-again-2D79456036

17 Conrad, Ryan, Chávez, Karma, Nair, Yasmin, and Loeffler, Deena, *Against Equality: Queer Revolution, Not Mere Inclusion* (Against Equality Press, 2014), pp. 45–6.

18 https://queerkidssaynomarriage.wordpress.com/

19 Nair, Yasmin. 'Against Equality, Against Marriage: An Introduction' in Ryan Conrad (ed.), *Against Equality: Queer Critiques of Gay Marriage* (Against Equality Press, 2010), pp. 7–15.

20 ibid.

21 https://www.legislation.gov.uk/ukpga/2013/30/schedule/5

22 https://www.legislation.gov.uk/ukpga/2004/7/contents

23 https://assets.publishing.service.gov.uk/government/uploads/system/uploads/attachment_data/file/721642/GEO-LGBT-factsheet.pdf

24 https://www.gov.uk/government/news/gender-recognition-certificate-fee-reduced

25 https://www.thepinknews.com/2023/02/01/trans-self-id-laws-gender-recognition-reform-scotland-ireland/; https://www.scottishtrans.org/wp-content/uploads/2022/10/5-Reasons-To-Support-Gender-Recognition-Reform-Booklet.pdf

26 https://www.theguardian.com/world/2023/jan/10/tories-review-lgbtq-gender-recognition-certificate-deal

27 https://www.thepinknews.com/2023/12/08/conservative-approved-list-gender-recognition-sterilisation/

28 https://www.instituteforgovernment.org.uk/explainer/section-35-scotland-gender-recognition-bill; https://www.bbc.co.uk/news/articles/c97zv90d77do

29 https://inews.co.uk/opinion/marry-bride-reminder-unequal-trans-rights-still-are-400587

30 https://commonslibrary.parliament.uk/research-briefings/cbp-9515/#:~:text=No%20legal%20recognition,recognition%20of%20any%20other%20gender; https://inews.co.uk/news/non-binary-

american-uk-stuck-legal-limbo-gender-2242643; https://www.dazed-digital.com/politics/article/52914/1/the-uk-government-will-not-legally-recognize-non-binary-as-a-gender-identity

31  https://gayiceland.is/2017/non-binary-couple-tie-knot-protest-laws-marriage/

32  https://metro.co.uk/2023/11/28/partner-protest-wedding-cant-real-thing-19888865/

33  https://www.legislation.gov.uk/ukpga/2020/11/contents/enacted

34  https://www.legislation.gov.uk/ukpga/1973/18/section/12

35  https://www.equalityhumanrights.com/human-rights/human-rights-act/article-8-respect-your-private-and-family-life

36  https://www.legislation.gov.uk/ukpga/2013/30/schedule/5/enacted

37  https://www.bbc.co.uk/news/uk-politics-22779586

38  https://novaramedia.com/2023/02/20/welcome-to-terf-island-how-anti-trans-hate-skyrocketed-156-in-four-years/; https://www.thepinknews.com/2021/10/01/transphobia-uk-terf-island-tiktok/; https://www.compactmag.com/article/welcome-to-terf-island/

39  https://www.vice.com/en/article/jg8znx/uk-equalities-minister-kemi-badenoch-goes-on-anti-lgbtq-rant-in-leaked-audio

40  https://www.ons.gov.uk/peoplepopulationandcommunity/cultural-identity/genderidentity/bulletins/genderidentityenglandandwales/census2021

41  https://www.ipso.co.uk/media/1986/mediatique-report-on-coverage-of-transgender-issues.pdf; https://www.ipso.co.uk/news-analysis/new-research-on-reporting-of-trans-issues-shows-400-increase-in-coverage-and-varying-perceptions-on-broader-editorial-standards/

42  https://www.newyorker.com/news/q-and-a/sasha-issenberg-on-the-fight-for-marriage-equality

43  https://glaad.org/publications/victims-or-villains-examining-ten-years-transgender-images-television/

44  https://time.com/5947032/elliot-page-2/; https://time.com/magazine/us/135460/june-9th-2014-vol-183-no-22-u-s/

45  Schulman, Sarah, *The Gentrification of the Mind* (University of California Press, 2013).

46  https://www.theguardian.com/society/2024/mar/29/two-english-couples-10-years-equal-marriage-england-wales

## Chapter 2. Home Sweet Home?

1 https://www.stonewall.org.uk/lgbtq-facts-and-figures
2 https://england.shelter.org.uk/media/press_release/at_least_309000_people_homeless_in_england_today
3 https://www.standard.co.uk/homesandproperty/renting/london-rent-crisis-asking-rents-per-month-rise-rightmove-b1095788.html
4 https://england.shelter.org.uk/media/press_release/half_of_working_renters_only_one_pay_cheque_away_from_losing_their_home_
5 https://ec.europa.eu/eurostat/statistics-explained/index.php?title=Living_conditions_in_Europe_-_housing
6 https://england.shelter.org.uk/media/press_release/17_5million_people_now_impacted_by_the_housing_emergency_
7 https://hqnetwork.co.uk/news/one-in-five-lgbtq-private-renters-experienced-discrimination-from-a-landlord-or-letting-agent/
8 https://england.shelter.org.uk/media/press_release/private_renters_who_complain_about_disrepair_more_than_twice_as_likely_to_be_slapped_with_an_eviction_notice
9 https://bills.parliament.uk/bills/3462; https://www.bbc.co.uk/news/articles/c19dd1v00jro#:~:text=This%20allows%20landlords%20to%20evict,with%20a%20Section%2021%20notice.
10 https://www.generationrent.org/2022/06/28/i-didnt-feel-safe-being-my-full-self/
11 https://williamsinstitute.law.ucla.edu/publications/lgbt-poverty-us/; https://lgbtq-economics.org/issues/wealth-gap/income-savings-gap/
12 https://www.stonewall.org.uk/resources/lgbt-britain-trans-report-2018
13 https://jrf.org.uk/housing/whats-causing-structural-racism-in-housing; https://www.ethnicity-facts-figures.service.gov.uk/housing/owning-and-renting/renting-from-a-private-landlord/latest/; https://www.ethnicity-facts-figures.service.gov.uk/housing/owning-and-renting/renting-from-a-private-landlord/latest/
14 ibid.
15 https://www.ons.gov.uk/peoplepopulationandcommunity/populationandmigration/populationestimates/articles/moreadultslivingwiththeirparents/2023-05-10
16 https://www.justlikeus.org/blog/2023/04/19/new-research-shows-almost-half-of-lgbt-adults-are-estranged-from-family-and-a-third-not-confident-their-parents-will-accept-them/

17  https://www.houseproud-lgbt.com/about-us
18  https://www.surrey.ac.uk/research-projects/housing-pride-working-together-create-lgbtq-inclusive-social-housing
19  https://www.insidehousing.co.uk/insight/lgbtq-homelessness-the-data-hole-that-undermines-services-74552
20  https://www.housing.org.uk/news-and-blogs/blogs/jotepreet-bhandal/tackling-the-lgbtq-youth-homelessness-crisis/
21  https://www.crisis.org.uk/about-us/media-centre/councils-across-england-running-out-of-options-as-demand-from-households-facing-homelessness-soars/
22  https://www.akt.org.uk/wp-content/uploads/2023/07/akt-thelgbtqyouthhomelessnessreport2021.pdf
23  https://www.akt.org.uk/wp-content/uploads/2023/07/akt-thelgbtqyouthhomelessnessreport2021.pdf

### Chapter 3. Edu-gay-tion

 1  https://www.legislation.gov.uk/ukpga/1988/9/section/28/enacted
 2  https://mckellen.com/writings/activism/8807section28.htm
 3  https://www.independent.co.uk/news/world/americas/iphone-science-trans-woman-lynn-conway-b2458269.html
 4  https://www.bbc.com/news/technology-18419691
 5  https://www.independent.co.uk/life-style/alan-tu-ring-new-ps50-banknote-gay-codebreaker-mathematician-sexuality-pardon-a9005086.html
 6  https://www.justlikeus.org/wp-content/uploads/2021/11/Just-Like-Us-2021-report-Growing-Up-LGBT.pdf
 7  https://www.lgbtmap.org/equality-maps/criminaljustice/drag_restrictions
 8   https://edition.cnn.com/2023/09/27/politics/texas-drag-show-ban-unconstitutional-free-speech/index.html
 9  https://www.them.us/story/anti-drag-legislation-trans-community-drag-queens
10  https://www.bbc.co.uk/news/newsbeat-40340177
11   https://daily.jstor.org/parents-rights-sex-and-race-in-1970s-florida
12   https://www.flsenate.gov/Session/Bill/2022/1557
13  https://www.nea.org/sites/default/files/2023-06/30424-know-your-rights_web_v4.pdf

14 https://www.bbc.co.uk/news/uk-england-manchester-67729418
15 https://www.lbc.co.uk/news/teenage-transgender-girl-stabbed-14-times-attempted-murder/)
16 https://educationhub.blog.gov.uk/2023/12/19/gender-questioning-children-guidance-schools-colleges/
17  https://www.bbc.co.uk/news/articles/cxxx821l57go
18 https://learning.nspcc.org.uk/safeguarding-child-protection/lgbtq-children-young-people
19 https://galop.org.uk/wp-content/uploads/2022/04/Galop-LGBT-Experiences-of-Abuse-from-Family-Members.pdf
20 https://www.gov.uk/government/news/age-limits-introduced-to-protect-children-in-rshe
21 https://journal.nds.ox.ac.uk/index.php/JNDS/article/view/176
22 https://www.acog.org/clinical/clinical-guidance/committee-opinion/articles/2016/11/comprehensive-sexuality-education; https://www.fpa.org.uk/rshe-for-teachers/sex-education-benefits-and-statistics/
23  https://assets.childrenscommissioner.gov.uk/wpuploads/2023/02/cc-a-lot-of-it-is-actually-just-abuse-young-people-and-pornography-updated.pdf
24 https://neu.org.uk/press-releases/teachers-feel-severely-underpaid
25 https://www.bbc.co.uk/news/uk-england-london-67126160
26 https://www.bbc.co.uk/news/uk-england-london-67101982; https://www.theguardian.com/society/2024/feb/27/health-emergency-15-of-uk-households-went-hungry-last-month-data-shows
27 https://www.washingtonpost.com/education/interactive/school-shootings-database/
28 https://www.rcpch.ac.uk/news-events/news/paediatricians-step-more-children-experiencing-mental-health-crisis-end-their

### Chapter 4. Health Conscious

1 https://www.bbc.co.uk/news/health-66994133
2 https://translucent.org.uk/womens-single-sex-spaces-in-hospitals/
3 https://www.stonewall.org.uk/about-us/news/new-data-rise-hate-crime-against-lgbtq-people-continues-stonewall-slams-uk-gov-
4 https://www.cam.ac.uk/research/news/lesbian-gay-and-bisexual-men-and-women-report-poorer-health-and-experiences-of-nhs
5 https://jamanetwork.com/journals/jama/article-abstract/2818061

6    https://www.apa.org/pubs/journals/releases/hea-hea0001067.pdf

7    https://issuu.com/moiremarketing/docs/gwu8110_2021_progress_
     report_final_web

8    https://www.who.int/news-room/fact-sheets/detail/human-rights-
     and-health

9    https://www.gov.uk/government/publications/national-lgbt-survey-
     summary-report

10   https://www.england.nhs.uk/about/equality/equality-hub/
     patient-equalities-programme/lgbt-health/

11   https://lgbt.foundation/wp-content/uploads/2023/10/LGBTQ-
     Patient-Experiences-in-Primary-Care.pdf

12   https://transactual.org.uk/wp-content/uploads/
     TransLivesSurvey2021.pdf

13   https://www.ncbi.nlm.nih.gov/pmc/articles/PMC10052488/

14   https://transharmreduction.org/blood-tests

15   https://www.news-medical.net/health/Do-We-Need-Transgender-
     specific-Reference-Ranges-for-Common-Laboratory-Tests.aspx

16   https://cks.nice.org.uk/topics/rheumatoid-arthritis/background-
     information/prevalence-incidence/; https://assets.publishing.service.
     gov.uk/media/5b3a478240f0b64603fc181b/GEO-LGBT-factsheet.
     pdf

17   https://www.english-heritage.org.uk/visit/blue-plaques/blue-plaque-
     stories/eugenics; https://blog.nationalarchives.gov.
     uk/20speople-improving-the-nations-stock-for-great-and-greater-
     britain-eugenics-in-the-1920s/; https://wellcomecollection.org/
     articles/YxW0VhEAACEAi6qc

18   https://www.history.com/topics/european-history/eugenics; https://
     www.genome.gov/about-genomics/fact-sheets/Eugenics-and-
     Scientific-Racism#:~:text=Eugenicists%20worldwide%20believed%20
     that%20they,by%20them%20to%20be%20unfit.

19    https://bpr.studentorg.berkeley.edu/2020/11/04/americas-forgotten-
     history-of-forced-sterilization/

20   https://blog.petrieflom.law.harvard.edu/2021/07/23/covid-eugenics-
     health-based-discrimination/; https://rabble.ca/health/dont-look-
     away-from-the-implicit-eugenics-of-living-with-covid/

21   Shufeldt, R. W., 'The Medico-Legal Consideration of Perverts and
     Inverts,' *Pacific Medical Journal* 48 (July 1905): 385–93.

22   https://www.bmj.com/content/bmj/328/7437/427.full.pdf

23  https://assets.publishing.service.gov.uk/media/64b-
14c0d07d4b800133472e9/LGBT_Veterans_Independent_Review.pdf

24  https://www.cdc.gov/mmwr/preview/mmwrhtml/june_5.htm

25  https://www.cdc.gov/museum/online/story-of-cdc/aids/index.html

26  https://www.hiv.gov/hiv-basics/overview/history/hiv-and-aids-
timeline#year-1981

27  https://www.historyextra.com/period/20th-century/aids-hiv-epidemic-
changed-britain-how/

28  https://www.tht.org.uk/news/heterosexual-hiv-diagnoses-over-
take-those-gay-men-first-time-decade#:~:text=For%20the%20
first%20time%20in,in%20gay%20and%20bisexual%20men.

29  https://www.sfaf.org/collections/beta/what-is-aids-survivor-syndrome/

30  https://www.tht.org.uk/news/impact-its-sin-one-year

31  https://www.gov.uk/government/publications/towards-zero-the-
hiv-action-plan-for-england-2022-to-2025/towards-zero-an-action-
plan-towards-ending-hiv-transmission-aids-and-hiv-related-deaths-
in-england-2022-to-2025

32  https://www.bmj.com/content/343/bmj.d5604

33  https://www.nhsbt.nhs.uk/news/landmark-change-to-blood-donation-
eligibility-rules-on-today-s-world-blood-donor-day/

34  https://bmcpublichealth.biomedcentral.com/articles/10.1186/s12889-
021-11000-7

35  https://www.england.nhs.uk/2019/06/fake-news-putting-50000-
lesbian-gay-and-bisexual-women-at-risk-of-cancer/

36  https://transactual.org.uk/wp-content/uploads/
TransLivesSurvey2021.pdf

37  https://www.consortium.lgbt/wp-content/uploads/2019/07/A-Guide-
to-Lesbian-Bisexual-and-Trans-Womens-Health.pdf; https://www.
england.nhs.uk/2019/06/fake-news-putting-50000-lesbian-gay-and-
bisexual-women-at-risk-of-cancer/

38  https://www.thepinknews.com/2022/03/01/trans-nhs-london-assembly-
health-committee-sadiq-khan/

39  https://www.london.gov.uk/sites/default/files/health_committee_-_
report_-_trans_health_matters.pdf

40  https://raceequalityfoundation.org.uk/wp-content/uploads/2022/10/
Better-Health-41-Trans-NB-final.pdf

41  https://medicalhealthhumanities.com/2023/10/16/equitable-
representation-in-medical-textbooks/

## Chapter 5. Mental Healthcare

1  https://www.magonlinelibrary.com/doi/abs/10.12968/bjmh.2015.4.1.31

2  https://www.attitude.co.uk/news/corei-hall-gofundme-451301/

3  Shay Patten Walker was a trans activist who worked as gender story consultant on series four of *Sex Education*, who sadly died by suicide at the age of twenty-four in 2022.

4   https://digital.nhs.uk/news/2021/lgb-health-statistics; https://committees.parliament.uk/writtenevidence/95714/html/

5  https://www.stonewall.org.uk/system/files/lgbt_in_britain_health.pdf

6  https://www.gaytimes.com/life/lgbtq-youth-are-three-times-more-likely-to-have-an-eating-disorder

7   https://www.thetrevorproject.org/survey-2024/

8  https://www.theguardian.com/society/2023/jan/25/young-people-england-wales-twice-likely-identify-lgb-overall-population

9  https://www.justlikeus.org/blog/2021/11/25/lgbt-young-people-twice-likely-depression-anxiety-panic-attacks/

10  https://www.rethink.org/news-and-stories/media-centre/2024/06/new-survey-reveals-stark-impact-of-nhs-mental-health-treatment-waiting-times/?whatsnew

11  https://www.rcpsych.ac.uk/news-and-features/latest-news/detail/2022/10/10/hidden-waits-force-more-than-three-quarters-of-mental-health-patients-to-seek-help-from-emergency-services

12  https://www.kff.org/report-section/lgbt-peoples-health-and-experiences-accessing-care-report/; https://core.ac.uk/download/pdf/74372485.pdf

13  https://assets.publishing.service.gov.uk/government/uploads/system/uploads/attachment_data/file/852924/t451-eng.pdf

14  https://www.bbc.co.uk/news/uk-england-bristol-61605588

15  Even now, you need the sign off of two GPs in the UK; https://jaapl.org/content/jaapl/50/4/494.full.pdf

16  Frazer-Carroll, Micha, *Mad World, The Politics of Mental Health* (Pluto Press, 2023).

17  https://transactual.org.uk/transition-access-22/

18  https://www.independent.co.uk/news/health/mental-health-nhs-patient-deaths-b2148501.html; https://www.bbc.co.uk/news/uk-

england-cambridgeshire-67664310; https://www.bbc.co.uk/news/
uk-england-cambridgeshire-67664310; https://www.bbc.co.uk/
news/uk-63045298; https://www.inquest.org.uk/jury-find-gross-
neglect-by-privately-run-mental-health-hospital-caused-patients-
death

19  https://www.madinamerica.com/2020/03/report-psychiatric-
interventions-torture/
20  https://disabilityvisibilityproject.com/2020/07/22/abolition-must-
include-psychiatry/
21  Frazer-Carroll, Micha, *Mad World, The Politics of Mental Health*
(Pluto Press, 2023).
22  https://goodlawproject.org/case/nhs-cyp-guidance
23  https://goodlawproject.org/crowdfunder/nhs-cyp-guidance/
24  Peschey, Ben, *The Book of Non-Binary Joy* (Jessica Kingsley
Publishers, 2022) and Peschey, Ben, *Your Gender Book* (Jessica
Kingsley Publishers, 2023).

### Chapter 6. The Life-changing Magic of Gender-affirming Care

1  https://nypost.com/2023/06/22/gender-affirming-surgery-puts-a-feel-
good-phrase-on-child-butchery/
2  https://www.nhs.uk/medicines/spironolactone/common-questions-
about-spironolactone/
3  https://www.nhs.uk/conditions/gender-dysphoria/treatment/
4  https://www.ncbi.nlm.nih.gov/pmc/articles/PMC3667985/
5  https://edition.cnn.com/2023/06/06/politics/states-banned-medical-
transitioning-for-transgender-youth-dg
6  https://whatweknow.inequality.cornell.edu/topics/lgbt-equality/what-
does-the-scholarly-research-say-about-the-wellbeing-of-transgender-
people/; https://whatweknow.inequality.cornell.edu/about/
selection-methodology/
7   https://whatweknow.inequality.cornell.edu/topics/lgbt-equality/
what-does-the-scholarly-research-say-about-the-well-being-of-
transgender-people/; https://www.thelancet.com/journals/lanchi/
article/PIIS2352-4642(22)00254-1/abstract?fbclid=IwAR0o-
PrdHaj48V_v1Db-_mwm1EVYDx4BzDTkQ9yyyta0uxI04W0G-
CAj-hxQ
8   https://www.ncbi.nlm.nih.gov/pmc/articles/PMC6961288/

9    https://pubmed.ncbi.nlm.nih.gov/34812198

10   https://pubmed.ncbi.nlm.nih.gov/28243695

11   https://www.msn.com/en-gb/lifestyle/relationships/72-of-men-and-54-of-women-have-regrets-about-getting-married/ar-BB1izoDw

12   https://pubmed.ncbi.nlm.nih.gov/37796606

13   https://transactual.org.uk/wp-content/uploads/TransitionAccessSurvey2022.pdf

14   https://www.bbc.co.uk/news/uk-england-bristol-61605588

15   https://www.opendemocracy.net/en/nhs-a-and-e-delays-austerity-emergency-care-hospitals-hunt-hancock-lansley/

16   https://transactual.org.uk/whats-happening-with-nhs-phallo-and-meta

17   https://www.leighday.co.uk/news/news/2023-news/trans-men-left-in-limbo-between-gender-affirming-surgeries-take-legal-action/

18   https://www.leighday.co.uk/news/news/2023-news/trans-men-left-in-limbo-between-gender-affirming-surgeries-take-legal-action/#:~:text=Another%20client%2C%20who%20we%20have,travel%2C%20or%20gain%20new%20employment.

19   https://transactual.org.uk/wp-content/uploads/TransitionAccessSurvey2022.pdf

20   https://transactual.org.uk/wp-content/uploads/TransitionAccessSurvey2022.pdf

21   https://www.pointofpride.org/; https://www.gofundme.com/c/gender-confirmation-surgery-fundraising; https://www.theokraproject.com/resources

22   James, S. E., Herman, J. L., Rankin, S., Keisling, M., Mottet, L., and Anafi, M., Executive Summary of the Report of the 2015 U.S. Transgender Survey, 2016.

23   https://www.blacktranshub.co.uk/about

24   https://pubmed.ncbi.nlm.nih.gov/30375233

25   https://transactual.org.uk/wp-content/uploads/TransLivesSurvey2021.pdf

26   https://edition.cnn.com/2023/06/06/politics/states-banned-medical-transitioning-for-transgender-youth-dg

27   https://www.lgbtmap.org/equality-maps/medicaid

28   https://williamsinstitute.law.ucla.edu/publications/medicaid-trans-health-care

29   https://www.amnesty.org.uk/press-releases/uk-cass-review-gender-identity-being-weaponized-anti-trans-groups

30  https://novaramedia.com/2024/04/15/spare-a-thought-for-hilary-cass/
31  https://patha.nz/News/13341582
32  https://www.independent.co.uk/voices/cass-report-trans-guidance-children-nhs-failures-b2526357.html
33   https://cass.independent-review.uk/about-the-review/assurance-group/
34  https://www.thenational.scot/news/24250632.cass-review-must-greeted-caution-scotland-say-academics/; https://www.wpath.org/media/cms/Documents/Public%20Policies/2024/17.05.24%20Response%20Cass%20Review%20FINAL%20with%20ed%20note.pdf?_t=1716075965
35  https://transactual.org.uk/wp-content/uploads/TransActual-Briefing-on-Cass-Review.pdf
36  https://www.wpath.org/soc8
37  https://link.springer.com/chapter/10.1007/978-1-4684-4784-2_4
38  https://learning.nspcc.org.uk/child-protection-system/gillick-competence-fraser-guidelines
39  https://www.healthcareethicsandlaw.co.uk/dentalconsent/gillick
40  https://www.gov.uk/government/news/new-restrictions-on-puberty-blockers
41  https://goodlawproject.org/dark-money-anti-abortion-group-ramps-up-activity-in-the-uk/
42  https://www.epfweb.org/sites/default/files/2021-08/Tip%20of%20the%20Iceberg%20August%202021%20Final.pdf
43  https://supreme.justia.com/cases/federal/us/597/19-1392/
44  https://www.nytimes.com/2022/07/22/us/politics/after-roe-republicans-sharpen-attacks-on-gay-and-transgender-rights.html
45  https://www.frc.org/get.cfm?i=WL22E01
46  https://www.dailymail.co.uk/health/article-13126473/Trans-influencer-BBC-actor-moved-London.html
47  https://transactual.org.uk/transition-access-22/
48  https://www.radcliffe.harvard.edu/event/2023-jules-gill-peterson-fellow-presentation-virtual; https://thebaffler.com/salvos/doctors-who-gill-peterson; https://www.thecrimson.com/article/2023/11/4/Jules-Gill-Peterson-15Q/
49  In addition to the fact that when you take medication, you tend to be monitored.

50   https://transactual.org.uk/wp-content/uploads/
     TransActualBridgingPrescriptions.pdf
51   https://thebaffler.com/salvos/doctors-who-gill-peterson

### Chapter 7. Safe Space

1   https://osf.io/preprints/socarxiv/4uw6j
2   https://www.bbc.co.uk/news/uk-england-london-68226196
3   https://www.smh.com.au/national/nsw/sydney-s-oxford-street-in-
    identity-crisis-as-crowd-changes-and-cost-of-living-bites-20230607-
    p5den3.html
4   https://corklgbtarchive.com/items/show/150
5   https://www.lgbthero.org.uk/loneliness-and-being-lgbtq-2
6   https://blog.britishnewspaperarchive.co.uk/2020/06/19/18th-century-
    molly-houses-londons-gay-subculture
7   https://historicengland.org.uk/research/inclusive-heritage/lgbtq-
    heritage-project/meeting-and-socialising/pubs-and-clubs/
8   https://www.stonewall.org.uk/about-us/news/new-data-rise-hate-
    crime-against-lgbtq-people-continues-stonewall-slams-uk-gov-
9   https://www.youtube.com/watch?v=C2F2R2vGE98
10  https://www.dazeddigital.com/life-culture/article/62084/1/la-camion-
    era-london-lesbian-bar-founders-interview
11  https://www.pxssypalace.com/policy
12  https://www.theguardian.com/books/2019/dec/06/britain-has-closed-
    almost-800-libraries-since-2010-figures-show
13  https://londonlgbtqcentre.org/wp-content/uploads/2022/11/A-New-
    Queer-London-LGBTQ-Communities-and-Spaces-beyond-Covid-19.pdf
14  https://theinitiativeforequalrights.org/2019-survey-released/
15  https://www.bbc.co.uk/news/world-us-canada-36511778
16  https://www.opendemocracy.net/en/5050/honor-oak-pub-forest-
    hill-drag-queen-story-hour-police-far-right-amardeep-singh-
    dhillon/; https://www.theguardian.com/world/2023/may/07/
    met-accused-of-siding-with-far-right-group-in-anti-drag-act-protest;
    https://socialistworker.co.uk/news/police-cracked-my-rib-at-
    honor-oak-says-south-london-anti-fascist/; https://transsafety.
    network/posts/far-right-attack-on-honour-oak/; https://socialist-
    worker.co.uk/news/anti-fascists-outnumber-far-right-bigots-at-honor-
    oak-pub/

Chapter 8. Queer Families

1   https://www.rightsofwomen.org.uk/about-us/our-herstory/
2   https://lccn.loc.gov/86674013
3   https://www.liverpoolmuseums.org.uk/stories/sandi-hughes-recorded-history
4   https://www.legislation.gov.uk/ukpga/2002/38/contents
5   https://www.lesbianvisibilityweek.com/_files/ugd/6818aa_5ceb7dbf5e8d4d18b128f815ed475fe5.pdf
6   https://www.hrw.org/news/2022/09/22/england-end-lbq-discrimination-access-fertility-services
7   https://www.leighday.co.uk/news/news/2021-news/same-sex-couple-issues-judicial-review-against-discriminatory-ivf-policy
8   https://www.gov.uk/government/publications/womens-health-strategy-for-england/womens-health-strategy-for-england
9   https://www.stonewall.org.uk/our-work/campaigns/make-access-ivf-equal-lgbtq-people
10  https://inews.co.uk/news/same-sex-couples-remortgaging-sacrificing-heating-eating-fertility-treatment-2716370?srsltid=AfmBOoqhnw8X-EnPokRQ47jlIgNejRvvushiu159k10l4d8byu-DloV-
11  https://www.londonspermbank.com/catalogue/prices/
12  https://www.stonewall.org.uk/our-work/campaigns/make-access-ivf-equal-lgbtq-people
13  https://helpwithchildarrangements.service.justice.gov.uk/parental-responsibility
14  https://www.hfea.gov.uk/treatments/explore-all-treatments/becoming-the-legal-parents-of-your-child/
15  https://www.glamourmagazine.co.uk/article/logan-brown-interview-2023
16  https://www.reuters.com/article/fact-check/the-nhs-has-not-removed-the-word-woman-from-its-website-idUSL1N35L1P2; https://www.independent.co.uk/life-style/women/nhs-women-menopause-inclusive-language-b2111916.html
17  https://www.legislation.gov.uk/ukpga/Eliz2/1-2/20
18  https://www.theguardian.com/society/2019/jul/16/transgender-man-who-gave-birth-loses-high-court-privacy-case-fred-mcconnell
19  https://academic.oup.com/icon/article/21/2/603/7194654
20  https://www.independent.co.uk/news/uk/home-news/lgbt-family-children-research-b2567392.html

21 https://www.kantar.com/Inspiration/Equality/The-generational-shift-in-LGBTQI-women-coming-out
22 https://www.justlikeus.org/wp-content/uploads/2024/06/LGBT-parents-report-2024-by-Just-Like-Us.pdf
23 https://www.forbes.com/sites/roberthart/2023/03/06/kids-raised-by-same-sex-parents-fare-same-as-or-better-than-kids-of-straight-couples-research-finds/
24 https://www.flsenate.gov/Session/Bill/2022/1557
25 https://www.spuc.org.uk/Article/383931/No-outsiders-More-like-no-parents-rights
26 https://www.ala.org/news/2024/03/american-library-association-reports-record-number-unique-book-titles
27 https://pen.org/press-release/new-report-find-unprecedented-surge-in-school-books-bans/; https://www.washingtonpost.com/education/2023/05/23/lgbtq-book-ban-challengers/
28 https://www.npr.org/2024/04/16/1245037718/book-bans-2023-pen-america
29 https://gnet-research.org/2023/11/15/we-dont-co-parent-with-the-government-gender-ideology-as-a-global-culture-war/
30 Nash, Catherine, and Browne, Kath, *Heteroactivism: Resisting Lesbian, Gay, Bisexual and Trans Rights and Equalities,* 1st ed. (Zed Books, 2020).
31 https://cris.brighton.ac.uk/ws/portalfiles/portal/396829/GPC%20revised%20_.v5%20no%20comments%20(1).pdf
32 https://getpenfold.com/news/childcare-cost

### Chapter 9. Don't Stop Moving

1 https://www.nhs.uk/live-well/exercise/exercise-health-benefits/
2 https://lgbt.foundation/help/hidden-figures-lgbt-health-inequalities-in-the-uk/
3 https://www.glsen.org/research/school-climate-survey
4 https://equality-network.org/wp-content/uploads/2013/03/Out-for-Sport-Report.pdf
5 https://www.stonewall.org.uk/lgbtq-facts-and-figures
6 https://www.nbcnews.com/nbc-out/out-news/openly-gay-paralympian-mar-gunnarsson-embraces-multifaceted-identity-rcna169324#

7  https://www.dailymail.co.uk/news/article-13656413/SHARRON-
   DAVIES-missed-Olympic-gold-East-German-rivals-illegal-doping-
   female-athletes-face-conned-medals-transgender-competitors-
   cowardice-misanthropy.html ?
8  https://bjsm.bmj.com/content/bjsports/early/2024/04/10/
   bjsports-2023-108029.full.pdf
9  https://stillmed.olympics.com/media/Documents/Beyond-the-Games/
   Human-Rights/IOC-Framework-Fairness-Inclusion-Non-discrimination-
   2021.pdf
10 https://www.washingtonpost.com/lifestyle/style/we-celebrated-
   michael-phelpss-genetic-differences-why-punish-caster-semenya-for-
   hers/2019/05/02/93d08c8c-6c2b-11e9-be3a-33217240a539_story.
   html
11 https://www.hrc.org/resources/the-real-threat-to-womens-sports-
   isnt-transgender-athletes-its-underfunding-and-lack-of-resources
12 https://www.kpbs.org/news/national/2021/10/27/the-ncaa-spends-more-
   on-mens-sports-than-womens-another-gender-equity-report-finds
13 https://www.flgov.com/2021/06/01/governor-ron-desantis-signs-
   fairness-in-womens-sports-act/
14 https://www.theadvocate.com/baton_rouge/news/politics/legislature/
   as-transgender-sports-bill-advances-louisiana-lawmaker-cant-cite-
   local-example-of-issue/article_f64eb566-a921-11eb-b863-
   3f74137b00c9.html
15 https://www.roundersengland.co.uk/content/uploads/2024/06/Trans-
   Non-binary-Players-Policy-and-Procedures-in-Rounders-2024.pdf

## Chapter 10. A Place of Refuge

1  https://news.sky.com/story/inhuman-suella-braverman-condemned-
   by-lgbt-asylum-seekers-who-say-they-cannot-leave-uk-12970533
2   https://news.sky.com/story/illegal-migration-bill-government-
   accused-of-ignoring-international-law-during-house-of-lords-
   defeats-12911388
3  https://www.bbc.co.uk/news/uk-politics-66919416
4  https://inews.co.uk/news/i-morning-briefing-the-backlash-against-
   suella-bravermans-refugee-speech-2645150
5  https://www.channel4.com/news/uk-immigration-whats-labours-
   alternative-to-scrapped-rwanda-policy

6 https://www.independent.co.uk/news/uk/politics/bibby-stockholm-report-small-boats-b2533434.html; https://www.theguardian.com/uk-news/2023/oct/29/this-is-a-prison-men-tell-of-distressing-conditions-on-bibby-stockholm

7 https://www.wsws.org/en/articles/2024/08/21/ccbl-a21.html

8 https://www.humandignitytrust.org/lgbt-the-law/map-of-criminalisation/?type_filter=crim_gender_exp

9 https://metro.co.uk/2021/01/19/i-couldnt-come-out-as-a-lesbian-until-i-moved-to-the-uk-13901545/

10 https://www.theguardian.com/uk-news/2014/feb/08/home-office-gay-asylum-seekers-questioning; https://www.bbc.co.uk/news/stories-51636642; https://www.rainbowmigration.org.uk/wp-content/uploads/2022/03/Missing-the-Mark-Oct-13_0.pdf

11 https://bills.parliament.uk/publications/44460/documents/1174

12 https://www.thepinknews.com/2020/01/30/home-office-gay-asylum-link-yew-fook-sam-malaysia-refugee-pride-high-court/

13 https://www.independent.co.uk/news/uk/home-news/lgbt-asylum-seekers-home-office-uk-applications-2018-a8658951.html

14 https://www.stonewall.org.uk/system/files/no_safe_refuge.pdf

15 https://www.gov.uk/government/statistics/immigration-system-statistics-year-ending-june-2023/asylum-claims-on-the-basis-of-sexual-orientation-2022

16 https://www.stonewall.org.uk/system/files/no_safe_refuge.pdf

17 https://www.judiciary.uk/wp-content/uploads/2015/07/lord-chancellor-v-detention-action-judgment.pdf

18 https://www.gov.uk/government/collections/immigration-statistics-quarterly-release; https://www.stonewall.org.uk/system/files/no_safe_refuge.pdf

19 https://www.unhcr.org/uk/sites/uk/files/2023-08/UNHCR%252520-%252520Alternatives%252520to%252520Detention%252520-%2525 2023%252520August%2525202023%252520-%252520for%2525 20publication.pdf

20 https://microrainbow.org/alternative-to-detention/

21 https://migrationobservatory.ox.ac.uk/resources/briefings/immigration-detention-in-the-uk/

22 https://www.theguardian.com/uk-news/2018/oct/10/private-contractors-paid-millions-uk-detention-centres-some-firms-making-30-percent-profit

23 https://www.unhcr.org/ke/kakuma-refugee-camp

24 https://www.thepinknews.com/2021/04/16/kenya-kakuma-refugee-camp-bomb-attack-chriton-atuhwera-trinidad-jerry/

25 https://www.vice.com/en/article/fear-and-violence-stalk-lgbtq-refugees-in-one-of-the-worlds-biggest-migrant-camps/

26 https://www.unhcr.org/ke/19859-unhcr-statement-on-the-situation-of-lgbtiq-refugees-in-kakuma-camp.html

27 https://www.amnesty.org.uk/press-releases/kenya-lgbti-refugees-risk-rape-and-violence-kakuma-refugee-camp-new-report

28 https://af02ef9f-eaff-4f16-a35c-9a7ea58a6250.filesusr.com/ugd/65cf98_db18b86c46744fb98648ccff1640e165.pdf

29 https://www.unhcr.org/media/framework-durable-solutions-refugees-and-persons-concern-0

30 https://onlinelibrary.wiley.com/doi/full/10.1111/disa.12447

31 https://www.bbc.co.uk/news/world-africa-48703112

### Chapter II. For God's Sake

1 https://www.nbcnews.com/feature/nbc-out/nearly-half-lgbtq-adults-are-religious-u-s-study-finds-n1249273

2 P. Califia, Sex changes: the politics of transgenderism (San Francisco, CA: Cleis Press, 1997), p. 89; https://cdn.unrisd.org/assets/library/papers/pdf-files/2023/wp-2023-4-anti-gender-movement.pdf; For more on this, see Gender Heretics.

3 https://www.birminghammail.co.uk/news/midlands-news/how-birmingham-reacted-parents-withdrawing-15910307

4 https://www.bbc.co.uk/news/uk-england-48351401

5 https://www.theguardian.com/uk-news/2018/oct/10/uk-supreme-court-backs-bakery-that-refused-to-make-gay-wedding-cake

6 https://www.standard.co.uk/news/london/turning-point-drag-story-time-protest-east-dulwich-pub-b1066453.html

7 https://cdn.unrisd.org/assets/library/papers/pdf-files/2023/wp-2023-4-anti-gender-movement.pdf

8 https://care.org.uk/cause/religious-liberty

9 https://christianconcern.com/ccpressreleases/university-accused-of-appalling-double-standards-over-lgbt-islam-and-christian-beliefs/

10 https://www.theguardian.com/world/2016/jan/12/angli-can-church-england-global-schism-homosexuality-gay-rights

11 https://www.icelandreview.com/society/ten-years-since-iceland-legalised-same-sex-marriage/

12 https://www.mahoningmatters.com/news/local/article277097118.html

13 https://www.bbc.com/news/uk-scotland-40190204

14 https://www.nbcnews.com/nbc-out/out-news/pope-says-church-open-everyone-gays-rules-rcna98613

15 https://www.myjewishlearning.com/article/same-sex-marriage/

16 https://www.hrc.org/resources/stances-of-faiths-on-lgbt-issues-orthodox-judaism

17 https://www.myjewishlearning.com/article/judaism-and-the-lgbtq-community-an-overview/

18 https://www.keshetonline.org/our-work/

19 https://www.hrc.org/resources/stances-of-faiths-on-lgbt-issues-islam

20 https://transreads.org/wp-content/uploads/2021/12/2021-12-23_61c4d74da4743_RoutledgeinternationalencyclopediaofqueerculturebyDavidA.Gerstnerz-lib.org_.pdf

21 https://transreads.org/wp-content/uploads/2021/12/2021-12-23_61c4d74da4743_RoutledgeinternationalencyclopediaofqueerculturebyDavidA.Gerstnerz-lib.org_.pdf

22 https://www.ijhssi.org/papers/vol7(1)/Version-1/K0701016265.pdf

23 https://www.sikhnet.com/news/how-sikhs-got-their-rehat-maryada

24 https://news.sky.com/story/politicians-criticised-for-toxic-language-as-religious-and-transgender-hate-crimes-increase-12977436

25 https://www.stonewall.org.uk/lgbtq-facts-and-figures

26 https://www.switchboard.org.uk/wp-content/uploads/2019/02/LGBTQ-Faith-Report_FINAL-EDITED.pdf

27 https://www.nazandmattfoundation.org/sdm_downloads/report-understanding-the-impact-of-coming-out-to-religious-parents-uk-2020/

28 https://www.advocate.com/religion/2022/12/17/how-bible-error-changed-history-and-turned-gays-pariahs

29 https://www.theguardian.com/film/2023/dec/01/christian-homophobia-bible-mistranslation-1946-documentary; https://www.1946themovie.com/

30 https://www.stonewall.org.uk/everything-you-need-know-about-conversion-therapy

31 https://www.gov.uk/government/publications/national-lgbt-survey-summary-report/national-lgbt-survey-summary-report

32 https://www.christian.org.uk/campaign/broad-conversion-therapy-ban/

33 https://ozanne.foundation/cooper_report/

34 https://time.com/3655718/leelah-alcorn-suicide-transgender-therapy/

35 https://www.fox19.com/story/30708054/cincinnati-becomes-first-city-to-ban-lgbt-conversion-therapy/

36 https://www.thepinknews.com/2015/12/10/cincinnati-becomes-second-us-city-to-ban-gay-cure-therapy/

37 https://www.mind.org.uk/news-campaigns/news/it-can-completely-destroy-a-person-how-mind-plans-to-make-mps-understand-the-devastating-effects-of-conversion-therapy/

38 https://assets.publishing.service.gov.uk/government/uploads/system/uploads/attachment_data/file/721367/GEO-LGBT-Action-Plan.pdf

39 https://news.sky.com/story/plans-to-ban-conversion-therapy-dropped-just-a-day-after-minister-said-government-wholly-committed-to-new-law-12579101

40 https://www.equalityhumanrights.com/our-work/equality-and-human-rights-monitor/equality-and-human-rights-monitor-2023

41 https://view.officeapps.live.com/op/view.aspx?src=https%25253A%25252F%25252Fwww.equalityhumanrights.com%25252Fsites%25252Fdefault%25252Ffiles%25252Fconsultation-response-banning-conversion-therapy-26-january-2022.docx&wd-Origin=BROWSELINK

42 https://www.vice.com/en/article/pkpym8/uk-government-officials-held-secret-meeting-with-ex-gay-conversion-therapy-providers

43 https://www.bbc.co.uk/news/uk-55326461

44 https://www.mshafsaqureshi.com/

## Chapter 12. Age-old Problems

1 https://jamanetwork.com/journals/jama/article-abstract/2818061

2 https://jamanetwork.com/journals/jamanetworkopen/fullarticle/2800814; https://www.bmj.com/content/bmj/374/bmj.n2169.full.pdf; https://www.hcplive.com/view/mortality-rate-higher-transgender-people

3  https://www.ncbi.nlm.nih.gov/pmc/articles/PMC3093261/

4  https://www.ageuk.org.uk/globalassets/age-uk/documents/
reports-and-publications/reports-and-briefings/equality-and-human-
rights/rb_may16_cpa_rapid_review_diversity_in_older_age_lgbt.pdf

5  https://swlondoner.shorthandstories.com/life-at-tonic-the-uks-first-
lgbtq-retirement-community/index.html

6  https://www.tonichousing.org.uk/bsc-2020-report

# Hello
## my name is

# OUTRAGE

# OUTRAGE

# RAGE

# OUTRAGE

# OUTRAGE

# OUTRAGE

# OUTRAGE